Additional Praise for

The eProcess Edge

"An unusual combination of insights and practical advice, this book goes beyond the hype to focus on the importance of both innovation and execution in the world of eCommerce. Managers will find it invaluable in helping to set a course for success in the increasingly competitive, Internet-driven, global business environment."

—**Donald J. McCubbrey, Ph.D., Director, Center for the Study of Electronic Commerce at Daniels College of Business, University of Denver**

"Collaboration is the core of business in the Internet economy. Keen and McDonald know this and they communicate their insights and expertise superbly."

—**Dr. Jerry Wagner, Founder and CEO, WebIQ, Inc.**

The eProcess Edge

The eProcess Edge

Creating Customer Value and Business Wealth in the Internet Era

Peter Keen
Mark McDonald

Osborne/**McGraw-Hill**

Berkeley ▶ New York ▶ St. Louis ▶ San Francisco ▶ Auckland ▶ Bogotá
Hamburg ▶ London ▶ Madrid ▶ Mexico City ▶ Milan ▶ Montreal ▶ New Delhi
Panama City ▶ Paris ▶ São Paulo ▶ Singapore ▶ Sydney ▶ Tokyo ▶ Toronto

Osborne/**McGraw-Hill**

2600 Tenth Street
Berkeley, California 94710
U.S.A.

For information on translations or book distributors outside the U.S.A., or
to arrange bulk purchase discounts for sales promotions, premiums, or
fund-raisers, please contact Osborne/**McGraw-Hill** at the above address.

*The eProcess Edge: Creating Customer Value and Business Wealth in the
Internet Era*

Printed in the United States of America

34567890DOC DOC019876543210

ISBN: 0-07-212626-4   **3 2280 00543 0699**

To Sherry, with love and gratitude
—Peter Keen

To Carolyn and the kids
—Mark McDonald

Contents

Acknowledgments

Acknowledgments often read like a roll call during the first day of school, listing the names of people whose involvement and contribution made a book possible. This makes it hard to communicate the sincerity of our thanks to our value network, which came together beautifully to create our book at eSpeed. These professionals collectively formed a real team, one we look forward to working with again.

The team members at Osborne/McGraw-Hill deserve recognition for their stellar work in bringing the book to life. Their focus and collaboration represent a new standard for publishing in the Internet era. Our gratitude and respect go to Roger Stewart, editorial director; David Zielonka, managing editor; Laurie Stewart, project manager; Lunaea Weatherstone, copy editor; and Maureen Forys, typesetter. They managed the publishing process with the grace of a ballerina dancing at a break-neck speed.

Our thanks to the team at *ComputerWorld*, including Peter Horan and Elaine Offenbach, for providing a platform for expressing our ideas as part of the IT Leadership Series. They deserve credit for recognizing that eCommerce is more than Web sites, networks, and routers, and for helping us reach the audience for our work.

The team at Keen Innovations responded superbly to the challenge to streamline a publishing process that typically takes many months into just a few weeks. Dale Garmon, Merry Richardson, Jennifer Hunter, Carey Colvin, Russell Hunter, and Sherry Keen took on a huge load in research, references and citations, and manuscript management. The quality of the book is a mark of their quality and energy.

The team at Andersen Consulting starts with the eProcess Development group, representing an outstanding set of professionals. In alphabetical order, our appreciation goes to Peter Bautista, Ellen Behm, Anson Gong, Takaaki Haraguchi, Lisa Hsu, Shaista Keating, Brad Kolar, Michael Leist, Andrew Marshall, Laurie Richmond, Sandy Stevens, Michael Stowell, Kristine Ward, Tammy Wedeking, Julian Weiss, and Xiao Yan Yu. Each played a role in developing and deploying the thoughts behind eProcess. This book reflects their hard work, research, and insight.

Laura Roberts and her team of Heather Dubes and Jennifer Peebler receive the persistence award for their efforts. Barrett Avigdor, Simon Maple, Diane Fitzgerald, Ajit Kambil, Jeannie Harris, Charles Doyle,

Kim Badland, and Pat Kovach deserve special mention for their expertise and assistance.

Pat Mullaney, Marc De Kegel, Peter Roberts, Glover Ferguson, Ron Anderson, and Ed Schreck deserve recognition for sponsoring this effort.

Finally, we would like to recognize the contributions of Bill Petrarca, Andrew Hunter, and Phyllis Kennedy. Their review of the manuscript and comments strengthened this book.

From Peter Keen

I've written more than 20 books. I've never enjoyed the entire process from ideas to book-in-hand so much as I have with *The eProcess Edge*. Mark has been a joy to work with in every aspect of the brainstorming and research we've done together, the writing, and the many complex follow-up activities involved in getting it into our readers' hands. His management talents are as extraordinary as his intellectual ones.

I can't ever thank my own Keen Innovations team enough. They halved my workload and more than halved my standard author's neurotic fits. Other friends helped me, too. Ron Williams sharpened many of the ideas in our frameworks, critiqued the manuscript drafts, and made many contributions to my thinking that don't show up directly in the book. Ron, you are among my best critics and a most generous colleague. My phone calls to Michael Schrage, author of two of the best books I know of on collaboration and prototyping, always generate something creative and provocative for me, and I value his creativity very much.

My wife, Sherry, makes everything special. Thanks, sweetheart. I love you and our life together more than just very much.

From Mark McDonald

My thanks go to Peter, who is a terrific collaborator and thinker. They also go to my colleagues and friends at Andersen Consulting for their ideas, reactions, and suggestions for improvement.

This is my first book, and while it is customary to thank your family for putting up with you during the writing of the book, I think few people understand what it is like to live with an author through the writing process. My deepest love and thanks go to my wife, Carolyn, and our children, Brian and Sarah.

Introduction

White Out!

Electronic commerce has been described as many things, including the single most disruptive technology and the engine for new wealth. It's been credited with creating the new economy and accused of driving the world to commoditization. One thing is for sure: eCommerce and the Internet are the subject of tremendous media and academic hype. This has created a "white out" where the blizzard of information and advertising blind executives from the fundamental actions they need to take for their customers and companies.

In writing this book, we wanted to get beyond the hype, the promises of instant wealth, and laments about the extinction of the old economy. We wanted to get to what really counts: how you use eCommerce to create customer value and wealth. During the past 18 months, we have looked at more than 80 eCommerce projects and companies both within and outside of Andersen Consulting to identify how they are addressing the commercial side of eCommerce. Focusing on how eCommerce changes business, we sought to identify the emerging business practices and principles that would guide companies in the future.

The market has legitimized our intention as it erased the meteoric rise of eCommerce market values in the first quarter of 2000. This replaced concern for share price and IPOs with concerns about profitability and made gaining an eProcess edge critical for success in eCommerce.

eProcess Fundamentals

An eProcess edge rests on understanding the fundamentals of eCommerce and how they apply to your business. These fundamentals begin with recognizing that eCommerce is first and foremost about commerce. A company wins through business performance that includes—but is not exclusively tied to—technological sophistication. This has never been more true, as you can lease your technology from an array of application service providers. eCommerce is about business first.

Commerce centers on relationships, involving the exchange of value between parties. Relationships are critical in eCommerce to overcome the high costs of customer acquisition, which can erase the company's profit potential. Relationships in this context mean more than just having a strong call center. It means designing and operating the business from the customer perspective and recognizing that all aspects of your operation affect the customer, including processes such as shipping that were traditionally viewed as being in the back office. eCommerce success rests on building relationships and repeat business.

Relationships are governed by business processes. Processes are the business rules, interfaces, and sourcing that define how the relationships flow. Processes establish how work gets done and how the relationship will work. A well-defined process, with clean rules, a usable interface, and backed by a fulfillment capability, builds customer trust and repeat businesses. Relationships, therefore, form the basis for the company's online brand.

Business rules define eCommerce processes and unlock the potential latent in new sourcing options. Rules are the foundation of the business model and operations as they define how the business will work. Traditional process design tends to bury rules deep within a work flow, focusing instead on completing forms such as an application or an order. Business rules rise to the surface in eCommerce, as the process work will be out-tasked to others. What remains is the definition and enforcement of business rules and relationships that ensure company economics. A strong set of business rules form the foundation of the company and its profit potential.

The eProcess Potential

eCommerce involves a fundamental shift in business because it changes business basics. The changes implied by eCommerce go to the core of how companies are created, operated, and managed. The scope of an eCommerce business extends beyond what it alone can do, to a network of suppliers, intermediaries, and others. This ability to change process sourcing is a significant factor in creating new levels of financial and customer performance.

The potential of this view is real. Perhaps the single key indicator of the immediate opportunity eProcess represents is a figure from a University of Texas survey of the Internet economy: revenues per employee. For U.S. business as a whole, this averages $165,000. For the Internet players, it's 65 percent higher.[1] This doesn't just apply to small and startup firms, whose stock-optioned employees basically live their lives at work. In April 2000, the *Washington Post* summarized the performance of America Online (AOL) in 1999: $4.8 billion in revenues and 14,000 employees.[2] That makes AOL's revenues per employee close to $350,000, double that of the U.S. average, so it's fully representative of the eSuccess firm. Just a month before the *Post*'s report, AOL became the first new economy player to join the *Fortune* 500, the old economy's measure of success. The question is, what must a company do achieve this level of performance?

Now, the eCommerce skeptic would point out that AOL and companies like it are Internet companies based on selling information over the Web. They would go on to ask, what about companies that over the Web. They would go on to ask, what about companies that do real commerce, serve real customers, and provide real products? What about them? Our review covered both Internet and traditional companies doing real commerce addressing real business challenges. In these cases, we found that companies can exploit eCommerce technologies and approaches to improve their performance as they strike a blend between vertical operations and virtual integration.

This eProcess edge involves identifying, sourcing, and managing the company's process base across the sourcing options shown in Figure I-1.

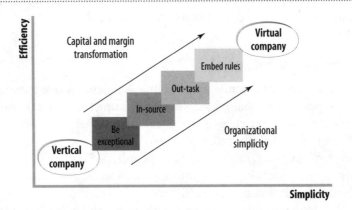

Figure I-1: eProcess sourcing options

These sourcing options center around key business design issues that define the desired outcome, responsibilities, and means to deliver the outcomes. Executives face a new set of choices in eCommerce as Internet technologies and a growing service supplier market expand traditional *build* versus *buy* decisions into the following options:

- Embed process rules in the software interface between the company and the customer

- Out-task processes and capabilities to others electronically

- In-source new capabilities electronically to strengthen relationships and brands

- Be exceptional in handling process exceptions through coordinated personnel and workflows

What Is in This Book

The critical issues facing executives center around how you source your capabilities, how you ensure the business rules, and how you manage a value network that extends outside of the company boundaries. The answers to these questions are addressed in this book.

Part I, "Defining the eProcess Edge," highlights the dynamics and responsibilities of process in the eCommerce and Internet era. Here we describe the new approaches to engineering eProcesses based on rules rather than traditional processes that concentrate on inputs-processes-outputs. Process excellence matters in eCommerce as you keep hard-won customers based on what happens after the click at the Web site.

Part II, "The Relationship Imperative," concentrates on techniques for targeting value network relationships, establishing new relationship types, and making capability sourcing decisions. These techniques define the company's eCommerce scope in terms of the breadth of its value network and the depth of each relationship in that network. These boundaries set the stage for tough decisions regarding the company's identity, priority, background, and mandated processes. This book builds on the value-centered focus found in Peter Keen's 1997 book, *The Process Edge*, extending that framework to address concerns of customer value and the enhanced sourcing options possible in eCommerce.

Part III, "Delivering eProcess Results," discusses how to build capabilities across each of the sourcing dimensions. This includes a discussion of what it means to embed business rules in software—a process that goes well beyond designing Web pages or a Web store. Out-tasking capability enables companies to access best-practice capabilities at speed and scale by leasing capability from value network players. Being exceptional at exceptions addresses how to handle the capabilities that guarantee the relationship by handling the non-routine, the exception with high touch and texture. Managing across multiple companies and channels introduces new challenges that are addressed through a service approach and an effort to harmonize the business across all of its channels.

The eProcess Executive Agenda

Business and technology executives looking for an eProcess edge must be willing to challenge their existing business models, their scope of control, and how they apply technology. They must recognize the importance of relationships in combating commoditization through Internet-based competition. They should understand the changing nature of competition and how they can use business rules and sourcing to create new businesses that compete on process excellence and customer value. They must recognize how to target the company's identity assets—the ones that matter most to their relationships and brand—in order to concentrate their scarce capital and attention. That attention needs to be refocused in terms of customer and value network relationships. Finally, business executives must understand management approaches for running a business that spans multiple value network players and channels.

Technology executives should use this book to move from recognizing the need to enable eCommerce to understanding the implications of integrating technology into the company's relationship and transaction base. Information technology is not a support function in an eCommerce company; it is the operational core. The difference is tangible and far reaching, as technology executives must become accountable for business results rather than just IT costs. These new responsibilities involve understanding the fit between business rules, capabilities, and technology that goes beyond a superficial acquaintance. IT executives therefore should look at what it means in business terms to establish a new eCommerce channel—one that involves embedded business rules, application program interfaces (APIs), and the accelerating move to component-based technologies and approaches.

Radical Conservatives

The eProcess Edge is a radically conservative book. It's radical in two ways. First, it challenges much of the core assumption of the eCommerce world: that this is all about Web sites and that the Web is the transformer of business. Our eProcess view is that the Web site is just the starting point that enables but does not in itself create the transformation of business. It's the relationship interface that creates a base for almost literally infinite expansion of the firm's value network. That's where the transformation will come across value networks rather than individual businesses. Put more bluntly, we believe that Web sites as such are a dead end. It's what you do with and behind the screens that makes the difference.

The second way in which this book is radical is in its entire reinterpretation of what a "business process" is. It's not workflows and activities. It's business rules and sourcing options. We hope you find this perspective one that helps your company get the best of all worlds: software, alliances via APIs and creative use of people through software embedding, out-tasking, in-sourcing, and exceptional handling of exceptions.

The eProcess Edge is as deeply conservative as it is radical— again, in two regards. The first is our view that every development in eCommerce reveals its roots in commerce. That's why it is so profoundly disruptive and destabilizing. It takes every basic of business and intensifies every trend behind it. For example, it intensifies the trend toward electronic logistics, which has been growing for around 20 years through electronic data interchange, point of sale, and quick response. It intensifies the worldwide moves to deregulation, globalization, and breakdown of industry barriers. It intensifies mass customization, multi-channel customer contacts (ten years ago, telemarketing was an innovation and toll-free numbers the luxury of large companies), and customer power. It intensifies the move toward ever more speed in every area of business. So we could easily take the position that there really is nothing new about eCommerce— it's commerce.

The second of our conservative views is that the eCommerce world belongs to well-run companies—companies that have achieved process excellence. That is, the better a company is in the old basics, the better it will do in eCommerce basics. That opinion demands a qualifier, though: the better it will do *if and only if it operates from a business model explicitly designed around the eCommerce realities*. Trying to make incremental add-ons to existing practices and clinging to old assumptions is just as much a dead end as thinking that a Web site makes you an effective eCommerce player.

Our Intention

When we began this project, we were asked by many people if we would report on what was happening in the eCommerce marketspace. We responded with a definitive **NO**. We are not chroniclers of what people have done; that's old news. Our intention was to go beyond what was happening to understand why it was happening in order to define the approaches companies can use to create their own value and wealth. *The eProcess Edge* is written for executives who want to understand how to take action and implement the solutions required to deliver eCommerce processes and capabilities to their customers and suppliers.

This book is about gaining an eProcess edge that is the response to the "innovate or die" imperative many companies face. Gaining that edge through taking action is the key to sustained eCommerce success. And that is not at all speculation. It's obvious—just ask your customers, just look at your competitors, just ask your employees. The move is on, from the first wave of Internet innovation to eProcess execution that builds relationships, customer value, and business wealth.

Part I

Defining the eProcess Edge

In this part

Chapter 1

From Internet Innovation to eProcess Execution

Innovate or die! That's the command to all businesses for the era of Internet eCommerce. The past five years have seen a surge of new Web companies, new business models, new alliances, new services, new technology, new brands, new pricing schemes—well, new everything—that have entirely changed the fundamentals of competition. But the Internet as yet amounts to only 1 percent of the U.S. economy. Look back on what that small percentage has already created and then look ahead to when it will be just 3 percent and on again to its becoming 5 percent. Maybe eCommerce will level out at 15 percent, as Amazon's founder, Jeff Bezos, believes, but even that relatively small figure means a continuing and urgent transformation for all businesses. The choice today is not whether to innovate, but how to innovate. As for when to do so, the answer is "now" and "do it fast." In the Internet era, businesses do not have time on their side.

But the command is incomplete. Yes, innovate or die. But also: *Execute or go broke*. As many Internet companies are finding out—and the market is telling them by bidding down their stock prices—the gap between innovation and execution is a tough one to close. An innovative business model, an innovative Web site, and innovative marketing get a company into the competitive game. Execution keeps it there; it is the basis for sustaining a competitive advantage in electronic commerce.

Execution rests on process excellence, just as it always has in "bricks and mortar" business. Quality management, coordination, procurement, inventory management, scheduling, organization, customer support, operations, logistics, finance, and marketing—all these traditional aspects of process excellence remain vital to eCommerce success. They are what lie behind the Web site and turn it from technology to business. Processes are what happen after the click at the Web site.

Here are just a few obvious examples of where process rather than Web site makes the competitive difference:

Retailing The winners generate high repeat business through their attention to building and sustaining trusted relationships, and by ensuring first-rate inventory management and fulfillment of orders. The losers attract customers through promotions, large discounts, and payments to such portals as Yahoo! and AOL, and then lose them through late delivery and poor (or no) response to queries.

Financial services The winners offer multiple channels for customers to choose between managing their own account on the Web, contact over the phone, and personal and immediate response to problems. The losers offer just transactions at a low cost with no relationship differentiation.

Manufacturing The winners maintain superb end-to-end logistics management—procurement, supply chain relationships, inventory management, credit and financing, distribution, and customer account management—that enables them to operate with half the working capital and half the overhead of their average competitor. The losers are in a permanent catch-up mode.

Travel services The winners provide new pricing processes, customized offers, cross-selling, and impeccable fulfillment of orders. The losers are going out of business fast, with the words "travel agent" beginning to stand for "office space to rent."

The losers often have Web sites that are the equal of the winners in terms of design, prices, ease of navigation, speed, and information resources—all the features associated with ".com" (dot-com). What they lack is eProcess: a strategy for leveraging the Web site through meticulous attention to the business processes that create the customer relationship. This strategy does more than just handle the online transaction—it transforms the company's operations and economics.

eProcess is primarily a matter of first prioritizing and then sourcing processes, using a combination of:

- ▶ Software to convert what used to be done by people into an interaction at the Web site

- ▶ Electronic links to partners, either to out-task functions such as shipping or financing to a best practice partner or to in-source a new capability that adds to the relationship

- ▶ People, workflows, and software that provide exceptional handling of the situations that make or break the consumer/business relationship

The easy wins in electronic commerce are over. It's hard, hard work to add execution to innovation. Achieving that creates the eProcess edge.

The eProcess Strategy

eProcess determines the nature of a company's capabilities and its core competencies for electronic commerce. It is the strategy by which a company:

- ▶ Prioritizes the process capabilities it must invest in to build its eCommerce relationship base—its value network. The value network is the source of competitive edge, not the enterprise as an isolated island in an ocean of Web sites. Think of the value network as all the resources behind the "click" on a Web page that the customer doesn't see, but that together create the value in the customer-company relationship—service, order fulfillment, shipping, financing, information, brokering, and access to other products and offers. An "island" Web site may in appearance look just like one that has a wide and strong value network behind it—but what a difference there is in process capabilities.

► Coordinates and sources those processes. The challenge is to combine best practice and best economics. The more that the business rules that constitute routine processes can be embedded in software, the better the service and the lower the costs. However, the more that the company at the very same time augments how it handles the routine with exceptional handling of exceptions, the stronger its brand becomes.

Sourcing is a key to being an eProcess company instead of a Web site and also to being an effective eCommerce player. Maximize your company's range of eProcess options. Use technology to provide your customer's convenience and sense of personal service while reducing your own costs—the "win-win" for both parties.

Use it also to out-task specific functions to a best practice provider, again creating a win-win. Out-task is our term for electronically passing a message to another online company that can completely carry out a task with no more communication or administration. It's not at all the same as out-sourcing, which is more a matter of having an outside organization take over a business department function.

Use the technology in a third way, which is to bring a capability into the organization by an electronic link in order to improve your relationship with the customer and strengthen your brand for eProcess; we term this in-sourcing.

Finally, combine the most powerful business resource of all—people leveraged by process design and technology—to handle the non-routine element of the relationship. In our phrase, that means being exceptional in handling exceptions.

Today, probably no more than one in ten of companies is fully positioned to build this portfolio of eProcess capabilities.[1]

Value Network Prioritization

An electronic business is much more than just a Web site. It is an operation that involves a network of players, with one of the major opportunities the Web provides being that a company can expand that network almost infinitely. It extends its reach across its supply chain, reducing its own costs of procurement while helping manufacturers better plan their production schedules through shared information. It adds the very best shippers, research information providers, insurers, financiers, or other service providers to its own site through an electronic link. It becomes part of their site, too, for advertising, referrals, or co-branding. It turns customers into collaborators and builds communities of interest. It links to new intermediaries such as agents, facilitators, and brokers. It seeks out complementors, companies that extend the company's appeal and value by providing products and services entirely outside its own sphere of operations and capabilities. It joins trading and auction hubs.

In all this, an electronic business uses the network power of the Internet to build new *value*. The Web site is only the interface to the network and to the value. The value network is what makes your online presence more than a Web page and the interaction more than just surfing or asking a search engine to locate, say, the lowest price for a product.

Collaboration across the value network establishes the total eProcess capabilities of your company. In other words, the value network makes the business, and eProcess makes the value network.

Source eProcesses

The fundamental management issue for *any* business process, offline or online, is how to coordinate the steps it involves and how to source it—whether to do it yourself within the company, obtain it from an outside service provider, or out-task it. eProcess offers a framework that exploits the truly unique opportunities the Internet provides in sourcing capabilities. There are four distinct options here that together comprise the company's eProcess value portfolio:

Embed process rules in the software interface Let the software handle the routine interactions between the company and the customer. Dell and Cisco have embedded an entire procurement department in the individualized Web sites they offer their customers. In the consumer area of eCommerce (often referred to as B2C—business to consumer), many MyXYZ sites such as MyAmazon, MySchwab, and My.Yahoo let the customers handle their own account details, queries, troubleshooting, reporting, and order tracking. In effect, they build a customer service department into the software.

Out-task processes and capabilities electronically Fender, the maker of guitars for professional musicians, is just one of the companies with a world-class logistics function it never sees. It's an electronic link to UPS, which handles just about every-thing, even including tuning the guitars, a key process that used to happen after the instrument was delivered. Gateway doesn't have a credit department for its Web business; that's handled by eCredit, a company that both assesses credit risk and locates financing. In both of these instances, out-tasking provides first-rate service to the customer and first-rate operational capabili-ties to the company without it having to build in-house skills and invest in facilities, training, and administration.

In-source new capabilities electronically The company strength-ens its relationships and brand by providing access to services and products that it brings from the outside to its own interaction with its customers. Fidelity Investments offers customers financial advisers, research information, tutorials, discussion groups, and many other value-adding capabilities. These are just an icon away, but they are not part of Fidelity as a company. They are very much part of Fidelity as a value network.

Be exceptional in handling exceptions Make sure that when the routine eProcesses either don't meet the customer's needs or some problem or breakdown occurs, there is a superb response process. Charles Schwab is able to charge more than three times the commission on a stock trade that competitors charge because when the online trade can't be made through software, it imme-diately puts people back in the loop. National Semiconductor makes handling of customer emails a priority, while most com-panies ignore them or send boilerplate answers.

Executive leadership uses these options to enable the company to build a portfolio of capabilities to deliver the right blend of opera-tional efficiency and relationship effectiveness. These options define how a company makes the transition from vertical to virtual integra-tion. The vertical company is the traditional model of the company as an organization of functions coordinated through the manage-ment structure. It's a pyramid, where coordination is largely up through the hierarchy. Many elements of finance—accounting and audit, for instance—are coordinated within Finance, which is very separate from Engineering. Most of the resources the organization needs are in-house, with some out-sourcing and use of contractors. All of this is very complex to coordinate and results in many necessary layers of administration and a heavy cost for communication.

That old model has been under attack for decades as lacking the flexibility and agility needed for a time of ever-changing change and essential for competing in a world where the customer is more and more in charge. Business process reengineering was an explicit and sometimes brutal attack on the vertical organization as the model for business. The growing emphasis on cross-functional teams was another recognition of its limitations. Out-sourcing was more and more used to simplify operations and reduce costs. Downsizing was the effort to tackle complexity and inefficiency head-on. The scale and range of such efforts were constrained by lack of what we now have for any company—the technology of the Internet. With this, the opportunities are almost unlimited. eProcess would be just a dream without this. Now, it's the obvious way to accomplish organizational simplification and reduction of waste and overhead and, at the same time, to create new levels of customer relationship.

Take a look at Figure 1-1. It shows the move from the complexity and overhead of the vertical organization to the efficiency and simplicity of virtual integration that is enabled by eProcess. It's the base for a very new model of business, where there is less and less need for "organization" and "administration." Coordination is handled in many instances by software. Resources that previously were part of the company, and thus added to complexity, are now handled through electronic out-tasking and in-sourcing links—hence our term virtual integration. Communication—including with customers and across the value network of suppliers, intermediaries such as agents and brokers, and business partners—is then a matter of electronic coordination, not organizational administration.

The shift from vertical company to virtual integration is not a matter of a single step, but rather a continuing evolution—reorganize, reengineer, and restart. The idea of the virtual company has been around for decades,[2] but the technology of the Internet enables companies today to reach a degree of virtual integration that was impractical then. In the past, a large organization was inherently complex and inefficient, creating limitations of speed and communication. Today, the startup Internet dot-com has an advantage of simplicity and efficiency.

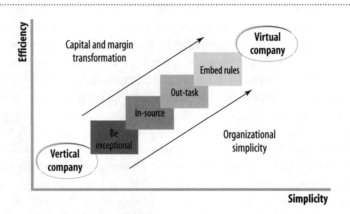

Figure 1-1: eProcess enabled sourcing options

The startup is limited in its offers if it's just a Web site where its business process rules are embedded in software—a small retailer, for instance. It needs many of the functions the vertical company has in-house. It must provide customer service without a call center, order fulfillment without a shipping department, and technology operations without a data center. It needs to broaden its offer beyond a small catalog of products for sale. So, it out-tasks to the many companies that provide access to call center capabilities, will handle shipping, and host data centers. The startup moves on as it builds collaborative arrangements to in-source capabilities, so that it looks to the customer more and more like a big company. It focuses its in-house skills on personal contact and responsiveness.

The startup benefits from moving from just being a Web site with processes embedded in software to one that has sourced an ever-wider range of eProcess capabilities. It's a value network now, not just a Web site. The established vertical company similarly fills out its portfolio of capabilities without adding more and more cost and complexity. The eProcess competitor is stronger than either the virtual company or the Web startup. It gains the eProcess edge.

The eProcess Advantage

Embed, out-task, in-source, and make the exception exceptional. They are the "Execute" complement to the command of "Innovate or die." These four options represent the portfolio of choices available to executives who lead their companies' eCommerce initiatives. But they have to lead. Otherwise, what is most likely to happen is that the allure of Web design will lead to a neglect of the processes behind it. There will be no enterprise perspective and driving force to move them up from functions independently handled as administrative overhead. The result is then the widely reported Christmas 1999 fiascoes in online retailing, where Web site successes in terms of sales were undermined by many failures in basic processes of fulfillment, inventory management, and after-sales service.

The flexibility and responsiveness created by eProcess sourcing creates an advantage, as the combination of process prioritization, value network, and choice of sourcing quite literally transform a company's relationships and economics. It gives an electronic commerce company a competitive edge that is extremely difficult to match. That edge can be seen in the greater asset and operational efficiencies enjoyed by leading electronic commerce players. Wal-Mart, the industry leader in pre-Internet eCommerce, turns its inventory an average of four times per year compared to Amazon.com's nine times per year. Translating Amazon's efficiency to Wal-Mart would increase Wal-Mart's cash flow by more than $7 billion dollars.[3]

There were plenty of signs in mid-2000 that Wal-Mart is positioning to make as aggressive a move on the Web as it did with point of sale, and in no way do we discount this superb process- and relationship-centered innovator. We offer the comparison with Amazon to show the extent to which online Web eProcesses can outperform even the best alternatives. It also highlights something that many commentators on Amazon overlook: it had to work very hard to achieve its eProcess edge (an edge that of course may be offset by Amazon's huge expenditures on marketing and sustained financial losses). In its early days as a dot-com, Amazon was routinely singled out as a model of online business because it did not need warehouses to store the millions of books it sold. It was then criticized for its unanticipated expenditures of around $300 million in warehouses and for its write-off of close to $40 million on excess inventory during the Christmas period in 1999.[4]

There's an alternative interpretation of these moves as sound eProcess practice, not dot-com aberration. Amazon had discovered just how important and complex order fulfillment and shipment are. It could no longer rely on intermediaries and distributors to handle these eProcesses and thus brought more and more of them in house. By stocking up on inventory, it was able to maintain a level of on-time delivery of over 99 percent while other retailers dropped below 90 percent and upset many customers who had relied on their gift being in stock and arriving before Christmas.[5] Amazon extended its many online "click" process strengths through these investments in "bricks."

The eProcess advantage comes from prioritizing the processes that matter and then designing and sourcing the needed capabilities in new ways. This advantage most obviously comes from taking routine processes that consume time, money, people, and organizational resources and turning them into software that does the work. Cisco, as much the Internet-era logistics leader as Wal-Mart has been in point of sale and store replenishment, shows the impact of this view of eProcesses. Table 1-1 lists figures on the payoff here.

Table 1-1: Cisco's eProcess Payoffs[6]

Logistics	First quarter, 2000 results:
	• Sales made online: 90%
	• Manufacturing: 75% of manufacturing contracted out electronically to Asian companies
	• Sales orders routed directly and immediately to a supplier who ships to the customer: 50%
	Orders reworked:
	• 1995: 33%
	• 1999: less than 1%
	Bookings per salesperson:
	• 1995: $5 million
	• 1999: $10 million
Capital efficiency and profitability	First quarter, 2000 results:
	• Return on invested capital: 87%
	• Gross margin: 65%
	• Net margin: 28%
	• $0.94 in annual cash flow for every $1 of balance sheet capital ever invested in the business
	• Of $20 billion in assets, only $1 billion (5%) is physical property and equipment
	• Generates $17 billion in sales on this base, with earnings of close to $4 billion

Table 1-1: Cisco's eProcess Payoffs *(continued)*

Payoffs from customer self-management	1997 results:
	• Documented savings: $550 million
	• Support: $175 million (Cisco estimates a saving of a thousand engineers)
	• Hiring: $8 million
	• Software distribution: $250 million
	• Documentation: $40 million
	• An average of 45,000 customer problems a week solved by customers collaborating
	• Access to order status: moved 70% of 7,000 calls a month at an average of $200 per call

The economic advantages Cisco has generated from its value network are extraordinary today, but they are becoming the target for other eProcess leaders and while they may not become standard practice, they surely set the benchmarks for all comparable companies. Execute or go broke. The eProcess leaders are racing to match or even exceed the benchmarks. Dell earns over 200 percent on its invested capital.[7]

Process Blindness

We could add many more examples of the eProcess advantage. It's so obvious to see. Why, then, don't companies exploit this opportunity? Why are they blind to process excellence? Blindness here means that they just don't see, not that they are incompetent. That the blindness is widespread is apparent in survey after survey. To take just one instance, the findings from the second annual review of medium-to-large U.S. companies—carried out by the Conference Board and reported in March 2000—are that many large companies still see eCommerce as detached from the mainstream of the business. Even though most of the 80 companies in the survey (90 percent of which earn more than $1 billion a year in revenues) are investing far more than last year in eCommerce, 25 percent admit that "they haven't established any adequate e-business functionality beyond that needed for "basic online brochureware." A primary author of the report concludes that "all the investment and management resources in the world don't amount to much if companies don't understand how their electronic business tracks with the rest of their business." Sixty percent don't have *any* electronic links between their own operations and key partners. Under 30 percent can process payments online. Yet 50 percent have full-time eCommerce development units, up from less 33 percent in the survey a year before.[8] Most businesses simply are not seeing eCommerce as about processes.

There are two main reasons for this. First, companies still tend to think of Internet business as "technology." The Web site then draws all their attention. That's understandable, given the complexity of designing, implementing, and operating a technology platform that must provide fast, reliable, secure, and easy-to-use service. But technology too easily and often diverts management attention from the basics of commerce. It also leads to the company's Internet service being isolated from many of the business units whose processes are critical to effective operations. So instead of a business strategy, we see an Internet strategy: plenty of information technology staff and marketing concentrating on the Web site design and operations. Who's even thinking about process?

The second factor creating process blindness among effective managers in first-rate companies is that it's not clear to them that a far-reaching impact of Internet business has been the extent to which processes that support or impede the customer relationship increasingly determine eCommerce success. When there are, for instance, more than 60,000 sites selling mutual funds over the Web, the site isn't the differentiator among them. When online players routinely cut prices by 10 to 15 percent compared to offline providers, price is less and less a differentiator. And when it costs $200 in marketing to attract a customer in financial services, the first business sale is bound to be a loss, so it is the repeat business that provides the margin.

These are now obvious in eCommerce just as it's obvious that it's the full customer experience that makes the difference, not just the experience at the Web site. But the obvious is missed again and again. Going back to our discussion of retailers, the 1999 holiday shopping season so clearly demonstrated the importance of back office fulfillment processes in electronic commerce. Companies rushed to spruce up their Web stores in anticipation of strong online sales. They were not disappointed. Business was up by a factor of four from the previous year for the same period, which in itself marked a fourfold growth from the year before that.

But while U.S. online holiday sales totaled more than $10.5 billion, the news that filled the newspapers concerned customers who could not get their orders on time, received the wrong goods, could not contact the company to get an explanation, and were incorrectly charged. This led to apologies, $100 vouchers, and at least one class action suit. The costs of process blindness are high when you consider that the crunch issue of 1999 was not the challenge of fulfilling orders during a record sales year. Rather, it was the fact that some online retailers fulfilled 80 to 95 percent of their orders on time and still disappointed their customers.[9] In particular, buyers were frustrated by the difficulties in dealing with the company beyond making the click to place the order. About a quarter of all eCommerce customers have some query—about payment, delivery, returns, or special needs, for instance. They then find out that the Web site is just a Web site—there's nothing behind it to help them.

The technology works. It helped generate record online orders for the 1999 holidays. But those orders were wasted in that customers aren't coming back, so the transactions are a loss instead of a loss leader for an ongoing relationship. The processes and operations were severely challenged, and the very best Web site design didn't compensate for that.

Online retailers are not alone in this gap between technology and process. In general, companies have been slow to recognize the eProcess opportunity. Figure 1-2 is an all-too-typical generic example taken from our own research and consulting experience in working with many companies. Our estimate is that well over two-thirds of companies are stuck in this mindset. As you read this, we suggest you ask what the fictional CEO who wrote the letter thinks are the drivers of eCommerce and who she thinks should take charge of them, plus what the chief information officer (CIO) thinks they are and who should take charge—and how. And what the hypothetical trade magazine it mentions thinks they are.

Memo

XYZ-CO Enterprises

To: Tom Carling, Chief Information Officer

From: Office of the President

Date: August 29, 2000

Subject: Our Web site

Thanks for your email telling me about the award we just got from *E-biz* magazine as one of its top ten Hot Web sites 2000. I suppose that's good news. But I have a big problem, and we can't pussyfoot about it any more. We are losing our shirts and possibly our jobs because of that site. I'm looking at a letter from yet another upset customer—he sent it registered snail mail because we never answer email. He placed his order July 10 and paid extra for next-day delivery. It's now August 29 and it still hasn't arrived. Why does this happen so often?

I talked with Jackson in marketing, and it's clear to me that he and operations never coordinate. Jackson's selling items we don't have in stock and Manufacturing doesn't know what to schedule for him. Meanwhile, Finance is dying from the extra workload XYZ.com's creating for them. Why didn't we agree on how to handle online credit authorization for new customers? I shouldn't have to spend my own time tracking down all the things that go wrong with our e-commerce business. I'm the CEO, not the Webmaster.

Oh, and one more thing. I took a look this morning at the original proposal for XYZ.com. Your staff stated very clearly, and I quote, that "The Web offers us a low-cost and reliable base for attracting thousands of new customers." It ain't low cost and it ain't reliable and it ain't bringing in business. We've been pouring out money for ads and slashing prices and we don't seem to be moving forward. That system crash last month is the third this year.

Obviously, the site isn't working. I now know what the "e" in e-commerce stands for: EXASPERATION!

Jane

Figure 1-2: Great site, bad business: A typical example

The hypothetical letter in Figure 1-2 from a CEO to her CIO captures the simple business reality of eCommerce: a great Web site does not mean great business. If Tom responds to Jane's memo by talking about improving the company's Web page—"Hey, we're adding one-click navigation and multimedia and we're going with XML"—he will have missed the point. More technology will not address this issue. If Jane in turn doesn't recognize that it's not her CIO's job to address all the process issues needed to rescue the situation, she'll continue looking for a technology fix for a business problem. In this example, process blindness will lead each to stumble around when the answer is clear: the processes are what matter.

The New Economy Is Not New Any More

Recall the famous line from the 1967 film *The Graduate* where Dustin Hoffman is cornered at a cocktail party and told the secret of the future: "Plastics!" If CEO Jane were at our party today, we'd whisper, "Process! eProcess!" We wouldn't shout "Internet!" That's old news. Indeed, our starting point in helping companies better manage their Internet business is that the Web is now integral to every company's competitive positioning and operations. We won't waste pages in our book urging our reader to get ready for the new economy, information economy, Web economy, wired economy, or the like. We take it as a given that the Internet is no longer a peripheral factor, but rather part of the emerging mainstream of business and a major driver of innovation. We don't know if Amazon will go broke or end up buying Wal-Mart, if the AOL and Time Warner merger is the end of the old economy, the start of the new economy, or just the economy. We can't tell you if Internet sales in 2002 will be $200 billion or $2 trillion or $20 gazillion. None of this changes the basic reality of our age: the Internet is as much part of everyday business as phones, fax, and personal computers.

It's not even useful to talk about the "new" economy any more. Do you mean by that term the old new economy—the economy of dot-com startups—or the new old economy, where more and more companies like General Electric, The Gap, and W.W. Grainger are moving to add online eProcess capabilities to their established commerce skills? Or do you mean the new new economy, which is so clearly the one where there's less and less distinction between clicks, bricks, clicks and bricks (established companies adding an online presence), and bricks and clicks (online companies such as AOL and Yahoo! making alliances with Wal-Mart and Kmart, respectively, to get a presence offline)?

Relationships! eProcesses! That's the new news for the new new economy that will lead to the new new new economy, which will be just "business." Online and Internet are old news. And "business" here means relationships, not transactions. The key to turning a Web site from a technical artifact to a business win is what lies behind the click—the business processes and capabilities that create customer trust, customer value, and, above all, customer retention. The winners in eCommerce are those that create a process edge that translates into process wealth through those relationships and repeat business.

In Internet business, relationships are *everything*. They form the new business capital of our age, the resources that generate profits, market valuation, brand, and sustainable competitive edge. What does this type of business look like?

A Sample eProcess Business

In this section, we show the profile of a hypothetical eProcess business, as eProcess smart as XYZ is process blind. (XYZ's the company we discussed earlier, whose CEO sent her CIO the letter that is quite likely to result in one of them moving on "to pursue other career interests.") It has elements of Dell, a leader in logistics processes, relationship management, and financial engineering; of Cisco, a leader in cost management and online relationships; of Amazon, whose repeat business rate is around 70 percent; of Yahoo!, which has built a relationship powerhouse, adding more and more personalization and customization; of AOL, a cash flow machine; of Charles Schwab, a winner in the online securities trading business despite having one of the highest commission fees; and of United Parcel Service, the company that has moved from a package delivery company to being in effect the entire logistics "department" of most online businesses. Well over half of all electronic commerce purchases of goods are handled by UPS, where handling means far more than just pick up and delivery. Its eCommerce services include warehousing, payment management, scheduling, and coordination of international trade documentation.

Here's the profile. We will call the company ePX, standing for eProcess Excellence. We've added some figures and examples from real companies that show that this is not a speculative fiction or fantasy. Every single characteristic of ePX is found in eProcess leaders. We provide some recent examples for each category of the eProcess success factor. The profile amounts to a to do list for eCommerce, as shown in Table 1-2.

Table 1-2: A To Do List for eCommerce

Things to Do	Instead of...
Design customer-centered processes	Running your online business over the established company-centered process base, centered on efficiency, administrative needs, standard operating procedures, and internal priorities
Focus on relationships	Transactions
Enable customer self-management of the relationship	Limiting customer interaction, making customer access complex and involving multiple contact points
Change incentive systems to reward contribution to the customer relationship and customer experience	Focusing staff on measures of functional unit performance, such as budgets and metrics that often encourage a local focus and discourage enterprise-wide collaboration on behalf of the customer
Expand relationships and make the Web site an interface to a wide and deep marketspace	Viewing the Web site as the company's isolated online storefront
Integrate the end-to-end supply chain	Viewing its components as individual responsibilities, separate functions, and disparate processes
Build collaboration and community	Build transactions, sales, and information

For each "to do" item in Table 1-2, we've added an "instead of" comparison. What's listed in the "Things to Do" column to some extent amounts to the business equivalent of New Year's resolutions. "This year I really will stop smoking" becomes the eCommerce resolution "We will be customer centered." Sure, but it's not that easy. It takes a lot of work. The items listed in the "Instead of..." column are what most companies really do, however pure their intent.

Design Customer-Centered Processes

ePX built a strong relationship base through careful attention to the processes that matter to *customers*. The company's Web site provides information and interaction in an intuitive and flexible manner. The site demonstrates a focus on designing the customer experience rather than on the customer being subordinate to the company's administration and operations. Fulfillment is impeccable, and when errors do occur, they are immediately recognized and fixed—every company makes errors and it's widely recorded that if it repairs them well, customer satisfaction is enhanced, not reduced. Exceptional handling of exceptions increases the trust that is at the core of the relationship and the basis for the brand.

Here are a few vignettes from leaders in customer-centered eProcess design:

> ▶ Patricia Seybold, author of the best seller *Customers.com*, states that online sales of her book were twice those of bookstores. "The traditional book industry has too many broken chains," Seybold continued. "When people look for a book and it is not on the shelf, the bookstore will offer to order it for you, but the sales clerks do not make a note of it and send it to headquarters. They lose too many sales because they don't close the loop."

> ▶ Sears makes it easy for new customers to apply for instant credit online, a process that in most companies takes days or even weeks and requires the applicant at the Web site to fill in and send information that will be processed offline. If approved, the customer can use the credit immediately.

> ▶ 1-800-flowers.com uses Net2Phone's technology so that customers can talk verbally with service representatives as they interact with the company at its Web site.

> ▶ Drugstore.com fills customer prescriptions online at a high price discount over pharmacies, but allows them to pick up their online purchases at a Rite-Aid pharmacy.

Focus on Relationships, Not Transactions

ePX views the Internet not in terms of Web "sites," but as the relationship interface between itself and its customers. This provides them with, in effect, their own private Web pages that are individually personalized. ePX maintains a constant two-way interaction with customers, alerting them to any problems and keeping them informed about the status of their orders. It provides customers with tools they use to manage their own accounts, configure their orders, and respond to offers customized to them. The result of these relationship ties is a 70 percent repeat business rate, which over time reduces the biggest single eCommerce investment cost: marketing and customer acquisition.

The following are examples of relationships versus transactions as the core of a company's eProcesses:

- ▶ If a trade is incorrectly processed or its network is down, a Charles Schwab account representative picks the problem up and solves it, at no cost to or effort by the client.

- ▶ MySchwab provides you with a personal Web page that can include information for you to review and manage your investments, customize your favorite sports news, check weather reports, and so on—and you don't have to be a Charles Schwab customer.

- ▶ Furniture.com has shown how to sell goods that most people assume need to be seen in a showroom. It provides access to online personal sales assistance and design consultants who will generate a "virtual showroom" for customers, displaying the goods according to their interest.

- ▶ Home Depot's Web site is really a project management consultancy service for small contractors. It helps them schedule planning and optimal delivery of items to the job site and even helps them locate electricians or carpenters.

Enable Customer Self-Management

A major win-win for both parties comes from enabling customers to be in charge of their own interactions with the company. This "self-management," which is a cornerstone of eProcess, saved ePX around half a billion dollars in administration and customer support in a single year. In passing, if that figure strikes you as implausible, it's very real. Cisco documented $550 million in savings in 1998 through customer self-management.[10] The implications are immense. The eProcess companies offer both best service and lowest cost. What Wal-Mart did to established retailers through this combination is surely what eSuccess companies in any business ecosystem will do to their established competitors.

The following are examples of the mutual benefits of self-management:

- ► MCI reports that its customers who manage their own account using its online tools are around 50 percent more profitable to the company and have a far higher retention rate.[11]

- ► Cisco has one customer who did more than $100 million of business with the company without a single human contact. The customer gets convenience, control, speed, and customization. Cisco reduces its own costs and gains a loyal customer who doesn't need handholding and is perfectly satisfied.

- ► It costs a company $10 to $20 to answer a query over the telephone, but only 10 cents to 20 cents to let the customer get an answer on the Web. The customer isn't left waiting on the phone or talking to an agent who may not fully understand the question or know how to answer it.

- ► W.W. Grainger sells $5 billion a year offline of machine maintenance and repair tools and around $150 million online. Its online customers are spending 20 percent a year more in total than they did when they made their orders by phone, fax, or mail, and their average order is twice as large.[12]

Change Incentives and Rewards

ePX had to rethink its entire incentive and reward systems to ensure coordination among its units *on behalf of the customer*. In most companies, these systems are designed on behalf of the company: performance against budgets, managing costs, and meeting schedules. At ePX, all business units now get a sizeable part of bonuses entirely based on customer-centered metrics. This includes sales reps, who were initially concerned that they would lose commissions as customers shifted their ordering to the Web; manufacturing, which was mainly rewarded on the basis of cost control and production efficiency; and finance, which in many ways had an incentive to provide customer and supplier disservice by being very rigorous—and slow—in credit evaluation and by stretching accounts payable.

The following are examples of companies recognizing and responding to the importance of making sure incentives encourage and reward a focus on the customer, not on internal priorities and functions:

- ▶ The former CEO of Marshall Industries, Jeff Rodin, says he believes the company's reward systems prevented rather than enhanced the customer relationship and that changing them was the single most urgent priority for online business.[13]

- ▶ American Airlines found collaboration across its business units to be its biggest challenge, requiring a culture change to encourage all business units to see its frequent flier Web service as a joint responsibility and opportunity.

Expand Relationships

As ePX built its relationship base, it added more and more services, exploiting both its brand strength and its technology platform. This strength makes it attractive to customers as well as a sought-after supplier of value-added services to other companies. ePX uses its information as an asset, offering its customers research information, shipping, access to financing, and many other services. The company sources these services through software links to other online businesses. In this way, it adds more and more capabilities, and strengthens the customer relationship, but with limited investments of capital and time.

The following are examples of companies extending their relationship span ever more widely from its original eCommerce offers:

- ▶ Yahoo! and AOL thrive on fees other companies pay it for a presence on their portal, such as $89 million from Drkoop.com for five years.

- ▶ AutoByTel announced in late January 2000 that it would sell cars online. It handles just about every aspect of car purchase: information, financing, insurance, extended warranties, and even delivery.

- ▶ Fidelity Investments sells thousands of mutual funds through its Web site, including its competitors' funds.

Integrate the End-to-End Supply Chain

More and more of ePX's process base is embedded in software, creating self-management capabilities for its customers and suppliers. In this way, it uses supply chain and trading partner hubs to reduce its supply chain costs substantially. It uses customized Web tools to do the same for its customers' processes, embedding business rules for purchasing and distribution into the relationship interface.

ePX relies on alliances and collaborations in its logistics and management of its technology platform, recognizing that no company can now go it alone and that it is only as strong as its weakest ally.

The following are examples of companies extending their supply chain logistics from single buying and selling transactions with individual companies to collaborative relationships across a value network:

▸ Ariba.com, an eProcurement software and services company, was launched in June 1999. By August of the same year, its trading hub was handling $100 billion of supply chain business between such companies as Hewlett-Packard, MCI, Cisco, and Dell.[14] It is moving rapidly to becoming a trading exchange rather than a buy-sell hub, adding electronic services such as contract management.

▸ Dell, Cisco, and Intel are companies selling more than a billion dollars of goods online, through customized sites that provide self-management for just about every element of their administrative processes. Their customer relationships and logistics value networks increasingly converge. Each drives the other. A customer order triggers the supply chain immediately and the supply chain generates the quality of customer service.

▸ Exodus Communications "hosts" "mission-critical" Internet operations for close to 2,000 eCommerce players. It has added consulting and technology alliances, including one with Andersen Consulting. Exodus charges customers about one-sixth of what it would cost these companies to operate their own facilities.

▸ When a consumer orders a personal computer from Gateway, Gateway doesn't ever touch the goods. UPS assembles the order from the contract manufacturer that makes the computer, and the other manufacturers and distributors for the printer, software, and monitor. It delivers the order and picks up the payment.

- A collaborative shared planning, forecasting, and replenishment initiative between Wegman's Food Markets and Nabisco increased sales by 40 percent and inventory turns by 29 percent.[15]

Build Collaboration and Community

ePX exploits every opportunity to make its site a vehicle for interaction with customers and for building community, including interest group forums, online tutorials, and seminars. It segments its relationships carefully, providing customized services according to the customer's profile and preferences. It backs up its Web operations with first-rate call center services, handled by well-trained staff. In addition, it links the Web site to sales and technical support staff, so that, for instance, if a customer encounters any problem, the site alerts someone to help immediately and directly.

ePX encourages interaction across its relationship base, with online seminars, discussion groups, and communication services, including news programs and online conferences.

The following are examples of a Web site becoming a meeting point for online collaboration and community:

- Buzzsaw.com brings together people in the highly fragmented construction industry. Architects, builders, and project partners can put an entire project online, posting documents and blueprints on a secure, private site, hash out details in online meeting rooms that include virtual whiteboards, and communicate flexibly and freely. One architectural company is using Buzzsaw for a project to build six casinos across the U.S. It began by posting the design blueprints for consultants to review.

- Marshall Industries has long been a leader in building customer relationships and communities online. Examples of its innovations include an electronic design center for customers to design chips online and simulate their performance, regular network seminars that bring customers and experts together to discuss specialized topics, and an online "chat" facility for its engineering communities. One of these seminars brought together engineers from 87 companies in 12 countries and resulted in Marshall selling several major development tools.

- The leading online financial service companies, such as E*Trade, Charles Schwab, and Fidelity Investments, all offer chat rooms, discussion groups, and tutorials. Customers build their own communities of shared interests.

eProcess Issues

ePX is the target profile for an eCommerce player to aim at. What are the management issues it must address to reach that target? If eProcess is the answer, what is the question?

After looking at and working with hundreds of companies, we see a set of questions:

- ▶ What exactly is eCommerce?

- ▶ What are the rules for the eCommerce economy?

- ▶ How much does eCommerce matter to businesses?

- ▶ What are the keys to eCommerce business success?

- ▶ What about the costs and payoffs?

- ▶ How does a company decide on what marketspace it should target?

- ▶ What executive and policy decisions do managers need to make?

- ▶ Are the answers to all these questions different for a startup company and an established company?

This book is our answer to all these questions. We begin our answers in the next chapter. Those answers start with understanding the economics of an eCommerce company, so we will end this first chapter with what we view as the long-term key to success in eCommerce: the financial structure of the online company.

The Economics of an eCommerce Company

For the past five years, business strategies for the Internet have focused on growth—in customers, revenues and, many skeptical managers would say, red ink. Now the urgency is not growth, but turning growth into profits. In this book, we focus on one of the key elements in this strategy: eProcess excellence. The other element is the company's business model—the basic framework for its Internet thrust in the coming years. The business model is the "Innovate or die" component, and eProcess is the business answer to "Execute or go broke." Of course, there is great opportunity to innovate within eProcess and much need to execute within the business model—

marketing, investment in technology infrastructures, alliances, and so on. But the focus of this book is helping leaders and executives at all levels of the organization move from business model to process base.

Economic Scenarios

There is a complex set of interactions between customer acquisition, margins, repeat business, and profitability. Understanding these relationships involves looking at different combinations in the form of scenarios. Each scenario depicts the economics facing one or more companies in eCommerce. These scenarios look at company margins, demonstrating the importance of striking a balance between the investments to build your business, your customer base, and your relationships.[16]

The Traditional Company

A traditional company experiences relatively low fixed cost and relatively low operating margins. In manufacturing, the pre-tax margin is typically around 5 percent. In financial services, it ranges between 7 and 12 percent. Figure 1-3 shows a simplified representation of the fixed operating cost base and the new margins for a company (revenues less variable operating costs and infrastructure and customer acquisition investments).

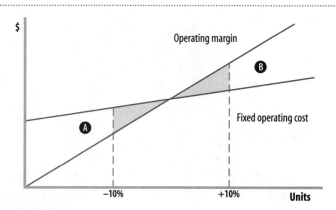

Figure 1-3: Traditional company margins

The stability of a traditional company, bounded in its assets, limits the value of significant investments in its operations or markets. It experiences relatively small losses when the business is 10 percent below its break-even point (area A in Figure 1-3). It also experiences relatively small gains when business goes above 10 percent of its break-even point (area B) because of the dominance of variable costs.

The dot-com Business

An online business is based on a different set of assumptions and assets. The company's fixed cost base largely consists of customer acquisition and technology costs as traditional assets are sourced to other value network players. Figure 1-4 shows the margin structure of a dot-com business. In general, an online business can expect an operating margin of 30 percent on its repeat business, with purely digital companies, such as auction sites, enjoying 70 to 85 percent margins. Compare Charles Schwab's use of $64 in assets to generate $1 of revenue to industry averages.[17] The catch for the dot-com player is that it has to spend money up front in large amounts before it can benefit from digital margins. But those margins are there!

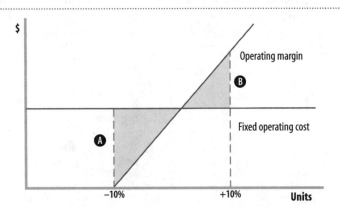

Figure 1-4: Online company margins

The online company operates at a substantial loss because it has to invest in marketing and infrastructures, which dramatically increase its fixed cost investments. Customer acquisition costs, which amount to anywhere between $50 and $200 per customer, depending on the type of eCommerce, easily overwhelm the revenue generated from these customers.[18] The costs can't be capitalized, and they appear as expenses on the company's profit and loss statement. This is not the disadvantage it may appear; if they are handled as depreciable capital, like a building, this hurts cash flow in that the company has to pay tax if it's profitable.

The online company looks like a disaster as long as customer acquisition costs exceed company revenues (area A in Figure 1-4). However, the company's revenues take off once they are able to operate above break-even, as the incremental margins on this business is huge (area B). Consider an online brokerage company with a customer acquisition cost of $200, a $10 trading fee, and 30 percent margins. That company would need the customer to trade 67 times, an average of five times per month, before trading revenues recouped the acquisition costs. Reaching this situation involves finding a way to generate additional incremental revenue without having to invest in acquiring new customers.

The Economics of eSuccess

The connection between relationships and eCommerce economic success rests in unlocking eCommerce margins through generating business without the burden of heavy customer acquisition investments. That happy situation arrives when a company generates repeat business from existing customers and decreases its fixed marketing costs, as illustrated in Figure 1-5.

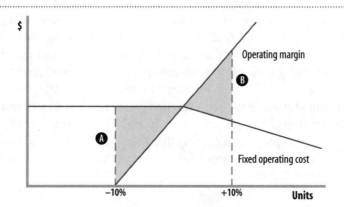

Figure 1-5: The margins of an eSuccess leverage the economics of repeat business

An eCommerce success involves building repeat and referral business. Repeat business provides a profitable revenue source unencumbered by the burden of customer acquisition costs. An eSuccess company enjoys network effects from an active customer base that generates referral business. Peer-to-peer or viral marketing relies on referrals and recommendations to lower customer acquisition costs as the network of customers reaches critical mass and becomes self-sustaining. It also relies on adding more and more services that do not have a high costs of goods or that are digital in form, such as information, fees for brokering, and payment for ads. Amazon may or may not make money in its retailing, but in a single week in late 1999 it signed up three promotional deals that will bring it $332.5 million in revenues over three to five years.[19]

The operating margin for this is about 80 percent. Amazon spent just $221 million in fixed assets through to February 2000. Barnes and Noble spent $472 million on its roughly 1,000 retail centers. Amazon's asset base scales up—that is, it can add huge volumes of digital revenue without significantly increasing fixed assets.[20] Think of this as CBS, NBC, and ABC for the Internet era. Amazon, Yahoo!, and AOL are operating on the same basis: build a giant franchise of repeat viewers/visitors and then make the money on Super Bowl ads/portal referrals.

The Economics of Disaster and Commoditization

Creating an eSuccess is the ambition of every eCommerce company. However, along the way to success the company must avoid creating an eCommerce disaster where company costs are above its marginal revenue. An eCommerce disaster occurs when the company is chasing customers so that its fixed costs keep growing without gaining the underlying business to generate operating revenues (illustrated by Figure 1-6). This is less a matter of reported financial losses on the profit and loss statement. You just plain run out of cash, and investors stop giving you any more. In early 2000, a number of companies started publicly reporting that they were not likely to have the cash to fund their operations for the rest of the year. There will be many more of these.

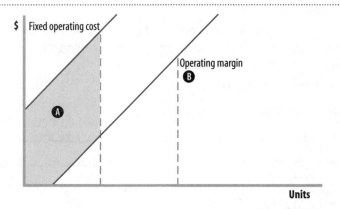

Figure 1-6: The margins of disaster

One indicator of a potential eCommerce disaster is where the company is spending an increasing rather than decreasing percentage of its total revenue on marketing and customer acquisition. The scene of this disaster is set as the company cuts prices and pays fees to portals to get business. This undercuts operating margins, and price cuts create their own game of commoditization as players seek to compete on price and little else. Obviously, the company will never get ahead, as it is spending hard marketing dollars to attract low-quality revenues. There are many Internet companies that reveal more than a slight likelihood of this being their fate.

Investors have been willing—even eager—to fund the ride, but when they decide to get off, the trip is over. Regardless of IPO money, a declining ratio of repeat business margin to customer acquisition expenditures is a disaster situation and is not sustainable. The company must find a way to break out of this cycle.

Create Success and Avoid Disaster

Avoiding an eCommerce disaster requires more than offering your products online. Setting up shop on the Web only broadcasts your prices and availability to the world, making you vulnerable to commoditization, razor-thin margins, and ever-increasing competitors. Competing on price alone is not the path to eCommerce success. To win in eCommerce, you need to offer more than product and price. You need to offer a relationship that builds trust and the value of your online brand.

How You Create an eSuccess

There are three core elements of eSuccess. The first is the company's business model. That must center on a combination of the six value imperatives that drive the eSuccess scenario:[21]

▶ Perfect your logistics.

▶ Perfect your long-term relationships.

▶ Harmonize your channels on behalf of the customer.

▶ Transform your capital and margin structures, as we described earlier.

▶ Build a power brand.

▶ Look to become a value-adding intermediary.

The second core eSuccess factor is to build the capabilities needed to exploit the business model. That rests on eProcess.

The third is to locate, retain, and mobilize the human and intellectual capital you need to fuse your business model and eProcess and to build a new entrepreneurial culture. That's another story and for another book. The story is only just unfolding in that companies are learning as they go how to mesh business, technology, and people. No one can reliably point to a blueprint for the eSuccess organization, beyond the obvious that it's built on speed and flexibility.

We do know the eSuccess business model and eProcess stories, though, and they are heads and tails of the same gold coin. Creating an eSuccess involves having an eProcess edge that focuses on issues of capability sourcing, process design, and relationship building. Intelligent sourcing establishes the asset flexibility and efficiencies necessary to create the operating margins of an online business that offset the marketing and technology infrastructure investments. Applying eProcess design principles creates a value network capability that centers on delivering customer commitments with speed, scale, and satisfaction. If executed well, your capabilities and processes foster ever-broader and ever-deeper relationships—relationships that transform your margins and build your eCommerce brand.

eCommerce success really does rest on building relationships and repeat business.

Chapter 2

Why Process Matters

At the end of Chapter 1, we listed eight questions that motivated the development of eProcess. Before we explore eProcess in detail, we need to answer those questions.

Question 1: What Exactly Is eCommerce?

There are many terms floating around for Internet-based online business: electronic commerce, e-business, e-services, Internet commerce, or even just "the Internet." We prefer "eCommerce" for three reasons. First, it's a reminder of what really matters: commerce and its correlated commercial relations. Second, it downplays the notion of this being electronic while still keeping the "e" as what distinguishes it from previous modes of commerce. Third, eCommerce signals that while the Internet is the core enabler of this new era of business, it includes many other information technology components, such as database management systems, corporate telecommunications networks, transaction processing software, enterprise resource planning (ERP) systems, packaged software, mainframe computers, personal computers, local area networks, firewalls, and servers. Making all these work together establishes the electronic commerce base; the Internet part of it has to be integrated with the rest.

Commerce is the issue. Commerce is the exchange of value between parties, and eCommerce is that exchange enabled via electronic means, though not confined to it—bricks now support clicks and vice versa. While this definition is bland, it does recognize that eCommerce is first and foremost about exchange, value, and relationships. Exchange creates a transaction relationship between the parties involved. Value opens up the possibility of relationships beyond the transaction: continued interaction, new forms of collaboration, repeat business, personal services, longer term contracts, accounts, and account management.

Commerce is conducted within a network of relationships governed by rules and implemented through interfaces between players and sourcing of responsibility among those players. eCommerce provides for new networks, new players, and new sourcing of responsibilities. It's all about connections. These connections may be summarized in the following sequence of statements, which add up to the syllogisms for the basic logic of eProcess:

  ▸ eCommerce is about *commerce*, not just "information" or "sales" or "hits."

  ▸ Commerce is built on *interaction*. It's a dialogue, a conversation for possibilities and commitments. The richer the interaction, the more the possibilities and the greater the scope of commitments.

▶ Value-based interactions become *relationships*—that is, they go beyond the transaction.

▶ Relationships depend on *processes* that cover both the routine and the exceptional. The quality of the routine processes is determined by efficiency, convenience, speed, and reliability. The quality of the exceptions is far more dependent on flexibility, judgment, and personal contact.

▶ eProcess defines the *priorities, rules, interfaces, and sourcing* of these processes, from routine to exceptional.

These statements provide a perspective on online business, which emphasizes the practices that make for successful relationships and profitable operations. Commerce rests on interaction rests on relationships rests on processes rests on prioritization and sourcing. That's eProcess in action.

That chain of logic places business processes at the very center of management. It views the Web site as the means to the business end, with sustainable competitive advantage coming from how the company leverages the site to support its processes, not the extent to which processes serve the site itself or are detached from it.

Question 2: What Are the Rules for the eCommerce Economy?

eCommerce connects customers, consumers, suppliers, and companies that previously could never be so interlinked. These connections define an electronic economy that is governed by new rules, many of which are only gradually becoming apparent. Rather than think of the Internet as a technical environment, it makes more sense to see it as the ultimate deregulation. It deregulates industries, for example. What "industry" is Amazon or AOL in? What is "banking" when any online player can provide some element of a traditional bank's services? What is a car "dealer" when CarBuy.com and AutoByTel act as information services and agents that handle more and more of the car selection, location, negotiation, financing, insurance, and delivery?

eCommerce bypasses and even mocks regulations about gambling, publishing, copyright, consumer protection, international politics, privacy, and taxation. That's a mix of good and bad, of course. There are very few binding regulations as yet in the Internet economy and where there are rules, many clever people are working on how to break them, most obviously in the area of security.

So at one level there are no rules, and many commentators compare the Internet to Dodge City and the western frontier. But there clearly are rules of good practice. Otherwise, there would be none of the consistent growth we've seen in eCommerce with no signs of any slowing down. Ordinary people of all ages, backgrounds, nationalities, technology knowledge and experience, and interests somehow find the deregulated eCommerce space a comfortable place to roam. They are still concerned about credit card and privacy risks, but they buy online and continue to do so. It's now harder for a business to stay offline than to go online.

There's one force that generates the rules of this unruly space: customer trust. That statement is more than a truism. What is truly unique about the Internet economy is that it is the first completely voluntary marketspace. No one *has* to be part of it. Consumers can live their lives without ever having to go to the Web. Electronic commerce—the eCommerce predecessor as represented by electronic data interchange links between large companies and their suppliers—was largely driven by an industry's power players. In effect, they forced their suppliers to adopt their systems and technology standards. Now, by and large, companies can do what they want in the business-to-business (B2B) space. It may not be a smart move not to go online, but it's not a requirement that your company do so. Even if you decide to be an online player, you have many choices of value network and partners.

Choice is what makes a customer. There have been many areas of business where there weren't any customers at all, and there still remain some. For example, if you are a small business seeking workers' compensation insurance or medical insurance, you beg more than buy. Until just a few years ago, telecommunications was dominated by regulation and monopolies, so businesses and consumers took what they were offered and were lucky if that was low-priced and high in quality—and it generally wasn't. The same was the case for the oligopolistic industries like banks, where you had a few choices within a very narrow range.

Here's our definition of "customer": a customer is someone who has choices, has the information to make those choices, is confident about doing so, and can't be prevented from making them. That's the Internet economy. It's marked by choices—price, range of products and services, information, and many more. Many of the new players that have shot to prominence in eCommerce did so because they created choices: eBay's auctions, Priceline's name-your-own-price, Amazon's massive book catalog, and the wide range of options for buying and selling stocks are just a few instances.

Other innovators provided the information and contacts needed to make choices. AutoByTel transformed the choice space for car buyers, for instance, and travel services sites such as Expedia and Travelocity empowered individuals and companies to decide for themselves what decisions to make about hotels and airplane bookings. B2B hubs did the same for businesses. Over time, customer confidence in making previously over-complex, unavailable, or risky choices has increased. Buying a car on the Web, applying for a mortgage, bidding on a contract, or ordering computers has become something routine.

And, of course, to the first three components of our definition of customer—choices, information to make the choices, and confidence in doing so—we must add the one that most matters: no one can stop you from selecting the choice for *you*, including the choice not to go near the Internet. The customer as well as eCommerce has been deregulated by the Internet economy.

What this adds up to is that customer trust sets the rules. Indeed, the electronic economy may be defined as the third phase in the evolution of the Trust Economy over the past 30 years. Up to the 1960s, customer choice was highly constrained. Banks were regulated in their offers, there was no telecommunications competition, airline prices and even routes were set by government rules, and most nations had largely nationalized their key industries and maintained tight trade barriers. In the U.S., the auto industry was collectively known as the Big Three.

Along came a piece of deregulation called Toyota and Honda. The Japanese car industry created choices other than the Big Three and niche foreign imports. Customers then showed what they would pay a premium for: trust in the product. The entire Total Quality movement centered on this, and U.S. carmakers and the consumer electronics industry faced an uphill struggle to recover trust. Now, while quality differences remain, all the main manufacturers offer excellent products. The trust premium shifted.

Information technology—ATMs, credit cards, toll-free numbers, and automated credit scoring—shifted that trust to the transaction and to convenience. We feel almost a constitutional right to a dialtone, always-available cash from the ATM, and fast delivery of pizza by phone. Ours has become the convenience society.

What happens when every company in a competitive sector offers plenty of choices, all of which are of high quality and equally convenient? The trust premium shifts again, to trust in the relationship. That's what "branding" means. A brand is a promise. Brand equity is the value created by customer trust in that promise. For most of this century, with manufacturing at the core of the economy, brands meant products: BMW, Nike, Coca-Cola, and IBM, for example. More recently, in the convenience society, brands mean services: McDonald's, Domino's, and Wal-Mart, for example.

And the brands of eCommerce? They are relationship brands. You can put many labels on them, such as portal, e-tailer, aggregator, Web site "stickiness," and the like, but they are fundamentally about relationship strength—and relationship is becoming everything in eCommerce. Amazon is a relationship brand; that's why it maintains its lead in book retailing, even though it rarely has the lowest available price.

So there really are plenty of rules in the electronic economy: rules of customer choices about the new trust premium, relationships. Transactions are cheap and the Internet makes them ever more so, through price competition, search engines, intermediaries, information, bots (software that roams the Web to locate the best deal), B2B hubs, electronic agents, and auctions. So transaction rules don't apply. Customers, not providers, decide what works, and there's rarely a transaction edge a company can sustain. There's no convenience edge, either. The Web is entirely about convenience as the minimum requirement for customer consideration. If you don't have it—and many companies don't—a more convenient competitor is just a few seconds away.

You thus can't win by transactions and convenience, though as eProcess firmly indicates, you can lose by lack of them. According to a survey published by Frederick Schneiders Research in November 1999, one in five users setting up a new online banking account doesn't complete the process. Why should they? It's not like the days when they had to put up with this "time-consuming red tape" because there was nowhere else in town to go to and the other banks were just as difficult to deal with.

The rules of customer choice and the relationship premium customers look for affect the structure and operation of the electronic economy and make the following the imperatives of relationship-building:

Build your company entirely around your customer. Customer loyalty is no longer a given. Customers now have easy access to low-cost competitors and can jump ship instantly. To bring those customers back—and to find and keep new ones—smart organizations are finding new ways to offer better value. With new data-gathering technologies, they are converting what they know about their customers into perfectly tailored goods and services. At the same time, they are maximizing convenience and transactional sources of transaction satisfaction—and becoming nearly indispensable to the customer.

Centering the company on the customer is a process issue in that how you treat the customer through your processes defines the dynamics and value potential of the relationship. Technology guarantees the integrity of online transactions in terms of handling them at speed, scale, and in a secure fashion. Your processes guarantee the integrity of the relationship as the company handles customers in "context," building relationships across time and, most importantly, providing superior service at times of customer crisis. Both technology and processes are necessary, as the failure of either jeopardizes the relationship.

Avoid the self-commoditization of your business that is an almost inevitable result of pushing products and services online. If you at this moment are the online provider with the best deal, that will change—and often change within the next few seconds. Your price will be matched. The emerging generation of software bots accelerates this. Dealtime enables shoppers to, in effect, park at the front door of a Web site. Shoppers inform Dealtime what they are willing to pay for an item offered by the site, and Dealtime's software watches until the time is right and sends an email with the information.

Build value networks that let you focus on your relationship strengths. No company is now an island. In the new economy, as the costs of forming electronic collaborations and online business alliances are dropping dramatically, an organization's ability to collaborate quickly and correctly becomes ever more critical. Where organizations once needed to own most or all of their value chain to compete, they can now quickly assemble virtual organizations from best-of-breed partners. When prudently crafted and managed, and when rapidly deployed, these collaborations lead to greater productivity, better cost-savings, and a degree of flexibility necessary for success in the new economy.

Think of your value network as a massive process factory that supports your key relationship strengths. If you are missing a relationship contributor, add it to your capability through electronic out-tasking and in-sourcing.

Design your enterprise for rapid growth. In an economy where value is virtual, old constraints on growth no longer apply. Unlike physical products, which require labor and resources each time they are produced, shipped, and sold, assets like information, intellectual property, and customer and partner relationships are virtually unlimited in growth and ultimate scale. Returns for traditional companies are based on the consumption and depletion of assets. Organizations can grow almost without limits, which means that even a new market can be dominated quickly by an entrepreneur who knows how to scale up fast.

Your experience and customer knowledge provide a reservoir of competitive advantage that grows in value as you apply it. Convert everything you know into revenue or market share. In the industrial economy, success went to those with the biggest physical assets. In an economy built on information, real value lies in knowledge-based assets such as brand, intellectual property, customer relationships, and partnerships. Once regarded as intangibles, these virtual assets can be leveraged quickly and cheaply across a global customer base. Correctly managed, these new assets become a freestanding source of revenue and lasting value—and the only credible path toward superior margins.

Information and experience now provide sources of this advantage as they enable companies to extend their products and services. This places a premium on the effectiveness and efficiency of your processes for developing and deploying new products and services.

As information becomes a new business currency, your processes will determine your ability to invest and apply that currency.

Connect with customers quickly before your competition does. Moving quickly has always been key in business, but in the new economy, being first to market is no longer enough. Whether introducing a new product to your external customers or a new way of doing business to your internal "customers," delivering value means delivering not just a product or service, but a focused, richly productive relationship with each customer.

Developing the capability to connect quickly is not easy. It requires more resources and energy than many companies are willing to commit. At a time when relationships matter more than ever, being able to build them fast is essential. This increases the importance of gaining process expertise and experience. Companies are no longer given time to shake out their customer service and production process, because in the new economy, coming in second may be the same as coming in last.

Process excellence is an entry condition as customers and the competition will not give you time to get it right.

Question 3: How Much Does eCommerce Matter to Businesses?

That's a question that has changed in the past year. It used to be "Does eCommerce matter?" with many managers agreeing it was important for some industries but not their own, or that it would be important sometime but not yet. Now there are very few managers who see it as not mattering at all. Given that eCommerce still comprises only 1 percent of the economy, that very few companies are making money, and that all the wild claims about it killing off traditional business have been invalidated by the convergence of clicks and bricks, their question now is "*How much* does it matter?"

There are many possible answers to this question, ranging from "The Web's the future of business" (the positive opportunity) to "Your competitors are online so you better be, too" (the defensive necessity). Those aren't very helpful for taking action because they don't provide guidelines for how to respond to the opportunity or the necessity. Those attitudes largely reinforce the view that it's the online element of Web business that is key.

We offer a different view. eCommerce matters because it opens a company to something unique: a degree of relationship intensity that provides for massive business expansion and innovation. eCommerce combines innovation with a degree of profitability that, while it is very hard to attain and very expensive in terms of up-front investment, is unmatched in modern business.

In other words, it's a commercial opportunity not to be missed.

Widening the Competitive Gap Between Relationship Leaders and Laggards

eCommerce matters because it radically accelerates the increase in variance among operating margins and performance. For the leaders, it is a massive opportunity. For the laggards, it is a long slide to the bottom. For the average performer, it is a choice of opportunity or slide. Again, this is not new. Wal-Mart almost slaying Kmart in retailing via point-of-sale technology, the great airline reservation systems wars, and the transformation of banking are all instances where industries were reshaped in a decade. Of the top 20 discount chains in 1980, just four were still in business in 1990. The airline leaders of 1980 are the quaint historical relics of 2000: Pan Am and Eastern. In both instances, technology was the force that most determined winners and losers.

One simple figure that illustrates the widening variance comes from the University of Texas's 1999 survey of the Internet economy. This well-grounded study calculates the average revenues per employee for U.S. business as a whole as $160,000, but for Internet players it's 65 percent higher. That's a formidable advantage. Again, it continues a long-established trend driven by the combination of technology and process. The gap between the per employee revenues and profits of the leaders and the median player in any industry is typically 50 percent.[1] What the Internet adds to this is a rate of change that compounds the gap. The University of Texas reports that the Internet economy grew by around 70 percent a year between 1997 and 1999.

So, eCommerce matters because we have seen all this before. What is different is the degree of change and the speed of change the Internet brings. While we do not know exactly what the business landscape will look like in 2010, any more than we knew in 1990 what that of 2000 would be, it is clear that it will be entirely reshaped. Given the past, we know the eCommerce redefinition of business will be greater. The technology that did the reshaping of banking, retailing, and airlines in the pre-Internet era was primitive, limited, expensive, and slow by comparison with that of the Internet.

So, too, was the degree and pace of change. Executives need to keep in mind that Amazon was founded in 1995, had changed the rules of book retailing by 1997, and was a mature company by 2000. eCommerce does not matter because it is new and all about the Internet. It matters because it is a continuation of the move of information technology from the periphery of business to its mainstream. It matters because this move is faster, bigger, and wider. It is so fast, so big, and so wide that already it has affected more customers, companies, services, sectors, channels, and nations in its first five years than the prior total historical investment in information technology.

Scale Fast and Big

eCommerce also matters because it scales so well. Can you think of any business that in five years built a customer base of 100 million? Yahoo! did. Can you think of any company that operates in the following markets, with a 70 percent repeat business rate: books, generic drugs, CDs, videos, auctions, and online shopping malls? Amazon, of course. How about a business with 80 percent operating margins? That's eBay. A billion dollars of after-tax cash flow on under $5 billion in sales? It is AOL. A billion dollars a *month* of online sales? Intel, which achieved that level in less than a year.

The relationship opportunity, the margin opportunity, and the scaling opportunity: these are the basic reasons why eCommerce matters.

Question 4: What Are the Keys to eCommerce Business Success?

Business models. Process excellence. Relationships. Being a first learner. eProcess. It is outside the scope of this book to review business models; they are the basic frameworks for the company's eCommerce strategies.[2] Whatever the model, its execution rests on the execution of its process capabilities. The credibility of the model plays a major role in determining what capital the company can attract from investors. Repaying that investment rests on process excellence, relationships, and being a first learner.

Process Excellence

Regardless of the business model and capital investment—the main components for "Innovate or die"—eProcess has to be the priority; it's the "Execute or go broke" piece. This is becoming more and more the case, for the obvious reason that there is no advantage in just a Web site. The market is so crowded with new entrants that adding a "me too" site only paves your way for commoditization as you compete on price. Success requires more than competing on price; it requires building something special based on your capabilities, because you are fighting for the relationship.

Relationships

Relationships provide the basis for repeat business and profitability necessary to create an eSuccess. Relationships do not happen by accident; they are constructed through the sourcing and design decisions that build your capabilities. Designing for relationships requires a customer-centered approach to your capabilities that recognizes the roles of technology and process in capability design and operations.

Transactions are the focal point of eCommerce technologies. Technology must ensure the integrity of the transaction concerning processing, data integrity, and security. These are substantive issues given the openness of electronic channels and their access to information. While individual transactions are important, a transaction does not, by itself, make a relationship.

Relationships build over time across multiple transactions. Building the relationship is the responsibility of your process capabilities that ensure customers are handled in context, crisis situations are handled properly, and commitments are fulfilled. A company builds relationships when it can handle all three of these obligations and as customers recognize the value of repeatedly doing business with your company. The resulting trust establishes the basis for your online brand.

Recognize that technology and process capabilities are interdependent, as failure of the transaction places the relationship at risk. Technical and process excellence are prerequisites to building relationships and creating value.

Be a First Learner Rather Than a First Mover

The old notion of "first mover advantage" was that whoever got the site up first gained a massive competitive edge. That's really a myth. Amazon, Yahoo!, and eBay certainly got there ahead of the pack, but they would easily have been displaced by others who tried to imitate them and had a stronger brand and more capital to spend, if all they had was a technology presence. Consider how Amazon has displaced many "first movers" as it adds new product categories. One of the companies it beat out as leader—in just four months—was CDNow, the first mover in selling compact discs online. In early 2000, CDNow was flagged in a controversial article in *Barron's*, the investment weekly periodical, as likely to run out of cash to fund its operations before the end of the year.

Even if there once was a natural first mover advantage, it mainly meant catching others by surprise. There's no surprise left. Many companies were blindsided by startups like Amazon and Ariba. They discounted their impact. Most of the *Fortune* 1000 were very slow to recognize the need to shift their business models to address the new competitive context, or they tried to move their existing business model online. There was a flurry of investment in dot-com subsidiaries and new startups. With so much going on and so little proven business experience to guide their efforts, established businesses continued to be taken unaware.

But now that's all changed. There is not a single large company left that is not on the Web and, of course, thousands of Web ventures are launched every week. Any successful new model is quickly copied and often improved upon. Consider just three of the main innovations of eCommerce: pricing schemes, B2B, trading hubs, and application service providers. There already are many hundreds of each of these. What will differentiate them? The site itself is not the critical success factor. It is more of a critical failure factor; a Web site must be reliable, easy to navigate, secure, and fast. Otherwise, customers stop accessing it.

Sustained advantage is based on being a first learner rather than first mover. The competition and rules change too fast in the electronic economy to guarantee the structural barriers and lock-out associated with first movers. The only sustainable advantage is through the relationships you build and what you learn from those relationships. If you are a first learner, you are able to bring new products and services to market faster than your competitors. This further strengthens your relationships as customers recognize your ability to learn and serve their needs. This establishes a virtuous cycle that is hard for others to match or displace.

The first learner is also the one most likely to be the first brander—that is, it gains the key advantage of all, that of becoming an Internet brand instead of just an online company. It's interesting to note that the many press reports concerning AOL moving onto the *Fortune* 100 list headlined it as the first Internet company to do so. But AOL is not an Internet company at all; it runs its own proprietary telecommunications network, which *connects* to the Web. That doesn't matter. It's an Internet brand and that gives it immense power and influence in the Internet space.

Question 5: What About the Costs and Payoffs?

The costs of Internet business are huge, often cripplingly so: spending 20 percent of revenues or more for marketing; about the same for building and operating technology and customer support infrastructures; price discounts of typically 10 to 15 percent; shipping costs averaging 11 percent for retailers that offset the advantage of no sales tax; fees for being positioned on a portal that consumes marketing budgets, $5 million a year on average and far higher for an alliance with one of the Internet power brands.

All this adds up to a heavy up-front investment demanding capital from investors and a long period before the company becomes profitable. Many will not ever be profitable. Just as much of first mover advantage was a myth, so is the notion that Internet business is low cost.

The eCommerce payoff comes from transforming margins. Despite the fact that most Internet companies are as yet not making any profits and it will be years before they do so, the evidence is clear that Internet business is incredibly profitable while at the same time providing a good deal for the customer.

Table 2-1 lists examples of that evidence. It includes figures from AOL, Yahoo!, and others. It's worth bearing in mind that it took AOL a decade and half a billion dollars in marketing before it broke even. Now it's generating $1.2 billion dollars a year in cash flow, at an annual "run rate" of around $6.5 billion in revenues.[3] Its marketing expenses as a percent of sales are falling as its repeat business increases. The cost of operating its network has dropped by 10 percent. One of the key issues in the economics of eProcess business is that relationships are expensive to build, but over time they shift the company from a high variable cost/low operating margin to a high fixed cost/very high operating margin on repeat business.

Table 2-1: Sample Financial Performance Measures

	Yahoo! 12/31/1999	eBay 12/31/1999	AOL 6/30/1999	Dell 1/31/2000	Cisco 10/30/1999
Revenue growth (3-year average)	291%	131%	94%	68%	63%
Gross margin (current FYE)	80%	74%	43%	21%	65%
Net margin (current FYE)	10.4%	4.8%	16%	6.6%	17%

It is worth remembering that Yahoo! has never charged subscribers—more than 100 million of them—for its services. In 1999, it charged advertisers $588 million dollars for access to those subscribers. Yahoo! and AOL have a special advantage as Internet companies that do not deal in physical goods. That advantage is operating margins of around 80 percent on its repeat business. We stress "operating margin" and "on repeat business" because its costs of customer acquisition represent an investment for the future more than a current expense. We consider those investments logically as a capital investment for the future and treat them like research and development when looking at the business model and financial performance. In looking at the economics of Internet business, the key issue is capital and margin. If capital outlays keep growing faster than operating margins and repeat business grow, the company will not make it. If it does, scale starts to work to its advantage.

Question 6: How Does a Company Decide on What Marketspace It Should Target?

This is the toughest question to answer. In this chapter, we will give what may appear to be a weaseling reply: it should segment its market on the basis of relationship and community opportunities, and it should personalize everything. In later chapters, we will expand on this concept, which is at the core of eProcess.

The Internet is self-segmenting. Customers have total control over their choices. They really can take it or leave it. There are two main and conflicting reasons they take it. The first is price and convenience; the Web is paradise for bargain hunters, a giant discount mall. Only a very, very few players can make money being an eCommerce commodity, and many that tried it are now gone. The costs of customer acquisition and technology infrastructures are just too high. The second reason customers choose to come back again and again is not value in the deal but value in the relationship, *on their own terms*. Much of that relationship value comes from personal and customized service backed by the processes that deliver customized service.

The flood of MyXYZ sites like My.Yahoo and MySchwab center on this. But there are many other sources of relationship value, such as communities of interest—personal, professional, political, social, family, etc. The "etc." might be rephrased as "as many as you can dream up."

There is a lot of dreaming up going on. A relationship-centered site has what the Internet trade calls "stickiness." It builds a brand, creates portal power, and above all begins to transform margin structures. Targeting the relationship and building, or joining up, with a very strong value network then helps deal with the capital investment challenge. The more focused the target market, the lower the cost of marketing. The stronger the value network, the higher the revenue per dollar from investment in technology infrastructures.

As the costs of acquiring customers get higher and higher, it makes more and more sense to focus expenditures very carefully. One of the main advantages of B2B eCommerce is that many of the relationships are self-defined already and do not demand massive ads. For example, the partners in a manufacturer's supply chain know about each other, know where to go to get industry information, and have plenty of reasons to join together. In addition, in B2B relationships, the hub at the center of a value network that brings buyers and sellers together has the advantage of digital margins. Auction hubs typically charge 1 to 10 percent as a fee. Electronic brokers charge 5 to 10 percent commission versus the 20 to 60 percent established intermediaries generally charge.

So, going back to our "weaseling" response, there's no cookbook answer about targeting your marketspace—relationship base plus value network—and it's in no way easy for any company to zero in on the right business model, aimed at the right customers, with the right marketing and the right execution. What is absolutely clear is that it's the customer who seals the relationship bond. Take it or leave it is the rule: take the relationship or leave the site. It is the customer's option.

Question 7: What Executive and Policy Decisions Do Managers Need to Make?

The executive responsibility is to take charge of all this change and recognize that eCommerce is about business. Executives must remove their "process blindfolds" and build the eCommerce capabilities that encompass technology, process, and organizational change. Executives cannot delegate this responsibility to the company's technology, other leaders, managers, or staff.

It is not the senior manager's job to handle all the eProcess details, but the business leadership must ensure that authority and accountability are meshed—that someone is in charge. Executives have to take command of the company's business model for eCommerce. No one else can. They must take a tough, company look at the company's incentive and reward systems. They must understand (as the CEO and CIO of XYZ-CO in Chapter 1 clearly did not) the nature of Internet economics. It is up to the executives to support line managers in building and operating the capabilities and value network required to create relationships and to deliver process excellence through flawless execution.

This requires them to make eProcess an enterprise-wide priority.

Question 8: Are the Answers to All These Questions Different for a Startup Company and an Established Company?

No.

Startups and established companies start their eCommerce business from the same basis—zero. Both have to build their business from this starting position, ensuring that company processes and operations attract customers, build relationships, and reach profitability.

While the answers are the same, existing companies face additional challenges around how to integrate their emerging online business with their existing operations. Startups can avoid issues such as channel harmonization and migrating existing customers. Recent performance suggests that existing companies face an uphill struggle when competing with online companies in the areas of order fulfillment and relationship building. Consider a study by Andersen Consulting that showed that pure e-retailers delivered their orders when promised 80 percent of the time compared with an existing company online performance of 20 percent.[4]

There are many areas of business where established companies retain advantages, of course. If, as seems almost certain in the longer term, Internet sales become subject to some form of tax, which most online companies don't have to charge today, the heavy burden of shipping costs will offset much of online sellers' low prices, and we'll see ordering online (clicks) complemented by picking up the goods at the store (bricks). Similarly, in areas where there are few online power brands, trusted names like The Gap have shown that consumers are likely to go to their online site if only because it's a familiar name or because they don't want to sort through all the masses of Internet companies with strange names overloading them with ads, offers, and noise.

Well-run companies win in eCommerce because they know how to exploit the commerce opportunity and eProcess priorities. Ones that rely only on the "e" in eCommerce lose.

eProcess as a Core Competence

The questions posed in our first chapter and answered in this second one are not really about the Internet. They relate to the capabilities and core competencies a company needs for the eCommerce era. A business is defined by what it *does*. In other words, its process capabilities determine its ability to take charge of change rather than react to it. Perhaps in the first few years of Internet business, technology capability may have been what most influenced its Internet readiness. Now, though, the company's best option is to source technology skills and resources through alliances and collaborations, with a small information technology group responsible for the design of its eCommerce technology platform (the Web site, links to internal systems and information resources, and the supporting operations base). The company must then build the new management, governance, and alliance processes needed to ensure the integrity of the platform.

It makes less and less sense to try and manage all the technology in-house. The priority for the company should be to focus all its efforts on the *commerce* elements of electronic commerce. That is in itself a huge job. Why make it harder by taking on technology operations? Technology governance, yes, but all the complexity of large-scale, multi-application integration real time? There are a relatively small number of companies that possess special technology capabilities that are a major core competence they should continue to build on. For most companies, the complexity of technology integration—telecommunications, databases, new eCommerce software for customer relationship management, existing transaction systems, external systems, and data resources—is escalating at a pace they cannot keep up with in terms of skills and ability to locate specialized expertise. The general imperative is to minimize the technology your company has to manage. That means technology alliance processes are ever more strategic.

eCommerce Capabilities

The challenges of eCommerce match the opportunities and vice versa. They require a new style of doing business. eProcess capability is the combination of tangible and intangible assets the company deploys in a part of its business. The tangible assets include its technology and, if it is an established company and not an Internet-only online company, its branches, operations, infrastructures, and facilities. The intangible assets are the information, processes, and organization that leverage the facilities and assets. The resulting capabilities form the building blocks for the company to mobilize for innovation, as depicted in Figure 2-1. Customer service, for instance, is a capability that involves technology, people, and process that must be integrated and must operate together. Add the Internet into the mix and the same requirements apply. The core process model provides a sample list of the capabilities required to be successful.

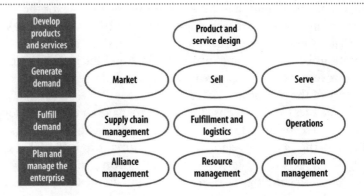

Figure 2-1: Core process capabilities

In the early days of eCommerce—roughly late 1995, the first year of Amazon's operations and the first full year of Netscape's Navigator browser—process was not only neglected, but also in many ways displaced by the Web. Observers pointed to Amazon's competitive advantage being in its having no warehouses to run, relying on distributors. The very idea of Web business was that it eliminated the need for physical operations. The metaphors of the era were those of cyberspace, wired, virtual, and info-somethings.

That era is well over, in just five years. Here are some of the lessons that Andersen Consulting and other progressive companies have learned:

► Marketing is key.

► Physical operations can matter as much as or more than online ones.

► Clicks and bricks (online plus offline channels) are the new game.

► Technology management processes require much more than merely setting up Web sites.

► Organizational capabilities and processes must change.

► The customer's perspective defines the value of a process.

Moving from the technology-centric "e" side of eCommerce to the business-centric "C" side involves looking at these factors and understanding how to build repeat business through relationships. These lessons serve as a way to recognize that there is a whole new economy with new rules and areas of focus.

Marketing Is Key

Originally, the assumption about Internet business was that a company could attract online customers through online ads, that the very size of the Web population of surfers would make it easy to gain hits, and that hits turned into customers. This has been termed the battle for eyeballs—get them to your site and the rest is easy. Of course, it was not and is not that easy.

The cost of customer acquisition makes marketing key to your success for both business-to-consumer and business-to-business Web sites. Effective marketing must be more than capturing eyeballs, it must target on and build repeat business. The challenge is considerable as studies show it takes more than 75 visitors to a Web site to generate a single repeat customer.[5] Ineffective or poor marketing sets the stage for the e-disaster as the company cannot gain the relationships and repeat business to reach escape velocity and break free of heavy customer acquisition costs.

Physical Operations Can Matter As Much As or More Than Online Ones

This might be called the holiday surprise. In 1998, consumer purchases over the Internet were four times those for the same holiday period in 1997, and customer satisfaction halved, mainly because of poor offline processes: order fulfillment, timeliness, inventory management, and liaison between marketing that handles the front-end Web site offers and operations that handles the back end. During the pre-holiday shopping season in 1998, there was little discussion of process; there were daily press reports on it in 1999.[6] In 2000, it became the main topic of discussion about e-tailers. This really should not have taken three years to discover.

The shift from site to process is symbolized by Amazon moving into the warehousing business on a very large scale. The trick here is to invest intelligently in physical operations, creating those that matter most to customer service and continuing to out-source the rest. The details of managing inventory, responding to customers, and handling shipments demands as much meticulous attention as does the technology. When physical operations don't fulfill Web-based commitments, the Web site design becomes irrelevant.

Clicks and Bricks—Online Plus Offline Channels—Are the New Game

Far from the growth of the Web meaning the disappearance of traditional "bricks and mortar" operations, increasingly companies see value in meshing physical channels, call centers, and branches/stores. What this means, of course, is that each offers special advantages to the customer and to the company. Even though 1-800-FLOWERS has been selling online since 1992 (through a deal with America Online) and has had its own Web site since 1995, only 15 percent of its orders are made online. An executive comments that "A lot of people browse through the selections online, but purchase using the telephone. Or they make an online purchase, but follow up over the telephone with questions about delivery. And customers want a consistent shopping experience, whether they log on to a Web site, call in an order, or walk into a store."[7] 1-800-FLOWERS sees the call center and Web as a single channel, not separate ones.

Technology Management Processes Require Much More Than Setting Up Web Sites

The term "scalability" has replaced "integration" in the vocabulary of information technology professionals. Scalability refers to the ability of a company to handle massive, unpredictable, and sudden increases in customers and transactions. Many online players thought all they had to do was set up a Web page at low cost and simple operation. They spent a few thousand dollars for the initial site, using designers who knew Web tools. They increased this investment to hundreds of thousands of dollars to add transaction processing, security, and network management. Crash!!! Overload!!! Cynics began to talk about WWW standing for World Wide Wait. Crash!!!

Far from it being easier to run a Web operation than the old in-house information technology platform, in practice, the demands for reliability, speed, security, and scalability strain both the technology and technology management capabilities. New processes have had to be invented almost on the fly, and new relationships and collaborations, too. In particular, companies need strong relationships with their technology providers. This is not a matter of customers and vendors or out-sourcers. The need is for tight bonds, close communication, and joint planning.

Organizational Capability Must Change

One of the main targets of reengineering was the "stovepipe" functions and processes of the vertical company. The trend of this and all the other process movements of the past decade has been to substitute for stovepipes self-managing teams, cross-functional processes, and worker empowerment. Much of this was merely good intentions or empty rhetoric, contradicted by the frequent reengineering/downsizing/firing link.

eProcess makes it essential, though. The stovepipes represent a process base designed to meet the company's own operational needs. eCommerce demands a process base designed to meet the customer's preferences. Here are just a few examples of companies that are leaders in eCommerce having to initiate major new organizational processes:

- ▶ Cisco's sales force was reluctant to lose direct contact with customers and to lose commissions from existing customers for business they do over the Web. Cisco adapted its reward systems so that the rep gets credit for any sale regardless of channel. It also created an "ambassador" position—a person who walks customers through their first online session.[8]

- ▶ American Airlines' many divisions had no incentive to keep its site for frequent flyers updated. The organizational change required getting some departments to actively promote American Airlines' products and services on the Web and provide and maintain accurate information. Now, 40 people across the company handle this new process and vie with each other to provide new content for the customer.

- ▶ AMR (a manufacturing company) sourcing demands new openness in information, communication, and contracting processes. Previously, the rule was you never shared demand or production information with suppliers because it gave them an unfair advantage. An executive comments that "you'd be fired for even suggesting it." Now, you should be fired for not making it happen.[9]

▶ The CEO of eToys emphasizes all the organizational processes his "virtual toy superstore" must have in place. "Inventory management is the great Web-commerce business process that no one seems to know much about. It is the true barrier to entry. Yet, on the back-end logistics side of things, you absolutely have to get it fit right for your business. If you do not get it to work, the exceptions will kill you because the exceptions, with their customer service expectations, will send your profit margins right out the window."[10]

The Customer's Perspective Defines the Value of a Process

This is the crunch issue. The customer, not the company, initiates electronic commerce. Customers are entirely in charge of eCommerce, and customers decide what's of value, not the company. There are many "background" processes the company may not view as a priority, but that are key for the customer. Many of the inconveniences and irritations customers report about Internet services often reflect process designs the company prefers for its own efficiency, costs, or just maintenance of the status quo and avoidance of new investments.

Retailers may view handling of returns as something to organize "efficiently" and not permit exchanges of goods bought online to be made in its local store. Customers, on the other hand, view easy returns as an important element in their decision to make a repeat purchase. Surveys regularly show that a majority of companies either do not accept emails from customers or simply ignore them. Responsiveness, however, is a significant contributor to deep customer relationships. A surprising number also do not link the Web site to their suppliers; orders made electronically are handled via paper documents and the existing workflow base, introducing delays, errors, and unreliability. These put the relationship at risk as well as build an unnecessary cost burden.

The eProcess Agenda

eCommerce requires eProcess. The days of just setting up a Web site are long over. This is all about commerce. It is easy to show that far from the Web site being in itself the core of eCommerce, it is the eProcess base that turns the site into an effective relationship interface, and it is the relationship that establishes eCommerce success. A

Web site is not in and of itself a relationship. It's just an interface between customer and provider or between businesses in a logistical chain. Workflow processes are not an interface in and of themselves. They are just an operational support to the company's relationships.

The eProcess company has a relationship advantage, a financial capital efficiency advantage, an organizational simplicity advantage, and an employee productivity advantage. That's what eCommerce is really about. The eProcess company manages by interface: the Web is the relationship interface it uses to embed processes in software, out-task, and in-source. It can choose how to source and coordinate all its processes. The traditional company does not have the choice—it must handle most of its processes in the traditional way.

Traditional companies make the transition to electronic commerce though giving themselves an eProcess edge. That edge concentrates on intelligently sourcing capabilities and process design that build relationships and repeat business. This edge raises asset and organization efficiency by concentrating on the capabilities that matter most to the customer and your online brand. Achieving this edge involves understanding the new role process plays in the Internet era and how you can use this role to create an eSuccess.

Chapter 3

Redefining "Process" for the Internet Era

Process, the second key factor we identified in eCommerce success, follows from and is driven by the first, relationships. Relationships are *the* issue. Companies therefore have no choice but to focus their efforts on processes in two main areas: deepening the customer bonds and reducing the costs of doing business. They must be cost efficient both to afford the substantial investments and price-cutting eCommerce requires and to run smoothly and reliably, as logistics is an indirect but integral part of the customer relationship.

These are obviously process issues, but not in the traditional sense of the term. eCommerce requires a new slant on exactly what a "process" is.

Process History

Historically, process has been defined mainly in terms of workflows, tasks, and activities. Processes in this sense are sequential and largely discrete linear steps, with a focus on transforming inputs into outputs. This mindset is apparent in many process movements, such as Total Quality Management (TQM) and reengineering. These strongly reflect the industrial engineering discipline that began with Frederick Taylor in the 1920s, continued through the quality movement and underlies the reengineering revolution—or disruption, depending on your viewpoint of its results. Business process reengineering sought to remove cost, improve performance through streamlining, and redesign the processes from this perspective.

Viewing process as input-process-output is a powerful conception but also a narrow one. How narrow is apparent in the typical diagrams you see in books on TQM and reengineering. They are packed with lines connecting boxes and diamonds that show questions and choices, like "Is this a new customer? If yes, then check credit record. If no, move on to step A102." Figure 3-1 shows an example of the order-to-cash process for a restaurant.

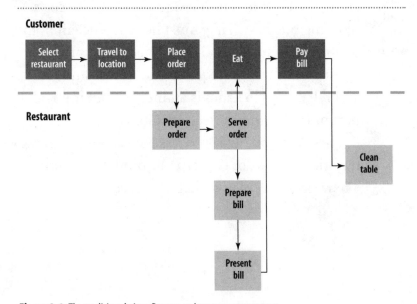

Figure 3-1: The traditional view: Process as input-process-output

This is a little like reading a textbook. You start at page 1 and work your way through to the end. You can skip pages or go back, but it's a fairly systematic process. You can engineer—via TQM—or reengineer the sequences. They have a beginning, middle, and end. Such representations and treatments are very well suited to structured routine activities, such as placing an order, handling a loan application, or shipping goods. And the clearer the steps and business rules, the easier it is to embed them in software. Indeed, much of the cost saving and improvement in customer service enabled by the Internet comes from simple transactions such as customers placing their own orders, with software asking questions and taking the needed steps, or applicants providing financial information, and software granting or declining a loan request. Software can initiate shipment of goods, issuing instructions about where, when, and how to send them, and so on.

The traditional process-as-workflow view is powerful, but it has its limitations. Look at all that's missing from Figure 3-1. Although the workflow representation of a waiter taking an order from a customer, the kitchen preparing the food, and the waiter delivering the order are very much the same for Joe's diner and Chez Basil, it doesn't capture anything about what makes one a better value and a better experience over the other. It's the difference between a textbook and an interactive multimedia experience, such as some of the superb Web sites for buying a car. There, you want to be able to jump in anywhere, move around, restart, get different types of display, check out financing while you're evaluating features, look at technical information, send email messages, ask questions, and perhaps talk to a salesperson while you're online at the Web site. It's an experience that's highly interactive, nonlinear, and involves many parties—for example, the site may offer extended warranties, financing, and insurance through its links to other online services. These all work together through interaction between you and the Web, with you making *your* choices. You're in control of the process. Rather than being a linear sequence, it's more of a hub and spoke, with you at the center, initiating questions and requests and receiving answers and offers.

Figure 3-1 reflects a solution looking for a problem. It can be applied to some of the eProcesses that the car site coordinates and provide highly streamlined workflows, but only some. That means at best it offers an incomplete blueprint for eProcess. The engineering tradition of process improvement focuses very much on those processes that can be streamlined and whose steps and activities can be sequenced. That's why TQM was so successful in manufacturing. It's also why reengineering cut out so much waste in administrative processes and customer service processes that involved a customer initiating a request and an agent walking through the steps to complete it. It's an input-process-output model.

But consider all the processes it can't incorporate. Try capturing the following important elements of the customer relationship with lines, boxes, and diamonds: the communication, advertising, pricing, product evaluation and selection, and community-building processes. Move on to the organizational processes that are so key to that relationship: motivation, incentive, hiring, collaborative, leadership, and training, for instance.

All the process movements highlight only the processes that fit into their fundamental conception of "process." That has the merit of greatly narrowing down the ones that companies focus their effort on. Therefore, some leaders of reengineering state that a company has just 10 to 20 "major" processes. Here's Michael Hammer and James Champy, for instance: "Hardly any company contains more than ten principal processes."[1]

Really? Let's see… To be a successful eCommerce company, here are just a few of the "principal" processes that come to mind: ordering, fulfillment, shipping, financing, marketing, security, privacy, supply chain management, communication, error handling, inventory management, returns, alliances (that takes the list up to 13 processes so far), technology operations, Web design, maintenance and updating, personalization, customization, community-building, internal collaboration (that's number 20), search and evaluation, channel management, call center support, forecasting, catalog management, new customer account opening, customer profiling, payments, portal management, contract management, technology integration and scaling, auditing and financial control, production scheduling, information management, customer relationship management, and market segmentation. That's 36 so far, and each of these—such as shipping and inventory management—breaks down into many more processes, in themselves complex and expensive. The list doesn't include all the principal organizational processes that must be coordinated in order to leverage these; that's surely more than ten.

The list covers so many different types of processes, with different management and skill demands, different combinations of people, workflows and technology, and above all different relative priorities. Can you skim through the list and decide which ones matter most? Least? The traditional process conceptions don't provide a base for prioritization. Therefore, TQM focuses on those with clearly defined workflows and concrete measures of quality. Reengineering zeroes in on wasteful and complex administrative workflows. Individual functional areas of business target the processes they understand and care about. Marketing thus highlights advertising, the use of customer data for market segmentation, and pricing. Production focuses on inventory management and supply chain coordination. Finance emphasizes credit, payments, and financial planning. eCommerce planners are most concerned with design, customer relationship management software, online interaction, collaboration, and community processes. Information technology (IT) concentrates on network operations, integration of the front-end Web site with back-end processing systems, databases, and security.

Very rarely is there anyone looking at the whole picture and fewer looking at it from the customer's perspective. Web site designers ignore or overlook inventory management from the customer's perspective. The IT organization overlooks account opening from the customer's perspective. Marketing overlooks credit and payment handling from the customer's perspective, and so on.

So it's no wonder that Web designers ignore the many lessons of TQM and reengineering, just as those who learned those lessons in production and customer service ignore many elements of effective management of customer interaction at the Web site.

Companies can achieve eProcess heights, but they won't do so without a different conception of "business process."

Processes in eCommerce

In the Internet era, business becomes more and more nonlinear, as companies form alliances, collaborate, and compete in the same markets. As market structures break down, traditional input-process-output operations become spread across the value network. The order process, for example, may include all the following and more. These elements are not a straight input-process-output sequence, but rather a flexible, interactive, and interweaving flow across an entire value network. This is the multimedia customer experience as compared to working through the textbook:

Access to online catalogs The company's catalogs as well as its allies' and even its competitors'. Behind this are many complex information management and coordination processes to keep the catalogs updated as goods are sold, orders placed, supplies received, prices changed, and so on. That coordination depends on many links between the buying and selling units of the value network to ensure accurate information, prices, inventory, and contracting.

Comparison shopping A fast link to services and information about products and providers, often via intermediaries.

Personalized offers Based on the customer profile and relationship history. This depends on coordination between the eCommerce unit, marketing, and sales.

Configuring the order Including confirmation of availability and delivery. This requires tight coordination between marketing, production, and eCommerce services.

Placing the order Via the Web, a switch to a call center, or even a visit to the company's store, dealership, and so on. Here, all the channels must coordinate their processes so there's no sudden discovery by the customer that the price has changed, the item isn't in stock, or the "special" personal deal made on the Web doesn't apply in the store.

Financing Links to registered lenders, perhaps for them to bid on the deal.

Confirming the order Including checking all details of fulfillment and delivery. This is where the detachment of the Web processes and the business process base is most common and damaging to the relationship. Procurement has this item backordered or the manufacturing schedule means it won't be available. A promise to the customer is about to be broken and trust damaged.

Shipment A link to UPS, the USPS, or Federal Express, who move their massive and superb process base into gear. (In passing, we would like to put in a good word for the U.S. Postal Service, which is outstanding in its Priority and Express Mail services, but too often gets the bum rap for stamp price increases, even though U.S. postal rates are among the lowest in the world. USPS is a logistics expert and that's why Amazon has chosen it as its primary shipper for smaller orders.)

Follow-up on customer inquiries A call to a toll-free number about the product, payment, shipping, and so forth. This applies to about a quarter of all Web transactions. The typical response is (1) the call center can't answer your question, (2) the Web site isn't set up to answer it, and (3) you can't get through to the people in the company who could help you solve in a few minutes what will take days of frustration, lack of response to email, and sitting on the phone.

Handling returns Roughly 5 percent of all Internet purchases, but closer to 20 percent for personal computers and clothing. Same situation as handling customer inquiries.

Updating the customer profile Any claim by a company about how much it values you as a customer loses credibility when your customer profile, including who you are and any orders you've made, isn't accurately reflected in its systems. For instance, when you sign on to the company's Web site and the site doesn't recognize you or when you phone the company's call center and the agent has your name and address but doesn't know anything about your recent order—the one that's two weeks late in delivery. CRM (customer relationship management) is the new field of business practice, plus data infrastructures and software tools, that focuses on making sure the company has the information to make the relationship real. It's the fastest growing component of consumer eCommerce—as it should be.

Problem-handling Automatically informing the customer if some problem occurs before the customer finds out: late shipment, unavailable product, and so on. This can only happen if *all* the physical processes across *all* the value network that are relevant to fulfillment and shipment are linked to the Web site and vice versa.

All this is just for the simple workflow equivalent of "Your order, please?" "Any information you need?" "Let me check that we can do this for you." "Done." "Have a nice day."

The entire nature of processes changes as the company becomes less vertically integrated—that is, it moves from handling all the processes from "Your order, please?" to "Done" internally and they become much less linear. In the simple example above, we haven't included some of the nonlinearities. For example, the order isn't being made directly from the company's own Web site, but is an electronic referral from another site, typically a portal. The customer started off comparison shopping on another site and is now placing the order on yours. As the ordering process moves ahead, software is working in the background to design special additional offers. Figure 3-1 has about as much relevance to this as transaction management does to relationship design—the old view of processes is just a subset of eProcess.

That statement obviously demands we answer the question: "Well, then, what *is* a 'process'?" The order placement example includes traditional processes that involve physical movement of goods, software doing the work that people used to do, software talking to software, and the customer not knowing or needing to know that your company doesn't even sell the goods being ordered but is just the portal that sends the referral or brokers the deal. All in less than five minutes. So it's a fair question. What *exactly* is a business process?

A business process is a recurrent set of business rules. It is linked to other processes through an interface. It is sourced through a combination of electronic links to many players in the value network and the company's internal capabilities. The key terms here are

Recurrent This is at the core of a process—if it's not recurrent, it's a decision or special case. The more recurrent and frequent a process is, the more a company can afford to invest resources in it and the more worthwhile it is to do it really well every day and every time.

Business rules This is the structure of a process, regardless of whether it's a workflow to be coordinated through steps and people handling them or a software application carrying out the very same steps. Rules define the terms of business: here's the request, here are the rules for meeting it, including how to handle questions and other element of the interaction, and here's what you asked for. They establish the roles and responsibilities that govern commerce: I send you the request, as per our agreements or as per your job responsibility, and you know what to do. I count on you—software, person, team, business—to carry out the process according to the highest standards; that's why I chose you to do it. Rules define what each player expects of the other as well as that player's responsibility. Each process provides value to the requester. Aggregating and integrating the processes through the Web site creates a value network.

Interfaces A business interface is the interaction link and media for conducting commerce. Processes execute across an interface where players exchange information and conduct business according to the rules. That is, I know exactly how to contact you and exactly what information to send you so you can play your role in our value network, and you know the same about me and my responsibility. Here's the catch: if there are multiple contact points with no clearly defined interface—and if there's no clear, consistent, and precise definition of the information to be passed across the interface—we will have a mess. I send you my order and it disappears into the organizational void. There are five departments involved, each of which uses different forms, procedures, and time tables. When I try to find out where the order is, none of you have a clue. You can't even link my order information to my credit history or to the production database.

The technology of eCommerce and the linking of eProcesses across the entire value network rests on management by interface. Cisco can exploit eProcess because when an order is placed by a customer, it sends a message across its Web interface to the contract manufacturer in Asia, to its shipper, and to its own internal information and transaction management systems.

The company with clean processes, clean process interfaces, and a technology platform designed around application program interfaces (APIs) is an eProcess player. The others are an organizational muddle that has to rely on layers of people and administrative procedures to get its work done.

Sourcing Sourcing determines who is responsible for the rules and processes. It determines the assets and the players involved in the transaction. Sourcing options are central to creating asset efficiency in eCommerce as processes can be housed with the most efficient player in the value network.

Well-defined business rules and clean interfaces mean a company can source an eProcess any way it wants. This goes well beyond outsourcing, where companies largely have an outside company handle functions that are not part of its core capabilities or strategic priorities. eProcess players may choose to out-task mission-critical strategic processes for the very reason that they are so vital. That's why UPS and other third-party logistics companies and Internet hosting companies like Exodus Communications are thriving. The eProcess company can choose to in-source dozens of companies' services— even competitors'—on its Web site because that strengthens its own brand, customer relationships, and value network benefits. It can choose...well, it can choose just about whatever it wants.

On the other hand, a company with poorly defined and ambiguous business rules, a company that uses multiple interfaces—this company can choose...well, not that much, actually. In fact, eCommerce is something it should avoid rather than seek out, whether as opportunity or necessity. The long history of information technology shows very clearly that if you try to automate a muddle, you get even more muddle. So, while the process-muddled and interface-muddled business can easily put up a Web site, all it's doing is raising customer expectations about service that it can't fulfill. It then has to spend even more money trying to fix this. For this reason, it should avoid eCommerce.

For eProcess, while traditional process design does not disappear, issues of input-process-output are replaced with concerns about rules, interfaces, and sources. These issues form the central process design decisions. These decisions determine the structure of your eCommerce operations as well as their performance potential.

Processes and Capabilities

eProcesses are, in effect, modular building blocks that link smoothly to each other. Modularity is critical to asset efficiency and flexibility, as modular capabilities can be easily sourced across customers, suppliers, and other third parties. Shipping is an obvious and instructive example. When Gateway sends a message from its eCommerce base to UPS, UPS becomes a module in Gateway's value network. It "attaches" cleanly to the value network with no need for either party to change its own organization, share facilities, or add staff to coordinate with each other. If you look at the typical company's operations, it lacks this modularity; it can't attach a new building block through a clear and clean interface.

This is again why eCommerce is not just about Web sites. The typical company can't use many of the opportunities to attach new modules to build a value network. It must first clean up its own process base. These changes come from looking at a business from a process perspective rather than from that of organizations or functions. Now, obviously, a company can't suddenly turn itself upside down and inside out and transform every process. Instead, it must step back and prioritize its processes in terms of their actual and potential contribution to eCommerce goals.

Processes as Assets and Liabilities

The starting point for valuing processes and for targeting those that will provide the most eCommerce value is to forget about their specific function or standard categorization, such as finance, customer service, or procurement, and look at them in terms of their value generation. We'll discuss this very briefly in the next few pages and then come back to it in more detail after presenting the single key step in the valuation process, which is to forget about your company. Truly forget about it.

Some processes are major business assets, and some may be a key part of the company's very identity. They are essentially the company's brand. Think of Federal Express and what immediately comes to mind is guaranteed on-time delivery. In eCommerce, Priceline.com's brand is its pricing processes, which it has patented. Other processes are priority assets in generating value on an everyday basis: store replenishment in retailing, trading in securities, and quality control in manufacturing. In eCommerce, common priority asset processes are pricing, portal management and promotion, personalization of the customer relationship, and logistics.

Asset processes create value. Conversely, other processes are liabilities and drain it. Many of these liability processes are part of the necessary background operations of your business; your company needs to carry them out, but no matter how well they are performed, they won't contribute directly to relationships and business growth. For instance, does your own company's telephone cost allocation process generate any value in your customer relationships or contribute to creating investor confidence and shareholder value? If the company were 50 times more efficient in charging business units for their calls, would that change at all? Obviously not. This is what eProcess terms a background liability process.

But what about your process for tracking a customer's order status? That, too, is an administrative nuisance and an expense that in itself doesn't add value to your business. It largely handles mistakes—by the sales department, suppliers, production, shipping, or even the customer. It mainly involves sitting on the phone trying to assuage an angry customer and chasing down information and paperwork. Clearly, it's also a background liability.

Although that last paragraph simply states facts about the business world of the past century, it's nonsense in the world of eCommerce. That's because it looks at the process from the company's perspective, not the customer's. For the customer, being able to reliably, simply, conveniently, and quickly get information about an order is one of the key needs in online business. More and more customer decisions as to which site to go to—and even more, their decisions about which ones to come back to—rest on after-sales service.

We use this example to illustrate why we said the key to eProcess valuation and prioritization is to forget about your company. The reason so many companies display major weaknesses in handling business processes for successful eCommerce is that they look at the Web site from the *customer* perspective, but at the business operations from the *company* perspective. When customers had limited choices, and regulation and oligopolies dominated many industries, the company could by and large set its own priorities of efficiency, cost control, and scheduling. In the eCommerce world, the customer defines efficiency. The primacy of customer choice as driver of the online economy invalidates many tried and true assumptions about the value of existing processes and the need for new ones.

In the example of tracking order status, the company is thinking in terms of customer *service*, not customer relationship. It needs the process to handle the occasional glitches that occur and it tries to be responsive, but its identity and its value generation don't rest on this background liability process. For eCommerce, the company has to make order tracking and status reporting a priority asset from the customer's perspective or it will lose business to those that customers see as responsive to them in providing immediate and personal service. That may result in new eProcess designs and new sourcing. For example, in this instance, the eSuccess player first out-tasks shipping to UPS or FedEx and adds a direct link to the package deliverer's Web site from its own. Instead of the customer having to call the company and the company having to access FedEx, the customer does so far more quickly and simply.

Next, the eSuccess company sets up collaborative processes inside the organization as well as new links from its internal computer systems and databases to the information system the Web site maintains about the customer and the order. This adds a new alerting capability so problems with an order are handled when they are discovered instead of being reacted to when the customer discovers them. The company sets up an automatic email service to keep the customer informed about any delay. It establishes a new process whereby customer email is guaranteed to get an answer within a given period (typically 24 hours). This exception-handling process may include software that screens the email looking for words to help determine the likely nature of the problem, then routes the message to an employee listed in a database of skills, knowledge, and responsibilities, such as sales, technical help, or payment and credit. That person must get an answer to the customer and has the authority to draw on anyone in the company if he or she can't solve the problem or answer the query.

That's eProcess. Is it worth the investment? That's not the right question. Any process that is key to the customer relationship must be treated as a priority and made an asset. Otherwise, if it's handled by the company as a background liability, it's just created a priority *liability* process. This erodes any relationship opportunity, thus draining eCommerce value. The issue is not whether to make the investment, but how to source the eProcess in a way that best generates value and is most cost efficient. In this instance, the company may in-source a new capability via electronic links to one of the companies that provide software to manage reverse logistics (returns and replacements) or that offer specialized call centers, with staff trained to diagnose problems and talk with the customer to choose the best option for resolving them.

This is eProcess thinking. It would have helped many companies avoid the most widely reported failures in eCommerce service: retailers who handle order fulfillment and returns as background processes for themselves, online security trading services that view the paperwork and administration involved in opening a new customer account

in the same way, and manufacturers who see their own costs, operations, and administration needs—not the customer relationship—as
driving production scheduling.

Process Investment

In *The Process Edge*, Peter Keen introduced his Process Investment
framework for handling business processes as economic assets and
liabilities, which we have briefly illustrated above. Asset processes
create economic value-added. Liability processes drain value, however well they are carried out. The original focus in Process Investment was on processes as invisible capital items that don't appear on
the balance sheet, but which represent large historical investments
and must be managed as such.

This has nothing to do with accounting. This is about management of shareholder value. Consider a process as apparently small in
scale as handling corporate travel arrangements and expense accounts.
This certainly doesn't look like something that affects shareholder
value nor does it look like a balance sheet capital item. Add up the
money spent over the past three to five years to build the process
capabilities, and the picture looks very different: office space, computer systems, staff hiring and training, direct staff costs (and indirect ones such as the often considerable time spent by executives and
their assistants on making requests to and coordinating with the
travel department, submitting and processing expense reports, and
others).

This is a background liability process, obviously. It makes most
sense to out-task as much of it as possible. That is why we are seeing
so many excellent corporate travel management services on the Web.
Our focus in this book is on processes that most affect eCommerce,
but the same logic about valuation and sourcing applies to internal
processes. Here, the opportunity is less the external Web interface to
a value network centered on customer relationships than the internal interface to the company's intranet and a value network centered
on the company's own productivity. To a degree, this book focuses on
the revenue-generation side of the Internet opportunity. Perhaps
our next book will be *The Intranet Edge: Using eProcess for Organizational Advantage*.

In extending the Process Investment to eCommerce, we downplay
the economic scale of processes. The business priority Keen focused

on was making sure that the large investments in processes were managed well. This was the era of the vertical company. What's new, just a very few years later, is a point we discussed in Chapter 2: the very smallest processes can be made into major assets, and processes can now be software. Earlier, we mentioned Dealtime, the Web service that will park a bot at a Web site and keep checking until the price of an item drops to a point at which the Dealtime customer is ready to buy it. That's a tiny piece of software that costs nothing to the customer, but it's equivalent to a human personal shopping assistant armed with a cell phone and paid by the hour.

This eProcess is a form of intellectual capital—the type of intangible asset we spoke of in Chapter 2. In the business era of *The Process Edge*, the Web opportunity was nascent and most business processes were heavily people dependent. Now, in the eCommerce economy, the Web is a major enabler of any eProcess combination of people and technology. It thus makes all intellectual capital a potential value generator. So, for eProcess, we relax the definition of process assets and liabilities from major financial capital items to major intellectual capital items, regardless of how much financial capital they represent. The key question is, are they assets (value building) or liabilities (value draining) and how can they be best leveraged through eProcess sourcing?

The second element of the Process Investment framework remains core to eProcess: the business impact of a process. Processes vary in their contribution based on the company's strategic intent. There are four distinct categories:

Identity The distinctive differentiator of the company

Priority The engine of everyday competitive performance

Background Support to operations

Mandated Carried out only because of regulation and law

Identity processes define the company to itself, its investors, its employees, and, above all, its customers. Examples include McDonald's processes that ensure absolute consistency in their service of a commodity product and, online, eBay's auction processes. Other companies sell fast food that really is nowhere near as different from McDonald's as customers believe. But McDonald's really is different. It's the combination of the product, price, management of logistics, training, and customer experience that creates McDonald's unique differentiation in the marketplace. In the online marketspace—the term for the invisible and virtual interlinking of value networks that replaces the physical marketplace—many companies similarly offer auctions, including Amazon and Yahoo!, but eBay is "the" auction player. Identity processes are tightly associated with company brand.

Indeed, in many instances identity processes are far more the brand than the products and services themselves. They can also be brand creators and brand obliterators. Ask a group of managers if they've bought a book from Amazon and plenty of hands go up. Then ask them to keep their hand up if they can recall the name of the publisher. It's very rare that you'll see wristwatches waving in the air. In many ways, the battle to be a portal or hub, to create "stickiness," and to aggressively market and promote a site is the Web component of an eProcess war: build the identity asset processes that differentiate the relationship, not the site.

Priority processes are the engine of everyday competitive performance: on-time arrival for airlines, replenishment for retailers, quality control for manufacturers, and customer service for banks. It's only as we have more and more experience of successes and failures in eCommerce—there are only a few years of examples to draw on even today—that it's becoming apparent what the priority asset processes are for in this very new customer-determined economy. As we've mentioned, many of them turn out to be background liability processes in the old economy. What is absolutely clear, of course, is that while many of the new priority processes relate to attracting customers to visit and to buy—with marketing being about the visit and pricing, and Web site features being about the buy—the processes that matter are the ones that keep the customer coming back. That is, priority asset processes and relationship building and maintaining are very closely interlinked.

Background processes are the ones that support operations. They have mainly been liabilities in the past: administration, accounting, procurement, operations, and the like. They constitute most of the bureaucracy of business—the heavy paperwork, document flows and copies, layers of staffing, time delays, errors, and so on.

Mandated processes are ones that are carried out only because of legal or regulatory requirements. They can seriously impede online service and responsiveness, but they have to be followed.

The Process Worth/Salience Matrix

Figure 3-2 shows the *Process Edge* Worth/Salience matrix that is the core of Process Investment. We'll explore it in more detail in later chapters. It shows the two dimensions of process value. Worth defines whether or not it is an asset that generates value and Salience defines its prominence in the company's strategic positioning. So, identity assets stand out as the very core of the company's branding, differentiation, and sustainable competitive strengths. At the other extreme of value, or rather non-value, background liability processes, are just that—in the background and an expense only.

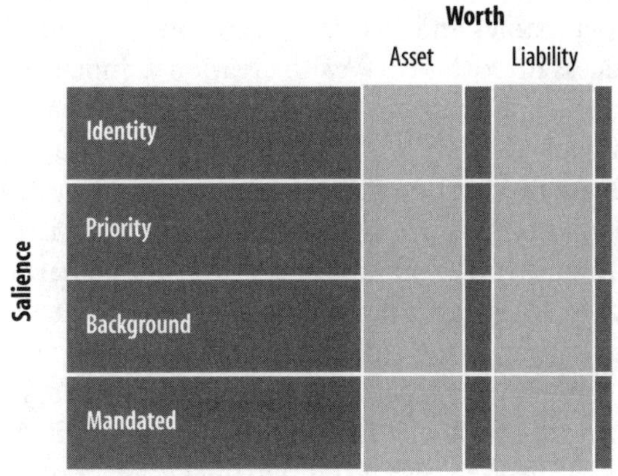

Figure 3-2: Worth/Salience matrix

Most companies look at Worth and Salience in terms of their own priorities. To continue to do so in the era of eProcess is process myopia rather than blindness. Companies must switch their perspective of value from themselves to their customer's perspective of value. If not, the company will view high-value customer processes, those critical to building trust, convenience, and service, as "administration." Process blindness is that you just can't see it. Process myopia is that you are very short sighted and choose not to put on eyeglasses.

Processes such as billing, account management, returns, and invoice reconciliation are not background to customers. They are a priority. For instance, many financial service companies handle account opening and administration as a background process. They market aggressively to get new clients to their Web site and walk them through the application process. So far, so good. Then comes the final step: the Web site instructs the new customer to print out and fax or mail a copy of the screen to the company. The account will then be activated "in four to six weeks." Clearly, the customer's expectations of online financial services as online are delayed until the administrative processes are resolved. The result? Some financial sectors report that only one in five people who begin to open an account complete the process.[2] That is not eCommerce. Rather, it's manual commerce in disguise.

Process Wealth and "Symmetry"

Wealth for companies and customers rests on symmetry in their view on process importance. Wealth creation dampens when there is asymmetry—an imbalance between how the company and its customers each view the process. We continue to find many examples in online companies. Many do not respond to email from customers, since for them it is an administrative nuisance, a side issue.[3] It would require them to spend extra money on staff and on new processes for ensuring the message is handled by the people most qualified to address it: a technical problem, incorrect order, missed shipment, and so on. The company considers this a background process; however, it is *always* a priority for the customer sending the email. Always. The very essence of the Web is that it is personal interaction, and by definition a relationship is personal. It's surely crazy to encourage the interaction through often very costly marketing, promotion, price discounts, and referral fees, and then make it clear there is nothing personal there at all.

Leading companies turn processes valued by the customer into priority assets that strengthen their reputation, which in turn strengthens its relationships. Amazon is very highly regarded here. It automatically keeps customers informed, confirming their orders, alerting them to items of personal interest to them, and providing fast replies (from a real person) to customer email. National Semiconductor, in the same way and for the same reasons—the relationship is primary to its profitability—has established formal processes combining software and people to ensure that customers always get a reply to an email about a problem within a given period.

Customer Priority Processes

Many companies do not seem to look at their business process base from the customer's perspective. What may be acceptable in offline operations can be a major blockage to effective relationship building in the online world. The company needs to turn its administrative processes into the customer's convenience processes. The Worth/ Salience matrix helped us spot one of the most powerful aspects of online relationship building that is win-win for the company and the customer. This is to turn the company's administration back-office expense (all background) into the customer's valued front-office asset through self-management. We can illustrate this with some simple examples:

- ▶ It costs American Airlines $10 to $20 to handle a call to its reservation and customer service centers. Fifty percent of the calls do not turn into a flight booking. One of the frequently asked questions (FAQs) is "What do I need to do to take my pet on the plane with me?" By providing customers with the opportunity to pose their question as a query at the Web site, where a software tool interprets it and provides the answer, American Airlines saves them time and inconvenience and saves itself money.

- ▶ Cisco saved $120,000 a month just by letting customers download copies of invoices.

- ▶ My.Yahoo helps its "customers" (it doesn't sell anything, and like CBS or *USA Today* makes its immense revenues from its relationship base of subscribers/viewers/readers) manage their own investment portfolios, personalize their own news feeds, and locate the best deals available on the Web. My.Yahoo has access to the individual's profile and pattern of purchases. The personal Web page can be configured for Yahoo to automatically download information about particular subjects and to bring attention to special offers in the customer's stated areas of interest.

These examples point to the huge payoff from enabling customers to manage their priority processes for themselves. When a Cisco customer needs a copy of an invoice, that's an immediate need—a priority—and the Web interface is an asset. As we will show in later chapters, self-management of the relationship is one of the most powerful and profitable moves a company can make. However, it also entirely changes the definition of what a business process is. The concept of a process as workflow/activity does not hold up. Consider, for instance, Dell's extension of relationship self-management to its corporate customers. It offers them customized "Premier Pages," which contain all the company's business rules for handling procurement of personal computers and servers: authorization procedures, configurations, software options, shipping, payment, accounting, and so on. What Dell has done is embed all those business processes in the relationship interface software.

Ariba, one of the leaders in helping companies manage their operating resource purchases (office supplies, contractor services, consumables, and the like), does the same; the software *is* the purchasing department. Increasingly, companies are linking to UPS, which in effect puts a world-class logistics department in the software. In the same way, Fidelity Investments and Charles Schwab provide first-rate financial advisory services and research—all of which are process dependent—via software links to other online providers.

eProcess: Prioritization, Coordination, and Sourcing

eProcess is a company's strategy for process prioritization, coordination, and sourcing, as well as a foundation for Internet electronic commerce success. An eCommerce company with an excellent technology platform and a solid business model for its Internet priorities has a range of options for designing, coordinating, and sourcing its processes that the traditional company lacks. In particular, it can attack the organizational enemy: complexity.

Efficiency and Simplicity

The immediate eProcess gain is one of efficiency and simplicity. eCommerce technologies enable companies to achieve new performance levels as they move from being vertically controlled to horizontally coordinated as capabilities are sourced across a value network. Sourcing options enable the company to choose the best partner for a particular capability from among its customers, suppliers, intermediaries, and other third parties. Sourcing reduces company workflow responsibilities that are organizationally complex to coordinate, that tie up capital, and that generate many indirect as well as direct costs. It makes sense to use people and workflows rather than services or software only when that adds value to the customer relationship.

The result is a radical reduction of organization and operation complexity. Sourcing gives companies access to leading-edge capability without investments in time and capital. Process design now starts with identifying the most appropriate source within the value network rather than assuming that all processes are internal command and control functions. Figure 3-3 shows the eProcess sourcing options and their relationship to company efficiency and simplicity.

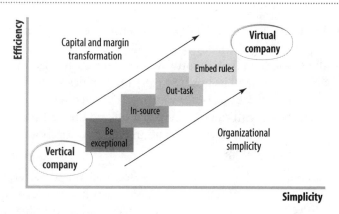

Figure 3-3: eProcess sourcing options

These sourcing options define the potential sources of your company's capability. There are many aspects of customer service, organizational communication, business partner relations, and decision making that demand the personal touch and perhaps always will. However, there are many aspects that can be far more effectively sourced through internal software and external links to other companies. The Dell, Ariba, and UPS approach transforms the cost and complexity of coordination of processes for their clients. This reduces capital costs and, hence, increases economic value-added and shareholder value. It is in that sense that we speak of eProcess as building process wealth.

eProcurement: An Example of Sourcing Efficiency and Simplicity

Consider, for example, procurement in the typical company. Most surveys report that it costs $50 to $120 to process—note the term—a simple purchase order. There are forms with multiple copies needed by different departments, delays, layers of supervisors, and so forth. Turnaround time is measured in days or even weeks. Inventory levels are not synchronized with demand. What is truly astonishing in our modern economy is just how inefficient supply chain management has been, even in the best companies. eProcurement creates a sourcing alternative for purchasing processes. The traditional process involves internal workflow coordination. eProcess solutions shift this workflow to embed the procurement processes in the form of rules enforced through Web site front-end software. Here are some typical examples:

▶ The Canadian Imperial Bank of Commerce (CIBC) improved its purchasing efficiency by some $50 million (Canadian) annually. CIBC used Ariba's software to build a customized Web site that contained all its business rules for purchasing supplies and standard service like office cleaning. This ensured that orders were placed with the suppliers that offered the best prices or that gave volume discounts, and that employees chose from particular catalogs.

▶ Cisco used to have some sort of inaccuracy on 20 percent of its orders. Now, it is 0.2 percent. All errors in an order, such as a missing delivery address or incorrect product number, are caught at the very beginning off the process and not discovered far later. Customer self-management makes it far more likely that the order will be accurate than if it is taken over the phone or by a salesperson writing it up on a paper form in the customer's office.

Create Simplicity Without Sacrificing Capability or Scale

The traditional company has to rethink its capabilities and sourcing in order to achieve these eProcess benefits. It can no longer accept the costs and complexity of process-as-workflow. An eProcess company by contrast can design its logistics processes, supply chain management processes, and most of its back-office processes to be sourced outside the company. This enables the company to reduce its invested assets and obtain leading-edge performance from the capabilities available in the value network. This is a rich set of options that extends the enterprise into being part networked company.

Capability Sourcing Options

The four sourcing options for eProcesses offer particular advantages and corresponding disadvantages: cost, reliability, flexibility, speed, impact on relationships, and so on. Together, they add up to a powerful combination that gets the best practical value for the company, customers, and value network players. These options require design and development of new eCommerce capabilities that harness process innovation and take advantage of available technologies.

Embed Processes in the eCommerce Software Interface

Perhaps the very first rule of eProcess is that any company should look for opportunities to substitute software for workflows. Think of a process as having the following characteristics. It is recurrent; otherwise it is not a process, but rather an exception or crisis. It consists of a set of business rules: "First check if this is a new customer. If so, then…." Carrying out these rules requires information and interaction with others: a customer, supplier, and staff in other parts of the business. It is very much a conversation. Judgment is needed. Exceptions must be handled appropriately.

eCommerce processes are very dynamic. Some of them can be automated. Indeed, more and more standard processes can be largely or even entirely automated as technology makes it practical to gather and apply the needed information to reach a decision. For instance, when you apply for a credit card or car loan, the entire decision can be handled through software, checking credit records and using statistical formula to rate creditworthiness.

Procedures and Conversations

Embedding processes in software involves applying business rules in a procedural fashion and maintaining the required interaction across the process. The company gains efficiency through procedurally applying business rules. The company builds a relationship through the "conversational" aspect of a process. The process must consider what happens if the procedure prevents any interaction. For example, a customer requesting a loan is rejected because of incorrect information in his or her credit file. The process design determines what must happen next: whether the customer is rejected outright or is contacted by a service representative to discuss the issue.

Internet technologies enable new forms of procedural and conversational communications via a Web site. New component- and object-based software tools make it easy to customize software in small and flexible applications. These "applets" link the Web-based conversation to the rules contained within large and generally inflexible transaction-processing applications. The power of these tools enables companies to combine the routine and the situational. The software can automate all the routine steps and pass the exceptions on to a service agent. This approach to process management greatly reduces complexity as well as capital and operations costs, and opens up major opportunities in building and sustaining relationships. Procurement and supply chain management are obvious examples with far-reaching impact on direct costs—the freeing up of working capital (inventory, especially), overhead reduction, prices, and scheduling. Just as far-reaching is customer self-management of processes that otherwise require intermediaries to handle workflows.

Out-Task Processes Through Application Program Interfaces (APIs)

Companies can also achieve greater efficiency and simplicity through sourcing capabilities to other companies in the value network. Companies out-task capabilities to gain scale and speed. Out-tasking is different from out-sourcing. Out-sourcing involves moving company resources to a third party and keeping a retained organization. When a company out-tasks, there is not a transfer of resources; it simply begins using the partner's capabilities directly.

Out-tasking is an extension of embedding a process in software as the company gains access through software links to the other company's capabilities. An obvious example of this opportunity is API links to UPS. (Think of an API as a structured message to another piece of software. It makes a request for a service and includes the information the recipient needs to meet the request.)

While UPS is an obvious opportunity for out-tasking, this offers more than handling simple delivery transactions. Consider UPS's relationship with Fender, the guitar maker. UPS provides logistics capabilities that include handling the tuning of Fender's guitars in its Netherlands shipping hub, through which all purchases of the guitars worldwide are routed. This process saves Fender weeks in delivery time by not having the guitars sent to a Fender location. It also reduces Fender's costs by 9 percent. The guitars can be taken out of the box by the customer and used immediately, instead of waiting for the expert tuner to arrive.[4]

Build a Virtual Process Base Using the Value Network

UPS is an electronic partner with Open Market, a leading Web commerce company, in a software venture that provides "end-to-end" Web transaction handling—from order to delivery to after-sales support. Hewlett-Packard and UPS have set up a collaborative partnership to ensure rapid transportation of electronics components from HP production plants in Asia to European customers. Fender, UPS, HP, and Open Market are separate companies, of course, but the electronic collaborations create something new: an eProcess base that no single company could afford the time or capital to create. This process base is the value generator of the network, where each party benefits. In particular, the enterprise adds process capability without adding complexity and capital and operations cost.

Turn Back-Office Processes into Front-Office Assets

Companies can unlock the value of back-office processes by making them available to other through out-tasking. Out-tasking through APIs provides an effective way to link new customers to your business process base without the cost associated with setting up a new business. Consider the challenge eBay faced in terms of guaranteeing the quality of the auction market's buyers and sellers. eBay has a fraud-monitoring department that immediately carries out background checks to guard against the likelihood of scams. The "department" is an API link to a highly sophisticated credit card monitoring system. eBay gains the world-class capability of the second largest credit card processor without building a real fraud-monitoring department. The credit card company, on the other hand, gains new revenue sources from one of its loss-prevention processes. Another example is eCredit.com, which provides an analogous service, again via an automatic and immediate API link, to handle credit analysis and approval based on its own business rules for new commercial customers. eCredit links to its network of online financing institutions, which offer individual terms and vehicles for the credit.

Note that in all these instances, the company is not simply outsourcing a function but is tightly coupling its own online service base to a process provider that is in itself a best practice company—otherwise, it makes no sense to choose it as partner. It is also strengthening its own brand in that, as in the examples of UPS, eBay, and eCredit, it is improving its own performance "seamlessly" and achieving a standard it could not afford or achieve otherwise.

The leaders in eCommerce build their brands using out-tasking and in-sourcing. AOL, Yahoo!, and Amazon are portals that own or are linked to many other product and service providers. Think of the process base they would need to build were they to try to grow a multibillion-dollar mega-conglomerate. It would be close to impossible. Consider how Amazon instead in-sourced many different types of retailers, auctions, and small businesses. Its zShops offer retailers low-cost Web sites on Amazon's own portal and provides them with one of Amazon's key processes embedded in its software: its patented "one-click" buying process.[5]

In-Source Processes and New Competencies

A company in-sources the capabilities that are essential to its identity or are critical to its operational performance. Once it has simplified its organizational complexity through the above process sourcing and coordination options, the company can then focus its investment on processes to be sourced internally and coordinated through people. Basically, the eProcess options discussed earlier address the routine—those where the business rules can be embedded in software—and those that are better handled by some other provider through out-tasking and in-sourcing.

All things being equal, it will always make more sense to shift a process from workflows and people to software and APIs. But, of course, all things are not equal, and there will always be areas of process excellence where it is people, judgment, personal contact, and conversation that matter. These will generally be targeted to the exceptional rather than routine components of relationships, to eCommerce innovation, and to differentiating the company from other online players.

The customer service reputation of Schwab rests on its combination of customer self-management using embedded software processes and call centers plus highly responsive customer care processes from its people in the branch offices. These are as much a part of Schwab's identity processes as its online capabilities, which, while excellent, are very much the same as those of its main competitors. An interview with Charles Schwab's director of corporate communications in a report by Beacon Research captures the company's operating philosophy:

> Our research shows that about half of our 4.9 million customers have visited one of our offices. And the fraction is higher for our more affluent customers. People want to feel close to their money—branch offices provide that. They also want to meet brokers and bounce ideas off them. And sometimes they need to pick up a check within a few hours. For all these reasons, we have strong incentives to keep our storefront a vital part of our services. So for us, online versus storefront is not a conflict. It is part of a mix of services that our customers are quickly getting used to. The mix is actually larger—customers also get 24-hour telephone access to humans as well as to speech-recognition and touch-tone telephone services…. We are always improving our personalization efforts.[6]

eBay: In-Sourcing Capabilities to Support a Virtual Business

eBay is about as close to a fully electronic process company as any. The company makes its auction markets by providing a relationship interface that is the base for not only handling auctions, but also payments and community interest groups' discussion groups over its Web site. Given the virtual and informational nature of eBay's business, one would assume little need to in-source capabilities beyond the design and support for its Web site and database.

However, eBay recognizes the value customers place on an open, fair auction market, which is one of its identity assets. In order to ensure the validity of buyers and sellers, the company created a mediation capability. eBay also hired a former federal prosecutor who works as eBay's "prosecutor, judge, jury and, if need be, executor" in watching out for fakes, fraud, and unacceptable or illegal items for auction. He describes himself as eBay's sheriff.[7] This new process relies on people rather than technology. eBay built this capability to help ensure reputation and profits—that is, to differentiate eBay from the many other auction sites on the Web. It's analogous to how McDonald's stands out among the many fast food restaurants.

eBay also has created new processes to involve its customers in ensuring the quality of its auction markets. These new capabilities leverage the strength of eBay's buyer and seller network. eBay made this eProcess investment without in any way changing its core business operations; it merely added eProcess investments. It provided an escrow capability by which payments were held by a third party, it offered insurance for larger purchases, and it added the "sheriff" mentioned above. These are not Web site features, though most of them are activated through software APIs. They are processes. It misses the business point to think of eCommerce in terms of technology features. eCommerce is about processes and the way in which the technology and the process are fused.

eProcess Is Redefining New Processes and Organizational Performance

eProcess is not a matter of reengineering and streamlining workflows. It is not a matter of substituting software for process. It is designing, sourcing, and coordinating the company's process portfolio in the best way. eProcess is process excellence for eCommerce. The challenge is to define the "best" way. We do this in terms of the two main determinants of value: the long-term customer relationship and the economics of the company's cost and capital structures. It is no news to any manager that the rapid and massive growth in most online players' Internet revenues has not as yet translated into profits. It is pretty clear that they will not unless the company's eProcess strategy changes the nature of its customers and assets. The company must first turn transactions into repeat business. Then it must build repeat business into a sustained relationship by fostering personalization, customization, collaboration, and community. Finally, the company must transform the structure of its balance sheet and operating costs through innovative capability sourcing.

That is what generates process wealth. Process really, really matters!

Part II

The Relationship Imperative

In this part

Chapter 4

Value Networks: Targeting eCommerce Relationships

Before you can hit a target, you need to know where it is. In the pre-eCommerce era, it was straight in front of you. Banks were banks and stores were stores. Industries were relatively well defined. Markets were international, national, regional, or local, and you knew which was which. Customers fell into tidy segments, largely marked by demographics—there were business travelers and leisure travelers and renters and homeowners. So, to target your business, you mainly had to keep your eyes on the road ahead of you.

With eCommerce, the target can be anyone, anywhere, anything, anytime, any price, any ally, any portal, and any other "any" you can think up. Targets are not always in front of you, so while you are looking ahead, you may get blindsided—"Amazoned"—by a company that's made your customers its own target. The power of the Web is that it opens up business worldwide, and that is also its weakness. The very breadth, scale, and variety of opportunity make it literally a hit or miss affair. In the early days of Internet commerce, this encouraged a very broad mass-marketing strategy: get your site up, get the ads out, and grab customers.

That may be termed the "China Fallacy." In the 1970s, as China opened up and became part of the global marketplace, would-be entrepreneurs built their dreams on the basis that China had a population of billions. The path to wealth in their minds rested on getting a market penetration of 1 percent. Just open up a Beijing or Shanghai office and wait for the money to come in. It is the same case in eCommerce, as new entrants talk about taking 3 or 4 percent of a target, say, $10 billion current market as the basis for their business case.

Matters were and are, of course, just a little more complex than that in entering the Chinese market. They are very much more complex with the Internet, too, and eCommerce is in no way a matter of just opening up a Web site and prospecting for customers. Companies have to define their target very clearly and aim carefully. But where do they start? Typically, they target specific customer segments, product, and service offerings, often on the basis of their existing business strengths, practices, and industry. New entrants target a niche opportunity. They observe trends, such as the rapid growth of business-to-business hubs and Application Service Providers, and look to exploit them. In all these instances, the primary focus is on the company itself.

We suggest a different focus: the wider set of relationships. The company associates itself with other companies to leverage its capabilities and opportunities in a way that attracts customers, keeps them, and grows associations of mutual benefit. Andersen Consulting calls this a value network. That term usefully captures the Internet business reality: that a Web site cannot be an isolated and independent node on the Internet. It requires relationships to leverage relationships.

Value Networks: Accelerating a Business Revolution

One of our major themes in this book is that eCommerce is about commerce first and technology second. We should modify that statement just a little: eCommerce is about what was happening in electronic commerce anyway, but the Internet opportunity moved it from an evolution to a revolution. There's only a single character different in those two words, and it's the "R" yet again—relationship. The Internet turned electronic commerce from T—transaction—to R. It also turned it from E meaning electronic to everywhere, everything, and everybody.

Prior to the Internet, the business opportunities of electronic commerce were available to most companies, but there were barriers. As a result, electronic commerce was a slow revolution, constrained mostly by the cost of technology and, thus, mostly driven by large companies. They had the clout to compel suppliers to link to them electronically through electronic data interchange or to build their own point of sale or reservation systems. They could enable industry consortia and fund collaborative services such as SWIFT (Society for Worldwide International Funds Transfer)—the banking network that revolutionized the movement of money—and comparable "clearing houses" in insurance, airlines, and retailing.

The Internet was like a gift from a fairy godmother. Whatever was happening in electronic commerce could now be extended in every way and to anywhere. Company size no longer determined technology opportunity. More important, electronic commerce networks like SWIFT were no longer closed ones—they could be made open to more and more parties. It took a few years for the old and the new worlds of electronic commerce to come together. The old one of electronic data interchange, point of sale, and reservation systems was very company centered and bounded by industry and contracts. The new eCommerce world is unbounded, relying on a wider set of relationships. The company associates itself with other companies to leverage its capabilities and opportunities in a way that attracts customers, keeps them, and grows associations of mutual benefit. Value network is the phrase that usefully captures the Internet business reality: A Web site cannot be an isolated and independent node on the Internet.

The simple statement that the new world of eCommerce requires relationships is revolutionary. Here are just a few of its implications for management:

- ▶ Relationships require that the company work in a broader context that extends beyond itself, as no one company can be world class at everything.

- ▶ Relationships make a company's value network the basis for competition rather than the company itself.

- ▶ The value network defines more than just how the company handles its business. It provides the portfolio of capabilities the company brings to customers and the market.

- ▶ The value network enables a level of capability through eProcess sourcing that was previously unattainable—embedding processes in software, out-tasking, and in-sourcing.

- ▶ Companies that do not recognize this shift will find themselves constrained to be a niche player.

From EDI to Value Network

Traditional commerce concentrated on a company's bilateral relationships with customers and suppliers. Those interactions were simple: the customer purchased your products and you purchased supplies. Business technology supported bilateral relationships. The costs and complexity of electronic data interchange (EDI) and labor-intensive alliances made it expensive and time consuming to run more than a few truly strategic relationships. Many banks, for instance, would have just a few tight relationships with major retailers to offer co-branded products. Manufacturers maintained close contractual ties with their "tier 1" suppliers. Brokers were barriers between customer and provider direct relationships and were relationship managers on their own behalf with each party.

Of course, companies had many trading party relationships, and of course they co-branded and made joint ventures. But, by and large, companies were fairly self-contained—hence the term "vertical organization." Business growth meant internal expansion in operations, employees and locations, and mergers and acquisitions (M&A).

Most M&A did not repay the purchase cost, as many studies show; the economic performance of the new combination decreased shareholder value. This reflects the complexity of meshing organizations, cultures, information systems, and business processes. (Looking ahead to our discussion of sourcing process capabilities in Part III, we note here that when a Gateway or a Cisco tightly bonds a shipper's third-party logistics to its eCommerce Web site, none of the above complexities apply.)

The vertical organization as the base of business started to change rapidly in the early 1980s, as large companies faced up to the problems of inertia, bureaucracy, inflexibility, and cost escalation that made many of them increasingly lag behind faster innovators. Out-sourcing began the shift from the vertical organization to the extended enterprise. Much of this was driven by fairly short-term negative pressures and motivations, such as downsizing and cost savings. It was accelerated by a major shift in supply chain management that combined reengineering—the streamlining of inefficient processes—and electronic data interchange—the originator of business-to-business (B2B) electronic commerce. Leading companies began to recognize the value of relationship-based associations rather than bargaining- and conflict-based win-lose negotiations with their suppliers. Toyota was the exemplar, where the parties worked closely together to create win-win opportunities through shared information, planning, and forecasting.

Companies such as Chrysler greatly reduced the number of suppliers they used and treated them as trading partners rather than playing them off against each other. Chrysler called this an "electronic keiretsu" after the Japanese trading companies such as Mitsubishi that had so transformed the rules of competition in the auto industry and consumer electronics and pushed U.S. manufacturers on a decade-long sustained defensive.[1] Time became the new currency of business—time to market, logistics speed, inventory turnover, stock replenishment, quick response (retailing), and financial payments speed.

EDI, electronic cash management, point of sale, electronic distribution systems, and global company telecommunications networks became the weapons in a new competitive game.[2] Even in the mid-1980s it was becoming obvious that telecommunications was a rapidly coming key to business innovation.[3] It lay behind the transformation of competitive positions in the airline industry. American Airlines and British Airways were using airline reservation systems to build relationship links with travel agents and the frequent flyer passengers who provided the bulk of their profits and to create an information edge in every area of customer service, pricing, logistics, and profit management. It was behind the rise of retailers like Wal-Mart, still the world giant in electronic commerce through its point of sale (POS) and information resources.

From 1986 through the mid-1990s, such innovation was largely the privilege of large companies. The cost of high-speed, high-capacity telecommunications was an expensive fixed cost smaller companies could not afford or manage. Value-added networks (VANs) sprung up in some industries to provide access to many players, anticipating B2B trading hubs. IVANS, for instance, served insurance brokers and agents; SWIFT, CHIPS, CHAPS, FEDWIRE, and other financial VANs transformed banking payments from bank notes to bits.[4] VANs, POS networks, and individual industry EDI services created early value networks. But for all the reported benefits, the expansion of electronic commerce was slow, expensive, and confined to a small number of industries.

The trends we see today are not new—indeed, the more you look at the Internet economy as commerce first and electronic second, the more you see it as the new old rather than the new new. EDI and bank payment systems remain by far the main vehicles of eCommerce in terms of industry practices, hubs, and procedures for agreeing on shared standards, terminology, and message formats.

Note that during the late 1980s to mid-1990s the Internet was already available and some companies were making use of it. They were mainly ones with scientific researchers and technology professionals who were familiar with its then pre-Web arcane commands and procedures. Schlumberger, Sun, and McDonnell Douglas were leaders here.

When the Internet first began to build momentum in 1996 to 1997 through personal computers, the Web, and Netscape's browser, business was seen as very much on the sidelines, with the Internet community intending to keep it there. Here's a quote from that far-off past that seems almost quaint:

> *Free. Egalitarian. Decentralize. Ad hoc. Open and peer-to-peer. Experimental. Autonomous. Anarchic.* These words make up the lexicon of the cyberspace frontier…. Notice, however, how sharply these words contrast with the hardheaded vocabulary of business and commerce: *For profit. Hierarchical. Systematized. Planned. Proprietary. Pragmatic. Accountable. Organized and Reliable.* There is more than simple word play here. There seems, in fact, to be a core conflict of values between the basic nature of the Internet and the demands of organized, large-scale commerce. One side or the other must give.[5]

This wasn't at all a minority view. Many groups organized to ward off any business intrusion—from their perspective—on the Internet. The view of business in the quote above is that of the stereotypical transaction- and production-centered company.

What changed so suddenly between 1995 and today? Business trends and the Internet came together and created an explosion. Business moved very much in the direction the authors of the above quote favor. Free, egalitarian, decentralized, ad hoc, open and peer to peer, experimental, autonomous, and, yes, even anarchic are all very applicable adjectives to the world of relationship-centered eCommerce. Business as usual largely did not work on the Web, but business as relationship did and that accelerated eCommerce. The existing trend toward electronic data interchange and electronic supply chain management in supply chain management were greatly accelerated by, most obviously, the availability worldwide of a toolkit that had a common software interface and set of standards. These included the browser, Internet Protocol (IP), and in more and more parts of the world, low-cost Internet service providers (ISPs) and low-cost or free local phone call access to the ISP. Thus, a well-established decade-long evolution suddenly exploded and EDI became B2B. Similarly, the application program interface (API) became a vehicle for first electronic out-sourcing and then linking your business to someone else's. The very idea of a vertical company made less and less sense. A Yahoo! or a business-to-business hub like Chemdex could grow *only* through extending its horizontal reach. Ones like Geocities were really nothing more than a site built on links to other peoples' sites—the start of the now commonplace term "portal."

And so it goes. *All this happened in five years.* Today, it's hard to even map all the relationship links of a company like Dell. UPS is "in" its organization, and when you place an order on the Dell Premier Page customized to your company's business rules, you're actually in Ariba's network. And perhaps in Sony's, Intel's, and how many others? Your order is being handled across multiple parties working in concert to create value for themselves and each other. eCommerce technologies have changed the need to collaborate across companies, as no one company now has the time or inclination to build an eCommerce vertical company.

There is thus an historical inevitability to what we are seeing today. Everything shaping eCommerce moves in the same direction. Business took over the Internet through relationships instead of the early transaction Web sites, and value came more and more from extending a company's presence out beyond the site itself, across evermore links and alliances. Value networks are now the catalysts of Internet eCommerce innovation.

The Relationship Web in a Value Network

eCommerce thus more and more involves a complex network of relationships to operate between the enterprise, its customers, intermediaries, complementors, and suppliers. This network covers consumer and business-to-business relationships, and eCommerce is applicable to any and all of the relationships within it, including those between different parts of the company. The many-to-many relationships possible in eCommerce make it important to clarify the role of each of the players in a company's value network. The network identifies both the players and the intent behind their relationships and, therefore, provides a basis for understanding the scope of eCommerce and potential actions.

If you think of the enterprise as the value center, there are four sets of relationship groupings, as shown in the following illustration: suppliers, intermediaries, complementors, and customers. The company uses its process-based links in building the nodes and relationships between nodes on the network.

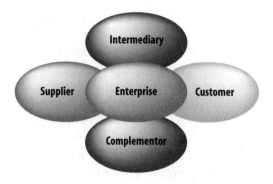

A value network takes advantage of eProcess best-practice provider options as your company sources the required capabilities across multiple companies.

The Enterprise

The enterprise is your company at the center of the network. The enterprise acts as the central point of execution and *responsibility* for the value network. The value network centers on the enterprise because it integrates and activates the network. It is accountable for its business viability and attractiveness. A poorly constructed or managed network will fail to attract the right capabilities, leaving the company as the hub of a wheel with missing or broken spokes. The enterprise is making a promise to the customer—that an item will be delivered on schedule, in good condition, and to price and quality specifications. The only advantage the vertical organization has here is that it controls most of the resources and organizational units that must deliver on the promise. If a supplier in the value network fails in its part of the interplay, the enterprise can't shift the blame to it.

The value network must operate with the efficiency of a vertical company. This requires managing the network from a process rather than an organizational basis. Companies at the center of a value network maintain the network through assessing the performance of the services exchanged among participants as these services link players together. This is why alliance processes are in themselves so key and why this is not traditional out-sourcing, where the company simply signs a contract for some service. The value network is an alliance eProcess complex of trading partner agreements, information sharing, collaboration, and joint ventures.

The enterprise holds the customer relationship, perhaps its most valuable asset. It is responsible for acquiring and maintaining that relationship. The enterprise is accountable for the activities and performance of suppliers and intermediaries in providing products and services. It's the hub and the value network partners are the spokes—for this particular customer relationship. For another customer relationship, the enterprise may play a spoke role as supplier, complementor, or any other role. Intel is thus a hub that sells a billion dollars of goods a month. It's part of supply chains where the hub may be one of the B2B leaders. It's a customer for companies it also sells to.

The Customers

Value networks exist to serve customers. They form the context for the value network as it seeks to align around customer needs and values. By customers, we're not just referring to individual consumers, but also businesses, associations, and other companies. Customers visit a site considering products and services in terms of price, quality, reputation, relationship, and so on. Their reaction to those offers and the extent to which they enter into a long-term relationship with the enterprise over time determines its revenue potential and investor assessments of its likely future growth.

Historically, you built your customer base mainly by being very good at what you did yourself. Now, you can become superb by always looking to include in your value network the very best of the best in any and every area that adds value to the customer. You don't have to do it yourself any more, and you couldn't even if you tried. It would take you many years to build all the capabilities you need, and time is never on your side now.

The Suppliers

Suppliers determine the enterprise's operational parameters and ability to keep promises to customers. Great companies need great suppliers, and great suppliers help make great companies. Suppliers provide products and services to the enterprise, which in turn, creates their products and services. The company's capabilities are bounded and unbounded to a large extent by their suppliers. Supplier performance is a significant determinate of the cost and performance boundaries, as they are a critical loop in the value network. An enterprise can't be fast and flexible if its end-to-end supply chain isn't both of these.

This has changed the very nature of supply chain and logistics—from contracts and transactions, with information something to hoard in order to get an edge in the next set of negotiations, to alliances and relationship investment, with information the base for optimizing the entire chain. The very term "supply chain management" is now obsolete. It's much more supply chain choreography.

The Intermediaries and Complementors

Obviously, in this choreography, more and more roles are played by intermediaries and complementors. These add services and products that expand the reach and range of a company's services and products. Intermediaries add services that are part of the enterprise's operational requirements and that the enterprise either cannot carry out for itself or should not even try to do so, in terms of quality and cost. There are multiple types of intermediaries:

Sales intermediaries These are companies that extend the enterprises' sales capability. They include resellers, distributors, channel partners, value-added partners, and channel resellers. Note that the same party may play a different role in a value network—the tidy old model of customer, broker/agent/distributor, and supplier, each with its clear-cut separation of identity, disappears.

Fulfillment intermediaries These are services that enable order fulfillment. These intermediaries generally center on logistics services (such as package distribution companies) and payment services (such as credit card payments).

Information and communication intermediaries These offer research information to customers, information for comparison shopping, technical data, catalog management, and vehicles for community building, such as discussion forums.

Complementors provide products and services that extend the appeal of the enterprise's offers and increase the scope of the value network. These are often co-branded with the enterprise. Yahoo! works with around 10,000 such co-providers. Let's restate that. Yahoo!'s value network has 10,000 value-generating players, a figure that can be scaled to 100,000 or 1 million, each of which is a value player itself and often linked to other value networks. They are each interactive and dynamic. Many of them are power brands themselves. To take just one example, one of the authors logged on to his My.Yahoo page while he was writing this chapter. The first item displayed on the screen was his stock portfolio, with prices updated every 15 minutes. Alongside was a rich range of complementors' information sources, including Reuters Internet newswire reports, News.com tech news, and E! Online news. There was an ad for e-stamp.com, which allows you to obtain USPS-approved electronic postage stamps.

Is this really an ad, though? It's a value network additional Yahoo! complementor service. Clicking the E-Stamp icon moves you to its page, which includes a link to, among others, the E-Stamp affiliates program. This program offers $10 for every visitor another site refers to e-stamp.com and who buys its Starter Kit package. The ad on Yahoo! initiates the response and interaction with E-Stamp, which makes it more than just an ad. The same is the case with the Reuters' complementor role in Yahoo!'s value network. It generates interaction with other companies' Web sites, ones that are mentioned in, say, a newswire item.

So a value network is a relationship in itself via the enterprise, a network of relationships through the enterprise link, and a network of relationships via the relationship links, and so on—if not ad infinitum, then at least in Yahoo!'s case, through myriads of combinations of interactions across its 10,000 complementors and their value network links.

The economics of Yahoo!'s value network are astounding in themselves. They are also an indicator of the degree of wealth generation the very best of the eCommerce players can create and how misleading earnings per share figures—historically, the main basis for investor valuation—are in themselves. Table 4-1 shows some information from Yahoo!'s first quarter 2000 earnings report. Is there any way in which a company that is not built as an Internet-based value network complex could in any way achieve Yahoo!'s growth in all the economic drivers of wealth?

Table 4-1: The Profit Opportunities of a Value Network: Yahoo!'s Financial Results, Quarter 1, 2000[6]

Sales for the quarter	$228 million, up by 120% over the previous year
Profits	$63 million, versus roughly break-even previous year
Operating costs (excluding marketing and sales) to generate these sales	$32 million; operating margin 85%
Cash generated	$214 million—on $228 million of sales!—with end of quarter cash and short-term investments $1.2 billion (cash flow is thus 238% higher than earnings)
Marketing and sales costs	$75 million; growth from previous year 76%, versus sales growth of 120%; cost per unit of revenue is now $0.33, versus $0.41
Number of advertisers	3,565 at an average contract of $64,000 (the $228 million in revenues); renewal rate 97%; average contract length 230 days versus 192 days for quarter 4, 1999
Number of merchants in Yahoo!'s value network	10,500, up from 9,000 quarter 4, 1999. Total merchant sales through the value network: $1 billion for the quarter versus $670 million quarter 4

One of the most interesting new elements of Yahoo!'s business model is its shift away from charging merchants a fixed price or rent. Rather, it shares in their growth through a fee for transactions with customers. Broadvision, the software company that gathers personal information to help companies customize sites and offers, similarly charges a fee per consumer profile. Exodus, the leader in Internet data center hosts, charges by the transaction too, and many other companies are moving toward a fee-based revenue model. The reason for this general trend is that, as partners in the value network grow, so do the fees they pay to Yahoo!, Broadvision, and Exodus. It's win-win. The profits come from the growth of the value network as a whole.

All this is far more than just designing a Web site. We suspect that within the next year, the discussion of electronic commerce will shift from the question, "What is the business model?" to "What is the value network?" Which B2B hub as a value network is your company part of? Which value network are you the portal for or spoke into the hub?

Target Relationships

As value networks form, grow, create brands, and sustain value, then clearly a major factor in eSuccess will be the electronic commerce company's choice of relationships. The enterprise-customer link will build repeat business; the enterprise-supplier and supply chain partners and hubs will ensure best-practice order fulfillment, quality, and logistics; and complementors will meet the broadest set of customer interests and needs. Targeting relationships rather than offering products and services within traditional industry boundaries generates flexibility, whereas any eCommerce strategy based on the latter is increasingly ineffective, for the simple but far-reaching reason that customers really do not care about industry boundaries and practices. Just try to describe the basics of Amazon in those terms. Is Amazon a retailer? A portal? A market maker? An auction house? Well, it is all of these now. In the future, it will be many other things; however, it will always concentrate on having the premier set of retail customer relationships. It's spending a fortune to do so, and its success entirely rests on achieving this.

Product, service, and industry labels are becoming irrelevant, as they do not give any sense of the eProcess demands of Amazon's or any other eCommerce value network. It's meaningless to talk about being in the car-selling "business," when that ranges from Priceline.com letting customers state their own price they're willing to pay for a car, AutoByTel and CarBuy offering information, location, delivery, financing, and so on. Selling "products" online has become more and more a matter of the links between the Web site as the enterprise-customer relationship interface and the enterprise-supplier eProcess relationship interface. "Customer service" in turn relates to process capabilities in many areas—financing, shipping, troubleshooting, handling of returns—that require very careful attention to choice of intermediaries and complementors.

Maintain an Outward Focus

Many companies still see the issues of eProcess and relationship as ones of transaction management: contracts, orders, and shipments. When viewed in this perspective, they think about conformance to the contract rather than thinking ahead to how to make the relationship work well for both parties. This inward focus on the company and its business rather than the health of the network is a cause of process blindness and myopia.

Companies all too often have this inward perspective in all elements of their commerce—on themselves as retailers concentrating on sales, inventory turns, and on the competition rather than the customer. Relationships provide the best approach for maintaining an outward focus that creates a bias toward enabling rather than controlling players in the design of products and services. Again, as with our earlier examples of the shift toward collaborative relationships in supply chain management and life event marketing, this is a general business trend in that the Internet both accelerates and enables new options. For example, out-sourcing is now commonplace as companies focus their efforts on core capabilities and get rid of peripheral processes. What is different between traditional out-sourcing and the eProcess approach to out-tasking and in-sourcing is the dynamic win-win view of the value network as the unit of eCommerce design, not the company in and of itself.

Define Roles Within the Network

The eCommerce target is value through relationships. A company creates and maintains its value network based on its value potential and value realized. A healthy value network concentrates on the roles companies and individuals can play in your network and/or that you can play in theirs. These roles—for them and for you—include that of customer, supplier, intermediary, and complementor. Your company can be a customer in one value network, an intermediary in another, and a supplier in yet another. The critical roles rest where you are the enterprise at the center, the hub for which the others are spokes.

The roles are not fixed; that's one of the shifts the value network approach brings. For example, "supplier" and "customer" imply a transaction interaction. Customers place orders and suppliers fill them. Historically, this had led to businesses carefully guarding information about their sales and playing suppliers off against each other. That's changed significantly over the past decade. The transaction and contract relationship has become a trading partner relationship. Manufacturers have learned to work closely with their suppliers in design, scheduling, and quality control. Retailers started to provide information so their suppliers could optimize production and delivery. They build value for each other through the relationship. The very terms "customer" and "supplier" lose their dichotomous us-you distinction.

Roles Blur the Lines Between Players

The Internet extends this trend and in some instances makes the customer-supplier label meaningless. For example, Amazon sells books to customers, but a customer may also be an Amazon Associate whose own Web site includes a link to Amazon's Web site. The customer is Amazon's broker, and in many ways, Amazon is the site's customer. For example, in the case of Peter Keen, his site includes extracts from his books. If someone accessing the site hits the link to Amazon and buys one of them online, Keen gets a commission from Amazon. Amazon here is his "customer," and he is Amazon's "supplier." Amazon has many thousands of such Associates, and they extend each other's value networks. Amazon also "hosts" retailers through its zShops; they may sell any type of goods to their customers. Amazon's software may refer its own customers to them.

eBay: An Example of a Networked Market

eBay is such a value network. Technically, the auction transaction is between a buyer or seller, but it's eBay as a value network that creates many value relationships: buyer to eBay, seller to eBay, buyer to seller, communities of interest that share forums, information and discussion, eBay to insurer, buyer and seller to insurer, and so on. eBay has often been described as the world's largest yard sale or flea market. That misses the point. If it were just that, it is unlikely that it would have grown as fast and as large as it has. A yard sale is just an anonymous transaction site. Much of eBay's success has rested on how it works to ensure what yard sales can't: both buyers and sales rating each other's reliability and honesty in the deal, thus building up reputations—almost a credibility record. When this is jeopardized, the company's relationships are at risk.

EXTEND OFFERINGS THROUGH RELATIONSHIPS

eBay continues to add electronic relationships to extend the value proposition to buyers and seller. It acquired Butterfield and Butterfield, a West Coast auction house established in 1865. The company operates offices in Europe and has a high-end clientele of around half a million. Both companies get a win-win situation here. They cross-refer would-be buyers and sellers to each other, and eBay continues to expand from its origins as an auction hub for small ticket items. Because it has such a large customer base, it's ideal for charity auctions. eBay sponsors Rosie O'Donnell's celebrity guest auctions online, for instance. To strengthen the sense of collaboration and community among its customer base, it provides My eBay personal pages and hosts chat rooms and news and announcement boards.

Other leading auction players have moved in very much the same way as eBay. Auctions are not a separate value network for Amazon and Yahoo!, but an extension of their already large, wide, and deep value networks. The same eProcess principles apply. Amazon in-sourced Sotheby's, the best known of all auction houses. It links auctions to all the other elements of its value network. For example, when customers access its zShop complex of retail stores—which in itself provides small businesses and home businesses an opportunity to become part of a value network they could never create by themselves—it alerts them to any auction offering the goods they are seeking.

PROCESSES: BEHIND THE SCREENS

It's easy to think of these as just Web site features, but that ignores the relationship dynamic and value network they are built on. This is eProcess in action. Many of the value network components are software embedded in eBay's own site. Its Safe Harbor feature, for instance, includes tools for "full service customer support and educational resources," such as the Feedback Forum. Safe Harbor also has out-tasked links to a buyer's insurance facility. It in-sources an online escrow service via a well-established insurance company and such extensions of its business as Butterfield and Butterfield.

Value Networks: A Basis for Organizing and Competing

This is the real competitive game—value networks, not Web sites. Our brief review of eBay could just as easily be a review of a leading business-to-business hub like Chemdex, personal computer retailers (Dell and Gateway), consumer portals (AutoByTel and AOL), manufacturers (Ford, IBM, and Cisco), financial service providers (Schwab, E*Trade, and Wells Fargo), community portals (iVillage), or just about every other type of online operation. Smaller offline companies are most likely to join a value network in order to gain access to eProcess capabilities, visibility, and customers. New entrants have based their business model on creating a new value network as a portal that brings together information and services for a target community (the many specialized sites designed for pet owners, for example) or as a business-to-business hub. Large online companies are value networks that can charge substantial fees for others to be part of them. AOL and Yahoo! are obvious instances here.

The Basic Company Model Utilizing Value Networks

There are value networks everywhere on the Internet: business-to-business supply chain management hubs, community-centered sites, and portals. They are, almost by definition, the natural and ever-evolving direction of the Web. They have to be, if value is the target—and it has to be if a company is interested in more than just having a Web site as a PR outlet or because companies now just have to be on the Web.

Value networks rely on a combination of the eProcess sourcing opportunities we outlined in Chapter 1: embedding, out-tasking, in-sourcing, and in-house processes. Those are the tools for building value networks. Relationships are the value generators. So design the relationship roles first and foremost. That's how to target the marketplace. Start with a blank slate. Leverage your business model not by designing a Web site, but by viewing the site as the relationship interface. Then define and source the process capabilities that provide the strongest value network. The technical components of the telecommunications, computer, and data complex are a relationship platform that can be expanded and extended over time.

Decide on the Value Network Roles and Relationships

Obviously, the primary relationship building blocks of the value network are the enterprise and its direct "exchange partners." These are the parties for which the value network exists. Commerce is about exchange of value. The most basic exchange relationship is direct buyer with direct provider as in, say, a Web site for ordering office products or for placing a request to a courier to pick up a package. The value on both sides of the relationship interface is limited. The seller still has a mass of in-house workflows to handle its own customer-supplier relationships, manage inventory, and all the paperwork associated with fulfillment of the order, payment, and so on. The value for the buyer is low price, convenience, and access to an online catalog. It is a transaction interface, the equivalent of the useful and skilled 7-Eleven chain of stores. Companies that stop at shopping and buying on the Web are just electronic convenience stores competing on price and creating commoditization.

Segment eCommerce Markets

So you need to look beyond the transaction at the relationships you want to build with exchange partners. Which ones? Everyone on the Web who gets to your site? Particular age groups? Communities? Small businesses? Specific industries? Supply chains? One of the most far-reaching and complex opportunities the Web has created relates to market segmentation, but not at all in traditional terms and tools. Standard demographics do not apply here. Web users choose the relationship based on their own self-segmentations. They don't have to fit into anyone's categories and indeed don't have to use the Web for anything. They choose. That means that everything about Web relationships is personal and has to be customized.

The question to answer in addressing target market and customer segmentation is not the obvious one of "Who is our customer?" but "What's going to make the customers we want to come back to us actually come back?" That question in itself expands to the ones below. Prefaced each question with "Given our business goals…"

- ▶ Who do we want as the players in our eCommerce value network? Which customers? Which suppliers? Which intermediaries? Which complementors?

- ▶ What roles do we want each of these to play in the value network?

- ▶ Why should they play those roles in our value network versus their own or someone else's?

- ▶ What type of relationships do we need with these players?

- ▶ What are the capabilities that build those relationships?

- ▶ What is the most effective way to source these capabilities?

The answers to these questions determine with whom you work and on what basis, what you do versus what they do, and where to invest time and capital. These answers set the executive agenda for eProcess investment.

Decide Who You Want in Your Value Network

Defining the value network means deciding who you want to be involved in your eCommerce business. All the relationships must leverage the end-customer. That's the value generator in a value network. In eProcess, the enterprise sources capabilities that will ensure value for its customers and for itself. It must ensure that it provides the very best customer-enterprise processes. It must examine its own enterprise-supplier and enterprise-intermediary options in that light. In general, those options will be driven by its operational needs. Clearly, supply chain and logistics are at the very core of the company, for reasons of both customer service and cost efficiency. The enterprise *must* choose and maintain relationships not so much with individual suppliers as with the value networks that are transforming the very nature of logistics.

To ignore these potential relationships is executive blindness and irresponsibility. It robs the company of an easy 5 to 10 percent reduction in the cost of many types of supplies—materials, operating resources, spare parts, and such. It could cut administrative and overhead costs by 10 to 20 percent and reduce working capital needs by 20 to 40 percent.[7] The reason for this is the many new value networks that address supply chain relationships within and across industries. They include trading partner hubs, vertical hubs, industrial auction sites, and new types of value-adding intermediaries that use the Internet to streamline information flows along the supply chain and broker deals and to manage many of the secondary transactions associated with supply chain management. These can include financing, reporting, shipping, and taxes.

Choose Complementors

The enterprise's choice of relationships with complementors is far more complex than that with suppliers and intermediaries. Suppliers and intermediaries provide core enterprise operations. Selecting these players involves identifying the best source of the capabilities required to support the operation. A company adds complementors to create a wider relationship. It is easy to illustrate this scenario in the securities trading business. Here, the core of the enterprise-customer relationship is the trade itself, management of the customer account, and provision of support services. The company relies on many intermediaries to process the trade. This is more complex than it may appear. There are vast differences in how quickly the trade can be made, through which dealers and which networks (many new ones have emerged that bypass the NYSE and NASDAQ), and at what "spread" between the quoted buy and sell price.

Companies such as Ameritrade, E*Trade, and Charles Schwab do not need complementors to carry out this basic business. But that basic business is just an $8 to $24 transaction. It's not a relationship, and it can be a way to lose money on a large scale in that the marketing cost to acquire a customer is $200 to $400.[8]

The way the leaders in online trading are building their relationship strengths is by adding more and more services through complementors. If you're a trader, you want the best securities research information, access to financial advisers, and ability to buy mutual funds and bonds, as well as stocks. The three companies mentioned are all building a financial investment and financial management value network in this way. Charles Schwab's latest moves have included strengthening the online relationship through offline meetings (for a fee) with a personal portfolio consultant.

The most powerful and profitable eCommerce brands rest on complementors. The more powerful the brand, the more it can charge a fee to them. AOL is an obvious example here. Through a combination of acquisitions, part-ownership, partnerships, and fees for a presence on its portal, it has built a $5 billion-a-year company. The complementors add to its brand and help it extend both its relationship base and its revenues per subscriber.

Define the Value Network: Creating Your Target

The capabilities within your value network define the breadth of your eCommerce capability and business. This breadth creates a vibrant framework for establishing the relationships that matter most to your business and capabilities. The resulting focus is necessary to determine and define the proper relationships between the players found within this network.

The value network is the basis for competition; it is far more effective to play on a team than to go it alone.

Chapter 5

Defining Relationships: Touch and Texture

Once a company targets its customer relationships, it needs to define the exact nature of each of them. The relationship type establishes the business requirements for its eProcess capabilities. It defines how and where to leverage *content* and manage *context* in the customer relationship interface. This establishes what eProcess terms the touch and texture of your relationships.

The Challenge of Online Relationships

It's hard enough to build and sustain relationships on a face-to-face basis. In the online world, it is harder to build relationships. It's harder in that the company is starting from scratch. It has a Web site. That's it. In most cases, it's just one of many sites offering very much the same transaction: a product or service. Initiating the relationships requires a reason for a customer or supplier to come to the site. The cheapest and least efficient way of doing this is registering with leading search engines and competing on price; that way, you have a chance of drawing hits by surfers. But to go beyond this is very expensive: heavy price discounts and giveaways, fees to portals such as Yahoo! and AOL, online advertising, and heavy marketing.

Marketing Is Not a Relationship

Even if these efforts pull in customers, what gets them coming back and back? They can always carry out another search, and there are plenty more great price deals to locate and accept. An ad on national Television during the Super Bowl may lead to hundreds of thousands of new potential customers accessing a site, but so what? A transaction isn't a relationship, and transactions don't in themselves turn into sustainable relationships. Unless there is a reason to return, most online companies will get stuck in the transaction trap as they compete on price. These companies must shift fast enough and grow large enough to recover the massive investment they make in marketing and the margin reduction that their price discounts and payments to portals and for referrals generate. You can't buy relationships.

Pure Transactions: The Commodity of Commerce

Relationships require touch and texture, which offer more than a pure transaction. Touch involves a degree of interaction between customers and suppliers. Texture describes the richness and personalization of information involved in this interaction. Texture and touch combine to define the characteristics of the relationship interface: how it uses information content and how it establishes the relationship context.

A pure transaction has zero touch, zero texture. "I will pay this price for that product. Thanks" is the extent of a transaction. We will call such transactions "zero-T." Such a simple zero-T conversation fundamentally excludes relationships. In eCommerce it is the online equivalent of a 7-Eleven—a convenience store where the customer looks at the options, picks one, handles payment, gives and gets a thank you, and leaves. We choose 7-Eleven as our analogy here because the chain carries out its processes superbly. It serves its purposes well, and customers get service and value. Thank you. Done.

The same may be the case for some Web sites: informational in purpose, intentionally small in scale, and offering a very straightforward service. That said, it's a dead end in that at best it's the result of a search engine request. There are a huge number of sites out on the Web that fit this zero-T profile, but their companies clearly have more ambitious aims for their eCommerce ventures and are paying an awful lot of money to build, run, and market them.

Automated Teller Machines: Pure Transactions

It may be worthwhile for these companies to keep in mind the history of the automated teller machine. Much of eCommerce is following its path. When Citibank launched the ATM in the late 1970s, it gained a competitive advantage because it created a new vehicle for customers to interact with the bank. The new technology opened up an opportunity for Citibank to deepen the relationship by adding credit cards, telephone banking, and other innovations. Customers gained a new level of convenience and service that did not exist beforehand. While it took years for ATM use to reach critical mass, little by little more and more banks made it a differentiator.

However, that's no longer the case; ATMs are a requirement that provides no differentiation. Customers wanted to be able to use their ATM anywhere, not just at a cash machine that handled only one bank's cards. Consortia like Cirrus and Plus offered networks that accepted cards from most banks, eroding the advantage the large institutions had in terms of large-scale telecommunications networks. Now, the ATM is taken for granted as an essential of everyday life. It handles transactions without building a relationship; unless you count the negative relationships created when customers go out of their way to use their own bank's ATM to avoid the $1 to $3 fee charged by others. For most people, transaction processes merely build a relationship with the network—whether with ATMs or, in the case of eCommerce, with the Internet itself, not a particular bank.

Transaction Factories: Islands of Automation

There are many studies that suggest—with, of course, the benefit of hindsight—that the banking industry might have been better advised not to build a mass of separate networks and systems[1] Customer demands made a value network inevitable, rather than what has been termed "islands of automation." In the end, the industry increased every player's technology costs as network transaction fees cut into bank profits without a resulting competitive advantage.

This is the limitation of transaction-centered Web sites. They may well generate an early "first mover" advantage, but only as islands. The more that customers, suppliers, and intermediaries are drawn into value networks, the faster the islands become little more than dropping-off points for handling the transaction, not the relationship. Almost all ATM transactions are zero texture and zero touch. Indeed, can you remember just which bank or ATM network's machine you last used to get cash? Do you ever walk past one because there is a special machine you must use? Substitute "Web site" for "ATM" in many standard and simple purchases, and the questions probably have the same answer. Zero-T means that only convenience counts.

Relationships: Establishing Context Through Personalizing Content

Building relationships is hard, far harder than the early Web business innovators ever expected. Companies have to get value from their marketing dollar by going beyond the transaction engine to building context and content. In the traditional economy, context and content accrued over time through personal relationships between your sales force and your customers' buyers. This made relationship sales and service an expensive endeavor to build and a valuable resource to nurture and keep. The same is the case for the Internet, but the scale and pace of innovation are so obviously far greater and far riskier.

Web-centered relationships are in some ways, though, easier to build than face-to-face ones. First, the technology itself helps. There's a growing toolkit for capturing information about customers to identify their interests and track their choices (and, alas, invade their privacy and in some instances misuse the data), for personalizing sites and customizing offers, and for ensuring a smooth, complete, and convenient interaction between the enterprise and customer. Customer relationship management (CRM) is the broad term for this toolkit and its uses. It is among the fastest-growing trends in eCommerce.[2]

Content: Information

Information is not in itself a relationship, any more than you have a relationship with a newspaper. And it's not an end in itself, something that far too many information technology professionals too easily ignore. They build databases for knowledge management, data warehousing, and information retrieval and wonder why so few people use them. Information is meaningful only when it enables communication, coordination, collaboration, community, and decision making. Then it can become enormously powerful.

Applied Knowledge Creates Relationships

"Content" is the broad term for information that is put to use: applied knowledge. The eProcess design question is, applied to *what*? The answer again is relationship building and relationship enhancement where relationship strength increases as content moves from the general to the personal. General knowledge such as stock prices, product catalogs, and news are a commodity with limited relationship potential. It may or may not be relevant to you. Personal knowledge includes preferences, product or service configuration, and profiles. It is directly relevant to you. General content is context independent; it's the same for me and for you. Personalized content is obviously completely context dependent, and that context is an individual, family, company, or community. The more specific the tailoring of the content, the more the shift from commodity to relationship. This involves

▶ Enabling customers to define their own preferences and profiles via the Web page software. These then drive the selection of "relevant" content.

▶ Presenting content based on those customer preferences and profiles instead of customers having to define their own requests and sort through a mass of catalogs, databases, and menu options.

▶ Fulfilling transactions such as ordering, financing, and shipping without the customer having to direct the process and provide information. The software should know what to do.

Context provides the basis for knowing who this customer or business partner is and how to personally respond instead of treating them as anonymous. The more customers provide information, the more the technology itself tracks choices, orders, interests, patterns, and indicators of individual choices that they themselves may be unaware of, and the more the Web site can personalize and customize every aspect of the relationship. (One of the main accelerating trends in eCommerce software is tools that gather data about customers' purchases and analyze it to infer what else they might be interested in.) And, of course, the more information the company provides—its own or information in-sourced from other companies—the more responsive, imaginative, and broad the offers it can bring to customers. Even more powerfully, the value network itself can generate information of value to all its parties. For example, suppliers learn about customer trends and are alerted to prospective new buyers.

Texture and Touch: Creating an Environment for Relationships

eCommerce tools that manage content are only as effective as their uses of that content, though. Customer data is not enough. Forget about Web "sites." Instead, think of the site as the *start* of the relationship. Think in terms of the two key factors that show up in how companies who have best built the relationship advantage have used the Web opportunity. We picked the terms we use for these two factors—texture and touch—to make sure that the very personal nature of relationships, whether online or offline, is at the forefront of eProcess design and doesn't get lost in the abstractions. These are shown in Figure 5-1, with two broad categories for each.

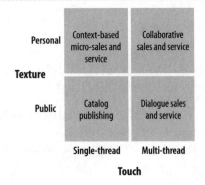

Figure 5-1: Texture and touch

Texture: The Nature of Information

Texture captures the nature of information and the feel of the online interaction—its substantive fabric of information, richness of presentation, originality, and other dimensions of the content. The question here is, how substantive is the offer? At the low end of the two extremes of texture is the thin and flimsy (and much-derided) corporate Web site that is little more than an online version of a company's brochure, or the retailer site that just publishes its catalog and provides basic ordering tools. At the high end are the sites that are rich in what Internet business insiders call "stickiness," material that brings customers back again and again because it is personalized to them. High texture creates the personalization called for to deliver micro-marketing, a longstanding promise of the Web.

Touch: Creating Context Through Dialogue

Touch captures the degree of interaction sought between the exchange partners—the type of contact—and relates to communication, collaboration, and community. Touch ranges from very *single-thread* take-it-or-leave-it interactions to *multi-thread* interactions where customers and the company co-create solutions and offers. Low-touch solutions are customer- and context-independent. It's what is in the library or on the shelves and available for everyone. It's low touch because the interaction is a single path from the company to the customer, with the essence of the dialogue being "try it out and take your pick." Personalization offers higher touch as content and services are tailored to your context. This requires multiple interactions creating a dialogue about you, your needs and interests, and perhaps some negotiations. The result is a rich texture of information and offers that are for you only, based on an exchange of ideas about deals where the provider partner can act as your agent. The difference between general (single-thread) and dynamic (multi-thread) is "Here's what *we* have" and "Let's see what we can do for *you*."

High Touch, High Texture: Co-Creation

If a simple transaction represents zero-texture and zero-touch, then co-creation is our best term for taking the relationships as far as it can go. "Co-" means "together," and many of the words relevant to touch begin with it: collaborate, cooperate, co-design, correspond, and coordinate, for instance. Others use the Latinate prefix "com-", meaning "with." Among these are communicate and community, which in themselves almost stand for a definition of value network. By choosing the verb "create," we are reminding managers of the new obvious: there's nothing routine, static, or obvious about building a high-touch relationship. It's a creative process that relies on innovation and invention—otherwise, it's just a commodity, the only negative "com-" word in the eCommerce vocabulary.

Relationship Types: Configurations of Texture and Touch

Relationships and their value potential are based on combinations of texture and touch. These combinations define the requirements for your business capabilities, Web interface, and value network. The *type* of relationship you support is an important eProcess decision that drives capability sourcing and process design. Companies that seek higher levels of texture and touch must build more sophisticated relationships and capabilities. These relationships take longer to build, as customers and suppliers build their level of trust and commitment to your eCommerce channel. The relationship types appear in Figure 5-2.

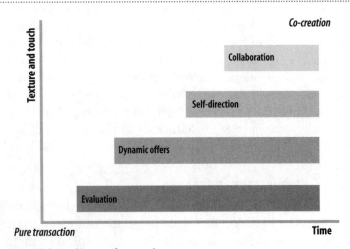

Figure 5-2: Relationship types framework

The relationship types cover the range from the pure transaction through co-creation. They build upon one another such that a self-direction relationship includes the capabilities required for dynamic offers and evaluation, and collaboration builds on self-direction. The four relationship types are

Evaluation Provides an exchange partner in the value network with tools to locate and assess offers and options. This relationship involves low texture and touch as publicly available information flows one way to the evaluator.

Dynamic offers Shapes offers to the exchange partner, based on a range of situational factors, including themselves (personalized deals and frequent buyer benefits), the market (brokers, agents, and auctions), or the value network itself (cooperative information sharing). This relationship type increases texture, moving from public to private information. However, it still keeps its low touch characteristics.

Self-direction Enables direct and personal management of the account, self-configuration of orders, transaction status tracking, individualized reporting, and so on. This is a high-touch relationship as the company responds to multi-threaded dialogue. However, the information remains in the public domain, giving low texture.

Collaboration "Co-" words appear everywhere as customers, suppliers, and your company work together to create solutions through their shared experience and knowledge. This is high texture and touch as people dialogue and share private information to accomplish tasks.

Evaluation: Shopping

Evaluation moves from the zero-T, 7-Eleven "walk in, buy, walk out" experience to build reasons to stride past shops and pick the one that offers something special. Typically, in the online environment—as in the offline world it complements, extends, and displaces—retailers use many tools to attract customers in, including storefront displays, ads in a range of media, catalogs, and special promotions. The major difference with the Web is the extraordinary range of information it can gather and display in seconds. Much of the early growth of consumer portals like AutoByTel, and more recently of B2B hubs, came from one simple reality: information has always been hard to find, expensive to get, difficult to process, and hard to validate.

It has also been largely non-interactive. It's been a form of goods rather than a relationship. In the world of information-searching, such a relationship has traditionally come from a broker—a travel agent, insurance agent, distributor, real estate agent, and the like. At their best, these are the information experts who are also trusted advisers; they work on your behalf to get you the best deal. Where that is indeed the case, you stay with the trusted advisers for their expertise and honesty, even if you could get the information to do the job yourself in many instances. However, you switch if any of these three conditions starts to apply:

► Your adviser doesn't have the best information.

► You don't feel you're getting the best deal.

► You feel confident you can do the job yourself and be better off as a result.

Here, it's not just a matter of information, but of how the information gets used. Information is everywhere. As the limitations of online search engines show, a simple question can generate total information overload. Skilled online eCommerce companies therefore place a premium on selecting information for you, organizing and displaying it and, more important, making sure you have access to the full range of relevant information. You don't want to be sold at; you want to be able to make an informed choice.

The Web is a wonderful vehicle for this, and as car dealers and travel agents know full well, there are plenty of services that will bring unbiased and comprehensive information to customers and meet their need for choice or for a specific combination of price, product, and provider. This shopping evaluation relationship builds on texture, focusing on the nature of the site content rather than on the nature of the interaction on the site. It is a relationship foundation, through the provision of general-purpose information and standard transactions (which are not necessarily just *at* the site; component software and bots are capable of seeking out deals and information for you dynamically and continuously). It provides for comparison shopping, purchases from catalogs, and Web site features such as mortgage payment calculations or comparisons of financing options. A shopping relationship rests on ease of navigation, search for products and prices, and other features that help customers research and evaluate your own offer.

This is the typical Web storefront retailer and information intermediary that provides searches and referrals. It's basically a catalog. It has several strengths but many limitations. The strengths are that it is informative, and a company can add more and more and more content and useful services that draw users back to it. That's also the limitation. Visitors come to many such sites to research and evaluate options, but then go elsewhere on the Web to make a purchase. In many instances, a popular evaluation site has to fund itself through advertising or referrals. This is the business model for many Web content publishers such as medical information sites (Drkoop.com and WebMD.com). The early search engines provide another example: AltaVista, Excite, Lycos, and Yahoo! In the case of Yahoo!, it has become a leader as it has increased its texture and touch through greater personalization of information and options.

Fiat Barchetta

Evaluation doesn't just mean looking at catalogs and making comparisons among product or service prices and features. Fiat Automotive provides an example of how to entice potential customers to take an in-depth look at a product and then move them on in the purchase process. Fiat used the Internet to generate excitement around its two-seater sports car, Barchetta (also known as Spider). The new model was available for evaluation and purchase over Fiat's Web site. While the site provided customers with an ability to review product specifications, choose colors, and gain other information, Fiat knew that evaluating a sports car involves more than looking at it; you have to drive it.

Fiat's Web site provided the relationship interface to its value network that enabled customers to arrange test drives through the Web site. The test drives, provided by a rental car company, offered customers the opportunity to evaluate the car without the pressures of a dealer environment. The rental car company maintained the cars and provided Fiat with geographic reach and the capability to handle individual appointments.

The Web Barchetta promotion lasted six weeks, generating more than 2,000,000 hits.[3] The result was a dramatic increase in consumer awareness of the new car and increased sales. Through the experience, Fiat learned how to provide the full evaluation relationship, meshing the clicks of its Web site with the bricks of the test drive. Since then, Fiat has added many new and deep collaborative innovations in its eCommerce relationships. When it wanted to test some new design ideas for its Punto car, it invited potential customers to select features for it on Fiat's Web site. Three thousand car lovers responded, a valuable source of information and feedback. Andersen Consulting describes this as co-creation: "Co-creation adds a new dynamic to the producer/customer relationship by engaging customers directly in the production or distribution of value. Customers, in other words, can get involved at just about any stage of the value chain."[4]

This example illustrates our recommendation that your eCommerce strategy recognize that evaluation is the starting point for relationship building, but only that. It is based on the texture and presentation of content from its own resources and its value network. The evaluation relationship supports shopping processes and is the weakest relationship type for eCommerce. This relationship is often the gateway to other, more sophisticated and valuable relationships. Building an effective evaluation relationship involves

- ▶ Enabling customers to research and acquire the information they need to make decisions

- ▶ Building credibility by providing information on all the products or services available in the market. Customers gain confidence in your offer by readily comparing it to others

- ▶ Providing a ready transition from research to selection of a particular product or service

While evaluation is the foundation of relationship building, companies have to move on or they will get stuck.

Dynamic Offers: Buying

Evaluation relationships typically quickly move to *dynamic offers*— they have to for eSuccess. This is high texture, but still relatively low touch. It remains transaction centered, but the offers are dynamic. For example, at Priceline.com, the customer chooses the price. On auction sites, buyers and sellers interactively establish the deal. Information about the customer may also be used by the product or service provider to offer a discount, a suggestion based on information gathered from software that profiles the customer, or a package deal. This is very much the equivalent of the best of retail stores. Note, though, that it is a store and has the limits of a store. The low touch here means that all shoppers are equal when they come in. They get special treatment if they have, say, a coupon or frequent buyer card. They can sign up for a rebate. They can perhaps bid on an item. But there's a limit to the degree of touch. It's a buyer-seller relationship: one-on-one marketing and relationship selling.

Organizations build their transaction relationship capabilities through generating and fulfilling customer requests at scale and speed. This involves bringing your demand generation and fulfillment capabilities together to ensure the necessary performance levels. The priorities here are to

- ▶ Enable customers to complete transactions via a clearly defined interface and process

- ▶ Provide information and activities in an intuitive way to build customers' confidence and commitment to the transaction

- ▶ Offer a standardized but customizable set of products and services to give customers choice within a range that is acceptable for your operations

- ▶ Enforce disciplined eProcesses to reduce errors, misunderstanding, and rework that destroy eCommerce efficiency

- ▶ Complete the transaction to the customer's satisfaction through strong back-office fulfillment capabilities

AutoByTel: Offering Total Service
AutoByTel has moved aggressively beyond being an information service for would-be car buyers (an evaluation relationship) to provide them with more and more personalized dynamic offers. Its advertisements now state that it will find you the car, get you the best price, arrange financing, and have the car delivered. In the early years of the Web, the dominant terms used to discuss opportunities were "information" and "content." There was plenty of talk about the information society, information superhighway, "content is king," and the like. Now, surely, it's more the collaboration society, the relationship superhighway, and "personalization is king."

Transaction and Evaluation: The Entry Criteria for eCommerce

It's noteworthy that of the many online startups that exploited the information opportunity the Web created, only those that have moved rapidly beyond being a search engine or just an intermediary between buyer and seller have prospered. Yahoo! and AutoByTel stand out in this regard, while AltaVista and Lycos have struggled, and Nets Inc., a promising forerunner of B2B hubs, went bankrupt. The same situation applies to the companies that focused on just transactions, like the many online malls sponsored by large companies such as IBM and MCI that came in quickly and disappeared quickly.

Transactions and the evaluation relationship represent the initial stage of many eCommerce implementations. However, handling transactions and providing research options do not necessarily build a relationship. Indeed, one consequence of the value network as the driving force in eCommerce is that they will rarely build a relationship in themselves. Companies expose themselves to commoditization as low price, high availability, and rich information sources generate escalating competition and online providers compete to gain customers. While a dynamic offer can generate eCommerce business, it is highly volatile because it is of value to the customer only on the spread between your prices and those of your competition. A stronger relationship than shopping and buying is necessary to generate sustained and profitable repeat business.

Self-Direction: Doing Business on Your Terms

Self-direction is perhaps the single most important element in moving from transactions to relationships. Here, *you* are in charge. You have your own personal site, customized to your own interests, priorities, and business rules. The site is likely to be named MyXYZ (My.Yahoo, MySchwab, and MyAmazon are examples). In business-to-business relationships, self-direction of just about every relevant eProcess is rapidly becoming the norm, with Dell's Premier Pages one of the best-known examples.

The reason for self-direction being absolutely critical in eCommerce evolution is that it adds a new level of touch to the customer relationship: personal service, customized offers, customer "intimacy," and other attributes of what professor Rik Maes of the University of Amsterdam terms the Emotion Economy—the ability to make choices entirely on the basis of how you feel and what you personally care about. This begins the transformation of the company's own cost structures.[5] It's this simultaneous win-win transition that makes eCommerce a true economic revolution.

Building self-direction capabilities rests on eProcess sourcing through embedding business rules in software. Here is a key to eCommerce success: high-touch customer relationship–bonding plus transformation of cost and service dynamics plus the new generation of eCommerce software. The priorities are to

▶ Transfer control and management of customer information and profiles to the customer. The customer is in charge. Of course, for that to happen, the consumer or business user has to want to take charge. There has to be personal benefit.

▶ Provide customer access to traditional back-office functions such as shipping and accounts payable, order tracking, and account status and reporting, troubleshooting, and any eProcess where the customer gains from do-it-yourself rather than phoning or emailing someone and waiting for a reply.

▶ Increase the depth and consistency of customer information across the enterprise through integrating Web site and enterprise applications—building the customer's value network.

▶ Embed knowledge management activities into the customer interface. This adds more and more intelligence. The system knows you, and you don't have to waste your time telling it who you are and what you want.

▶ Make skilled use of bots and agents to add more and more dynamic electronic workers in the background searching, dealing, reporting, and brokering on behalf of the customer.

Self-direction provides customers with greater involvement and control over the terms of business. The strength of a self-direction relationship rests with your ability to provide products and services that reflect the customer's preferences and profiles. This increases the value of having flexible and self-organizing processes. Companies that relinquish a degree of control to customers gain a strong relationship and a differentiating factor that increases customer repeat purchases.

Collaboration: Working Together

Collaboration extends self-direction from the personal management of your account—this is an account relationship and no longer a transactional interaction—to increasing degrees of collaboration. Here again, Amazon illustrates the trend among the eProcess leaders. Nothing happens on its site without it establishing a two-way interaction. For example, if you search on a book title, even if it can't locate it, it offers you the option to be automatically informed if it is later published or tells you about new books by the same author. If it finds the book, it also lists other books that people who are buying this one are also reading. It encourages readers to review books and authors to provide interviews. There are cross-links between its many types of offerings—books, consumer electronics, auctions, and so on. There are opportunities to meet with authors online and even such community competitions as writing a book in collaboration with well-known writers, where readers offer a paragraph that continues the story.

Business-to-Business Collaboration

In business-to-business relationships, collaboration includes "hosting" communities of interest interacting to solve technical problems, evaluate designs, and meet together in forums and workshops. The site offers many levels of relationship segmentation, so that, for example, procurement managers have their own site within the site that differs from that of engineers. The collaborations extend across the entire value network, with the hub providing forecasts and reports about supplier dynamics to buyers and about buyers to suppliers.

Marshall Industries provides an example of business-to-business collaboration among design engineers. The company supplies a design workspace for engineers to research its product catalog, collaborate with other design engineers, assemble virtual designs for electronic components, and test those designs through simulation. The engineers benefit from access to the latest electronic components, while

Marshall benefits as the engineers' component specifications represent potential future sales.[6]

Establishing a collaborative relationship requires the company to

- Create the electronic workspace to foster communication and knowledge sharing

- Support discussion groups by providing a wide range of products and services

- Be on the sideline and let participants resolve their own issues, unless they ask for assistance

- Learn from the discussions and resolutions created through the collaboration

- Expand the value network

Collaboration represents the strongest relationship between a customer and your online brand. A collaborative relationship draws customers together through your Web site. The connection with others who share similar interests and context defines a strong relationship and rationale for repeated use of your online brand.

If you consider any of the eProcess winners, they fill every cell in our touch-texture matrix, with collaboration forming the heart of the brand. This is the case with the supply chain and logistics winners such as Dell, Cisco, Marshall Industries, GE TPN, Ariba, Chemdex and many others, and with the top consumer mega-sites like AOL, Yahoo!, and Amazon that no longer fit into any industry classification. It's the same with their emerging equivalents in financial services, such as E*Trade, Fidelity, and Charles Schwab.

Relationships and Roles

Relationship types define the interaction style supported in the interface. That style is closely tied to the various roles present in the relationship between companies. Choosing relationship types occurs for each of the roles in eCommerce and not at the company level. Table 5-1 shows some sample roles, intents, and relationship types for the typical eCommerce company. Notice that different roles involve varying levels of touch and texture tied mostly to the roles intent in the business.

Table 5-1: Roles and Relationship Types

Role	Intent	Relationship Type				Actions
		Evaluation	Dynamic Offers	Self-Direction	Collaboration	
Purchasing agent	Evaluate and approve non-standard purchasing requests, define payment terms and profiles	X	X	X		Provide access to purchasing, inventory, and pricing information. Enable agents to maintain rules for what is a standard purchasing request
End user	Evaluate products and services, select items for purchase, initiate purchase request	X	X	X	X	Provide information based on end user profile (job responsibilities and purchasing authority). Link end user to customer recommendations and reviews
Customer service representative	Access customer information, order status, and FAQs	X	X			Provide the authority to resolve customer issues and update orders and profiles
Installer	Access product information, order status, and troubleshooting information	X	X		X	Provide product information, enable ordering, and access to FAQs and discussions on how to solve issues
Receivables manager	Create bills for service	X	X			Enable search of customer order and service information, generate invoices
Warehouse management	Assess inventory levels, demand, and manage logistics	X	X	X		Manage inventory levels and logistics through applying demand and production information
Shipping	Access order information, route orders to appropriate location	X				Review information, complete the shipping process

This sample worksheet helps define the specific actors and their responsibilities in the relationship to bring the flow of the business to life. Notice that collaboration at the relationship interface is required in just a few roles; behind the interface, it is vital, and the new organizational culture of eCommerce has to be built on collaborative competence. The starting point the spreadsheet illustrates is that the relationship interface must be designed not in terms of Web site features, but by understanding the roles involved in the day-to-day business and defining the intentions each role brings to the business. The actions summarize the business activities the relationship should support. Only then should the formal Web design work begin.

The Relationship Infrastructure

Building your relationship capabilities involves implementing a relationship substructure that provides texture through the Web site and touch through your service capabilities. Many Web sites still remain transaction sites, but most are moving in the direction of dynamic offers and self-direction. Once these relationship builders are fully in place and backed up with the strong eProcess base needed to build and retain the trust at the core of relationships, the solid foundation is there for extending both texture and touch to an expansive value network. Every step from zero-T pure transaction builds relationship capabilities and weaves the value network. While the transaction is not enough to achieve this, it's still the very base of an eCommerce capability: a company must be able to fulfill orders reliably and maintain its technology operations.

Build Your Infrastructure Piece by Piece

The relationship infrastructure consists of the building blocks for your business. The components of substructure build on top of each other to create a growing infrastructure. That superstructure must not collapse, and there are many, many eProcess requirements that must be met on a second-by-second basis. Behind the Web site is a complex of operations; to neglect them is to put everything at risk.

Unfortunately, speed to market, competition, and limited capital investments can lead to an unstable infrastructure. Two factors create this situation. The first is over-haste as companies rush to get into the market through cobbling together applications and operations to meet market windows. This creates an incentive to just do it now and worry about the consequences later. Improper reuse can also lead to infrastructure instability as companies seek to build their eCommerce channels on top of existing transaction processing systems. The result is operations that function, just barely, and that often topple when placed under growing business volumes or customer service demands. Figure 5-3 shows the relationship between infrastructure components that are patched together.

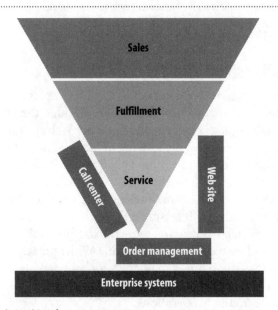

Figure 5-3: Relationship infrastructure components

Sales is detached from the call center and order management, and fulfillment is detached from order management. There are loose links between service, order management, and the call center. The call center doesn't integrate with the Web site, even though both are central to fulfillment. And so on. It's all unstable and likely to fall down.

A relationship infrastructure requires addressing the connections between your operational capabilities (sales, service, and fulfillment) and their supporting applications. Defining the components and their relationships establishes a basis for strong current operations and organizational flexibility. The value in an architected relationship infrastructure (illustrated in Figure 5-4) rests on its future maintainability and flexibility, which should offset the time it takes to define the architecture, as company Web operations will be under constant pressure to evolve.

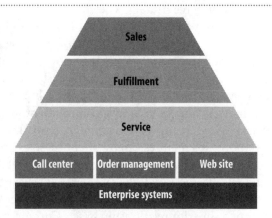

Figure 5-4: An architected relationship infrastructure

The higher and broader the superstructure, the more solid the base has to be, obviously. Very roughly, the eProcess management issue here is twofold:

▸ Who in the company guarantees the integrity of the relationships in the value network?

▸ Who guarantees the integrity of the transaction end to end?

The infrastructure addresses the technology issues needed to guarantee transaction integrity. These relate to technology and operations: network reliability, availability, security, and scalability. Process components and capabilities concentrate on the integrity of the relationship in the areas of sales, order fulfillment, and customer service. Those relating to the integrity of the relationship relate to technology and operations, but also to more "soft" issues, including information management, software customization, dynamic catalogs and pricing, and customer profiling in the area of technology use, in addition to marketing, alliances, and community building in operations. In all instances, eProcess capabilities must be sourced according to the relationship architecture. In all cases, they should be a mix of the eProcess portfolio options: embedding processes in software, out-tasking, in-sourcing, and exception management.

Choose a Relationship Type

The four relationship types we identify each require very careful attention to eProcess: evaluation, dynamic offers, self-management, and collaboration. The choice of which depth of relationship to aim for is central to eCommerce strategy. The choice defines the style of interactions within your value network and the scope and scale of that network. Note that we say "aim for"—there's nothing guaranteed here, since by definition a relationship is a two-way interaction. The company may say "Please join us," and the customer may reply "No, thanks." The very decision to aim for relationships rather than transactions is in itself a major executive commitment.

Direct relationships remain valid in an inter-networked world. Aiming for relationships requires careful attention to existing relationship mechanisms such as the customer sales force, retail stores, and other channels. It's too easy for eCommerce enthusiasts to overlook the many instances where the Web may offer a better transaction base, but not a superior relationship base. eCommerce is not for everybody, and trying to force players to conduct business via the Web may not be appropriate for all players or roles. Remember the relationship is in the eyes and at the discretion of the customer.

Relationships require the right blend of texture and touch. There are some instances where Web technology cannot as yet provide for this in sufficient levels of either to build the relationship. The Web presently cannot replace the texture and touch of direct human contact and reassurance. Such reassurance is necessary in situations of high-risk, big decisions or with choices that are highly personalized. Consider the real estate and travel industries, both of which involve large, long-established, and complex agency structures. In the case of travel agents, the lion's share of their business involves selling what is by now very much a commodity product: airline tickets, hotel reservations, and so forth. Their competitive advantage pre-eCommerce rested on access to information in the form of airline reservation systems. These agents lost considerable power and business when the Web eliminated this advantage. Perhaps no single industry has been so quickly and radically destabilized by eCommerce as travel agents, and the traditional players just don't have an edge to offset the simultaneous disintermediation—elimination of the middleman—through online customer evaluation and self-direction services and the creation of new intermediaries such as Expedia, Travelocity, and Priceline.

This is not a Darwinian sequence by which all agents are doomed, though. Many travel agencies were ravaged by this shift and the resulting pressure from airlines who have long tried to loosen the agents' key strength—the relationship with the passenger—and cut commissions. The survivors were those who broadened their services to include customized holiday planning and travel management for companies. These agents have increased the personalization of their relationships in order to recapture their market.

Rosenbluth Travel is a leading example. For decades, it has been an innovator in the use of information technology to build a unique value network that meshed many small agencies into its Global Information Alliance, which had the buying power (hotel and air fare prices, and commissions) of a mega-agency. Now it has moved the same innovative thinking onto the Web. Its corporate travel services include advising companies on the best time and place to hold a planned event that might involve many managers having to travel from many different points. It even recommends in some instances that it would be more effective to handle the meeting via videoconferencing, which Rosenbluth arranges through such low-cost public conferencing providers as Kinko's. A travel agent telling customers *not* to travel? That's how dinosaurs evolve into birds—they grow wings and fly.

While travel agencies have dramatically felt the effects of eCommerce, real estate agencies have experienced less disruption since eCommerce has not changed the size or personal nature of the real estate business. This is not to say that real estate has remained unscathed—far from it. eCommerce realty sites provide superior evaluation capabilities over newspapers and multiple-listing services. There eCommerce has changed the way people look around for housing. It has also changed the way home buyers transact the individual pieces of the home-buying process. Web-based lenders enable buyers to shop mortgage rates and terms, for instance.

But though eCommerce has entered the real estate market and changed evaluation and some transaction components of the industry value complex, it has not undermined the role of the agent as an advisor and integrator of the home-buying process. In this case, the value of the direct relationship exceeds the capability or willingness of homebuyers to manage the process for themselves in the majority of cases. That will also surely change over time, but the rule here is if you wish to displace an existing relationship base, you have to offer a better one.

Thus, while eCommerce rests on relationship building, it needs to recognize where that may be held back by the comforts of direct relationships. Including additional direct contact mechanisms is appropriate when the eCommerce situation may threaten to compromise the relationship. Direct relationships are appropriate in situations where demands for personal service and the need to build confidence are more important than the efficiency of the electronic channel. These call for direct contact as part of the *overall* relationship involving person-to-person exchanges through the customer contacting a call center, the company phoning the customer, or the customer visiting the office or branch. The importance of having a direct relationship is emerging in eCommerce as companies realize there are situations when people want to work with other people. Dell Computer provides an example of the need for this. Dell, which sells more than $30 million in products a day over its Web site, still conducts a significant part of its sales through a call center. Customers making a large purchase seek out confirmation that their order configuration will meet their needs. They want to talk to someone knowledgeable and helpful.

Texture and Touch: Determine the Type of Relationship

eProcess involves choosing the players in the value network and the type of relationships. These decisions define the scope of your eCommerce business and the requirements for your eProcess capabilities.

A relationship type defines company value potential and its basis for competition. High-touch relationships create deeper relationships through self-direction and collaboration. These provide greater "stickiness" as customers and suppliers bring their own profiles and preferences into the transaction. This increases their commitment to the relationship. It also raises performance demands as customers routinely expect to be handled in the context of their preferences and profiles. Failure to do so undercuts your brand and its promise.

High-texture relationships rely on the organization and presentation of content to serve customer needs. Evaluation and dynamic offer relationships are common in eCommerce; however, they are not always well tuned to the customer's intention and needs. Building evaluation and dynamic offer capabilities establishes the basis for eCommerce relationship evolution and will be standard to all eProcess companies. The challenge is not whether you can do business on the Web; a site, a big marketing budget, and a cheap price can always buy transactions. Rather, the issue is how you use the Web to build profitability through repeat business and relationships. Meeting that challenge requires a mix of capabilities that handle business transactions and relationship building. Figure 5-5 provides some guidelines on selecting the proper relationship type for each company and role in eCommerce.

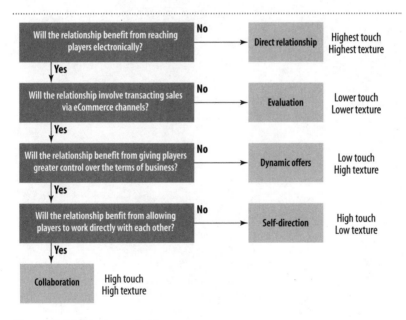

Figure 5-5: Relationship type decisions

How many Web site designers have asked and answered these questions?

Chapter 6

Valuing and Sourcing eProcess Capabilities

Once a company has identified its relationship targets, it then has to build the eProcess capabilities required to create, maintain, and expand the relationship. But how does it systematically choose which processes matter most for the relationship? And then how does it decide where and how to source those processes? This is at the core of execution of any eCommerce business model. The eProcess approach values capabilities based on the business model and primary relationships. These factors determine the most important capabilities to focus on and how to source them.

In our eProcess framework, there are four categories of priority: identity processes, priority processes, background processes, and mandated processes. Very roughly, identity means brand and competitive differentiation, priority means everyday competitive performance, background means support to operations, and mandated means legal requirements.

There are also four modes of sourcing processes: embedding them in software, out-tasking them, in-sourcing them, and building in-house capabilities. Embedding , out-tasking, and in-sourcing are what we term operational sourcing—that is, they address the routine elements of the company's eProcess base and rely on technology. The fourth category of sourcing addresses the non-routine exception handling. Here is a summary of the differences:

Embed processes in software Code the business rules for a process (for example, place an order, obtain account status information, or apply for credit) and implement them in the Web site software.

Out-task Take a specific task (for instance, shipping, financing, or catalog management) and link electronically via an API (application program interface) to a best practice provider that can perform that task superbly.

In-source Link via an API to a company for a service that augments your own capabilities and brand, such as research information, additional products, and referrals from its site to others.

Handle exceptions Complement all the other modes of sourcing the routine elements of eProcess with in-house capabilities that deal with the non-routine (for example, customer problems or personal interaction).

Out-tasking gets rid of something. In-sourcing adds something. In both instances, the goal is best practice at best cost.

eProcess Capability Matrix

The eProcess capability matrix shown in Figure 6-1 provides a simple framework for business managers to make the translation from relationship to capability. The left side of the matrix assesses process capabilities in terms of relationship importance that drives the capabilities value to the company. The right side assesses the best options for operational sourcing of them.

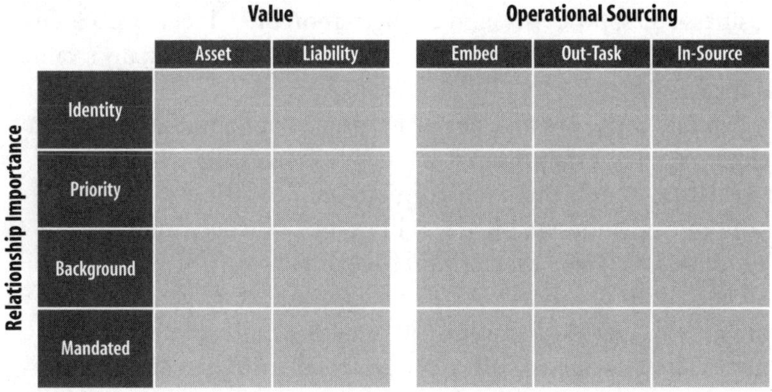

	Value			Operational Sourcing		
	Asset	Liability		Embed	Out-Task	In-Source
Identity						
Priority						
Background						
Mandated						

(Left axis label: Relationship Importance)

Figure 6-1: eProcess capability matrix

Think of the company's eProcess capability base as a portfolio of investments. Its goal is to build a set of eProcess assets—capital items that generate economic value through success in the value network relationships. Executives can rank eProcesses in terms of value to its customers, value to the company, and contribution to the relationship. The win-win combination is when its eProcess capability choice leverages all three of these.

Note that they are always potentially in conflict. For example, the company could easily maximize value to customers by giving its product away, or it could provide information that encourages them to access its Web site, use the information resources for evaluation, and then buy from somewhere else. Relationships are mutual exchanges of value; otherwise they are unstable and one of the parties will lose. When customers lose, they don't come back. When the company loses, it goes broke.

Value for the Company and Customer

Exchange value—what the customer gains and what the company earns—is an assessment of the contribution that an eProcess capability makes to the company's competitive and economic success, driven in part by the customer needs and priorities. Asset processes are value creating in terms of either strengthening the company's competitive positioning or contributing to its current or future profitability. They form an important part of company intellectual assets and process knowledge. This often leads a company to patent the business rules, processes, and configuration of its identity capabilities. They are assets because they contribute to the company's value to the customer.

Liability processes may be needed as part of the value network and relationship, but they drain value and resources. That is, the company has to handle them regardless of their contribution to its own economic positioning. Most liability processes cover more critical failure factors (CFF) than critical success factors (CSF). With a CSF, if you achieve it, you win. A CFF by contrast brings you little if anything if you succeed in meeting it, but kills you if you fail to do so. Many elements of back-office processes fall into this category: handling returns of goods, providing regulatory information, and billing are examples. Figure 6-2 highlights the relationship between customer and company views on the importance of their capabilities.

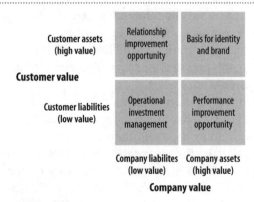

Figure 6-2: Customer and company values

Areas of high mutual customer and company value represent identity capabilities that are points of synergy and customer-company win-win opportunities. Situations where customer value exceeds company value represent opportunities to strengthen relationships by increasing attention to those operations or by offering additional products and services. For example, the move to customer self-direction begins with the company having to spend money on administration and service and over time ends up with the customer reducing its cost burden so that both parties benefit. This creates priority asset processes for the company out of its background liabilities.

The reverse situation is high company value and low customer value. In the eCommerce environment, that must raise red flags. It demands immediate eProcess performance improvements. These can be targeted to priority or background processes. The fact that the company sees a capability as something special to itself is irrelevant in the eCommerce economy; if customers don't care, they don't buy. Many aspects of product brand equity fall into this category. Companies that have built brand awareness and heavily promote their brand image are discovering that online buyers base their decisions on something else: the price an intermediary can get for them (Priceline), a referral (AOL or Yahoo!), or a value network offer (MySchwab).

Finally, there are eProcesses where both the company and its customers place low value on them. In these cases, doing a "good enough" job is good enough. These are mainly background and mandated processes. An example is entering the credit card and mailing address information required to transact an order. This is tedious to the customer and a vulnerable moment for the company, in that if it is complex and slow, many would-be buyers give up. Remember that roughly 30 percent of online purchase attempts fail.[1] Clearly these processes matter.

The obvious answer is software; make it fast and easy for the customer and cheap for the company. Amazon is a leader here; its patented one-click buying process for registered customers takes away a lot of hassle. What's worth noting is that Amazon chose this to patent and protected it in court. This has been a major value generator for Amazon—making the details of the buying process no big deal.

The eProcess capability matrix, in Figure 6-1, itself is nothing new; it's not a theory or methodology, just a reminder. It often produces new insights into the things the company should get right. Understanding how customers and companies value your capabilities defines relationship importance and value to the company. Many businesses take their processes as a given, instead of zero-basing their thinking. By zero-basing, we mean taking nothing as a given and going back to a clean start. It's worth keeping Amazon's one-click patent in mind. Here is something that on the surface looks really trivial—one-click ordering versus giving an online store clerk your credit card number and mailing address—but it's turned out to be a key competitive weapon. In the online economy, take nothing for granted.

Classify Capability

Electronic commerce thus may change everything about doing business. It introduces new rules and relationships that require reassessing the value and contribution of your capabilities, even if you have just completed a reengineering exercise and think you have an organization positioned for excellence within today's givens. The new and still emerging dynamics of eCommerce change the economic value of your capabilities, often undercutting the value of identity assets, such as product brand equity, and making background liabilities, like shipping and returns, into new sources of relationship value.

Benefiting from this shift rests on the new eProcess sourcing options enabled by the Internet and on zero-basing your company's analysis of the importance of the relationship in establishing the value contribution of your capabilities. The result is new opportunities for innovation, value creation, and asset efficiency—or new barriers to exploiting old process and relationship strengths.

The changing importance of eProcess capabilities in itself creates vertical disintegration as individual companies stake out and exploit a particular part of the value network. Companies such as Chem-Connect, Ariba, and Qpass have all positioned themselves in the emerging "sweet spots" created through vertical disintegration and changing capability values. They look for areas in a buyer-broker-seller relationship chain where information is one sided—such as the broker knowing which seller has product and which buyer needs it, but they don't jointly know the situation. They love inefficient and fragmented supply chains. As Rodrigo Flores, the founder of Celosis, told us: "If you are a profitable company in a fat and happy oligopoly, I am your worst enemy."[2] Ignore the impact of eCommerce innovators on eProcess capability value at your peril, as there is someone looking *now* to exploit the opportunity. So it's well worthwhile to step back and zero-base your thinking about eProcesses.

The eProcess capability matrix is built on the well-proven Process Investment framework introduced in Peter Keen's *The Process Edge*: identity, priority, background, and mandatory processes as the four value categories and as economic assets or liabilities. Each eProcess type is associated with its contribution to customer-company value, investment levels, and potential sourcing options. Classifying capabilities involves assessing your operations in terms of its relationship importance and its contribution to your operations.

Relationship Importance

The most strategic eProcess capabilities build identity: brand, differentiation, market strength, and reputation. The next category is priority capabilities—those that establish an operational performance advantage. Perform them 5 percent better every year relative to competitors and you draw ahead. Background processes are the ones that must be carried out to support the relationship, but do not in themselves make a strategic impact. Mandated processes are those that are required by regulation or law. Table 6-1 illustrates the connections between company value and relationships importance.

Table 6-1: Relationship Importance and Capability Value

	Asset	Liability
Identity	Capability is central to the business model.	Capability detracts or no longer fits with the business model.
	Capability is central to fulfilling customer commitments.	Capability is not involved with or no longer supports customer fulfillment.
	Resource requirements are less of a factor as the company will invest to bring identity capabilities to market.	Initial investment requirements are beyond company resources or no longer justified based on changes in transaction volumes or market conditions.
Priority	Capability contributes to operation of the business model, bringing speed, accuracy, and scale to the model.	Capability no longer directly supports the business model.
	Capability enables fulfillment of customer commitments.	Capability is not involved in meeting customer commitments.
	Resource requirements are manageable given its contribution to operations.	Changes in the market no longer make the capability economically feasible.

Table 6-1: Relationship Importance and Capability Value (*continued*)

	Asset	Liability
Background	Capability does not contribute to your business model, but is important to the model of another value network player. Capability supports fulfillment of customer commitments, generally in the form of improving the ability to manage priority and identity activities. Resource requirements are in line with the contribution to operations.	Capability is necessary to conduct business, but delivers little that directly improves priority and identity operations. Capability is not related to fulfilling customer commitments. Resource requirements to operate that capability at scale are excessive.
Mandatory	Capability contributes directly to the initial public offering process. Capability is central to building belief in the business model and its success. Resource requirements are appropriate.	Capability exists due to legal and regulatory requirements. Capability is not related to fulfilling customer commitments. Company does not have the resources or expertise to carry out the capability.

Capability Classifications

Relationship strength driven by customer and company value defines the relative importance of company capabilities, from highest to lowest: identity, priority, background, and mandatory. Each category represents a particular set of considerations that drives sourcing and operation of the capabilities. Figure 6-3 provides the key questions for assessing your capabilities.

Identity Capabilities

An identity capability supports the very core of the business model and commitments to customers and value network partners. It's the basis for differentiation and sustainable economic value. It forms the most important company assets and must have high executive importance. It shapes the eCommerce *brand*. Put more bluntly, a company without identity asset eProcesses is just a me-too competitor, which means that the more competition there is—and the more Rodrigo Flores–type innovators—the more it's at risk from the eCommerce revolution.

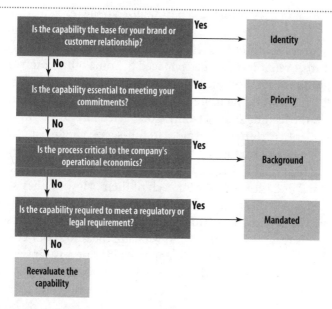

Figure 6-3: Critical questions for determining relationship importance

The companies without identity processes do not have the operations to live up to their brands. They are defenseless against commoditization. In the early days of the Internet, the Web site itself was very much the brand, because only a few companies aggressively targeted the electronic commerce opportunity and the leaders thus had the advantage of novelty and lack of competition. Today, that edge has totally disappeared. There's no novelty in a Web site, however well designed it is. Take any area of business and there are dozens of strong eCommerce competitors and often thousands of lesser ones, some of which may move to the top. Mortgages, furniture, auctions, travel, cars, office supplies, healthcare, computers…the list goes on and on. It's hard to stand out amid all the choices customers now have. That means most players do not have a real identity in the eCommerce marketspace.

Identity Assets

Identity assets have the strongest relationship value and form the basis for customer interest and repeat business. As an example, Charles Schwab's identity asset capabilities all center around service under all circumstances—face-to-face interaction at its branches for the many customers who want help in getting started online, links to brokers when anything goes wrong, and personalized free Web sites. Its most recent offers center on having a financial adviser (not a Schwab employee) collaboratively assess a customer's portfolio in terms of risk and return, even if most of it is managed by some other company.

Schwab's competitors are racing to match it. Schwab's leading rival, E*Trade, is adding more and more in-sourced services and has acquired the leading Internet-only bank, Telebank.[3] It's seeking to shift its identity from online trades to full-service financial relationships. There's a risk here that as all the leading players converge on the same relationship-driven strategies, with the same basic eProcess capabilities, identity will blur for each of them. How do they stand out now?

They will have to look harder and harder to find the eProcess edge in this regard. They must ask, what are the things our customers value that we have under-appreciated? The answer will not necessarily be dramatic, and it will not necessarily involve just the Internet. Indeed, the very fact that customers are in complete command—none of them have to use the Internet or have to do business with your company—makes it quite likely that it will be something the company itself previously discounted as just background. For instance, handling paper-work and payment processing (both background capabilities) have become identity assets for eProcurement companies such as Ariba and Commerce One. Another, perhaps more telling example, involves channel harmonization as a relationship builder. Here again Schwab leads the way as it offers multiple sales and service channels: online, broker, and telephone trades. These all are identity assets as well as the capability to define a consistent level of service across all these channels. Identity assets are not limited to what is visible at the Web site.

Warning: Identity Liabilities

We've discussed identity capabilities in terms of assets: value-generating eProcesses. What happens if an identity capability is a liability? Here is one of the major problems for many established companies entering the eCommerce space. Its very strengths can become potential liabilities. The brokerage business again provides an example. Many of the most venerable and esteemed security dealers rested their identity capability on full service. Brokers earned a high commission in return for expertise, advice, and research information. Well, much of that information is now online, freely available to anyone who wants to do a little research. The incremental value of this information decreases in the mind of the customer as it becomes readily accessible.

This leaves the full-service broker with rough parity in terms of eProcess capability, but with radically different price structures. The customer question is, should I go with the low-cost provider or the best relationship player? This is a potential liability situation based on the value the customer assigns to the availability of these full services. It boils down to the customer value of the capability and its importance to their perception of your brand.

When a company's identity assets become identity liabilities, it must take rapid and aggressive action, because its entire business is at risk. This happened with IBM in the early 1990s. Its powerful marketing, pricing, and cultural capabilities had moved over time from being what made IBM the dominant leader in the computer field to what made customers increasingly see it as arrogant, bureaucratic, and out of touch. It took new leadership and many years for IBM to create a set of new identity capabilities. Now, its very identity is no longer as a computer company, but as eCommerce. Its trademarked "e-business" is backed up by alliances, technology in all areas, consulting, and services that were foreign to it in its old identity.[4]

Identity and Brand

The company that has a strong set of identity assets has a branding advantage and a relationship opportunity by the very fact that it has a distinctive presence in a marketspace where many companies are the result of a search engine query. A startup dot-com company creates its own identity from scratch. While this has some advantages, there are some sizable disadvantages. The first among these is that it takes a lot of time and money to build a brand online. The most powerful players will often be the ones that successfully extend their identity asset capabilities in the way that Dell and Cisco have. They have always been leaders in logistics and supply chain management processes, and their reputation as major Internet eCommerce players remains very much the same in terms of identity. The company that lacks identity asset capabilities can only be a me-too competitor. It's this last point that poses most challenges in eCommerce in general. It can lead to a company being three clicks down some relationship leader's portal.

Priority Capabilities

Priority capabilities are the heart of a company's everyday operations, effectiveness, and efficiency. They represent the business core that, when performed well, creates positive economic returns and a competitive edge in terms of cost or asset efficiency. However, poorly executed priority capabilities restrict company growth and cash flow. They demand so much care, commitment, attention, organizational skills, and strong culture that they detract management attention and financial assets from their identity operations. Some familiar non-eCommerce examples are on-time arrival for airlines, stock replenishment for retailing, customer retention for financial service companies, and quality for manufacturing. For online services, they are—well, we don't as yet fully know. It's customers who decide what's priority, and in many instances we don't yet have a long enough experience base to derive clear lessons beyond the obvious importance of technology operations, order fulfillment, and after-sales customer service.

Technology Operations

Online service availability, network security, and platform scalability are the virtual bricks and mortar of an online business. Technology is responsible for handling transactions completely within availability, security, and scale requirements.

The highest level of availability operational standards are now standard in eCommerce. You need to be up and running 24/7 (and 365). Availability extends beyond simply being open for business. The target performance level for your Web site is around eight seconds per Web page; anything slower and the customer loses interest and clicks away from your site.[5] Think of process as the eCommerce infrastructure, relationships as the superstructure, and technology as the substructure that holds them both up.

Security is a broad term that involves issues of authentication, privacy, protection of the Web site and data from attack, and financial audit and control. It's a key part of the trust base on which any relationship depends. Scalability is the ability to handle increasing volumes, exchange partners, transactions, and communications smoothly and quickly. It is a critical issue for priority capabilities, since executives often overlook the need to build operational scale in the face of increasing demands for core business model investments. When the network is down for any reason, so is the customer relationship. When it goes down too often, so do the customer confidence and trust that underlie relationships. It's outside the scope of this book to address the many technology management processes essential to ensuring availability, scalability, and security, because they are such a specialized area in themselves. But in no way do we discount their importance. They are central to building customer trust.

Order Fulfillment

Order fulfillment has proven to be the Achilles heel for many eCommerce companies, not in terms of outbound logistics, but more broadly in many areas of supply chain management. Order fulfillment delivers on the customer commitment, making it at the very least a priority capability for any online business. Fulfillment issues involved in eCommerce center around the following:

Inventory management Inventory management addresses product availability and stock levels. This is the issue behind inventory stockouts and long shipping lead times. Inventory management requires the integration of inventory systems and the Web store. In many cases, this is as much a matter of organizational incentives for collaboration as links between the Web site, internal computer systems, and supply chain partners' systems.

Supplier performance Supplier performance defines the operational characteristics of the fulfillment capability and coordinates the performance of your own and your suppliers' interactions, which is a priority in meeting your commitments. It's your customer and your brand. When suppliers fail, you fail.

Logistics Logistics moves the product to your customer. An increasing majority of eCommerce companies out-source this aspect of order fulfillment, accessing the scale and performance of established players such as UPS, Federal Express, DHL, and the U.S. Postal Service. However, there are a number of companies that view logistics as an identity asset. Companies like Webvan, Shoplink, Kozmo, and others are building the processes and infrastructure to cover the proverbial "last mile" of the logistics chain.

Fulfilling orders correctly, on time, and cost-effectively delivers on the company's trust commitment created at the Web site. It is a priority capability that differentiates a company from the many other Web sites with comparable products and comparable prices. Fulfillment poses a challenge for online companies who were able to deliver only 80 percent of their orders on time, as well as traditional companies who faired worse at only 20 percent.[6] Companies that do it well support their relationships and brand based on fulfilled expectations.

Customer Service

Obviously the focus on relationships rather than just transactions makes customer service a priority in order to build trust, especially through handling individual customer concerns and responding to problems. eCommerce involves customers creating mutual commitments online rather than through a direct relationship, creating a potential lack of connection between your company and the customer. They worry that they may not be able to get through to you and be stuck in the Web site interaction—like being left on hold forever on the phone. That concern is why 80 percent of Dell's $30 million daily Internet sales are confirmed through its call center.[7]

Customer service involves handling customer crisis situations that represent the moments of truth in a relationship when the customer is in need of personal help. Providing customer service involves being able to proactively:

► Identify potential crisis situations, such as missed or lost deliveries, damaged goods, duplicate orders, and other transactions that are out of the ordinary

► Provide status on orders, shipments, and product availability via the Web site and call center

► Handle customers in the context of their own profiles, preferences, and specific context of their order

A customer interaction eProcess capability provides these services across call center, Internet, and direct service channels. The company builds trust through responding to queries and being there when the customer needs a personal contact; otherwise the very first time the transaction fails, the relationship is at risk.

Technology operations, order fulfillment, and customer service represent a minimum set of priority capabilities for an eCommerce company. These make obvious and direct contributions to the relationship and trust, through keeping customer information secure and private, responding to customer queries, and correcting customer errors. They build trust by honoring customer and company promises. These priority capabilities are obvious and serve as a checklist for an eCommerce business. The point of innovation and value creation is in finding your hidden priority liabilities and turning them into eProcess assets.

Hidden Priority Liabilities

Capabilities that the customer values more than the company does or where the company has insufficient capacity or competence represent hidden liabilities. Here is where the "gotchas" are in eCommerce, where your company fails to build relationships and repeat business. These are the liabilities that are holding you back. Many are not immediately apparent or cannot support the investment required to build them in-house.

What does the company do when the customer views an eProcess-based capability as a priority, but to the company it's a liability? Shipping is the most obvious example. To the company, once an order is placed and the goods sent out, it's done its work. But for customers, the job is incomplete until the items are in their hands. The company is not an expert in shipping and it also doesn't specialize in handling returns; that's expensive and a mess to arrange. The dilemma here is that this matters to the customer, but it's a drain on the company's resources and skills. Here's where sourcing may be key. Historically, out-sourcing has generally been confined to background processes, with companies being advised not to move core capabilities to outside companies. We argue that they should do just this in order to meet the customer's priorities eProcess demands.

Out-Task Priority Capabilities

Out-tasking the priority capabilities mentioned above all fits the bill where there is a strong market for third-party service providers. Application service providers and Internet service providers such as Exodus host eCommerce technology operations, replacing fixed IT investments with volume-based variable costs.[8] There are more and more third-party logistics companies offering order fulfillment capabilities that convert your overhead administration into a value-added service opportunity. Many companies provide full call center capabilities as they aggregate call traffic from multiple sites, achieving economies of scale that provide a cost-effective service. Out-tasking represents the most obvious choice in all these situations, as it involves finding the best of the best who treat the capability as an identity asset in its own eProcess base. It is not the only choice, though. Software may be the best eProcess sourcing.

Embed Priority Capabilities in Software

It may be practical to embed the priority capability in software, in effect transferring management of the eProcess from yourself to the customer or supplier by using the relationship interface. This has the effect of leveraging their capabilities by moving information across the value network. Consider a business rule a customer imposes on its staff that they must order specific office supplies only in bulk, to gain volume discounts, or that Product X must be bought from Company Y. Enforcing these rules is made convenient through linking the supplier's or your own inventory databases directly to your Web store and order management systems. The rules then limit customer catalog choices based upon the available items.

In-Source: Extend Your Brand

Customer value drives priority processes. Your limited performance of the capability makes it a liability, and your ability to source it in other ways enhances its asset value. This creates a dilemma concerning the capabilities your customer values the most. If you can't handle them well, you lose, but by the very fact that you don't perform them adequately, you have to go outside your company to do so. These liability eProcesses represent potential *assets* that can extend your brand and open new revenue streams. If this capability is something you need to add to your own brand, in-source it. Amazon offers an example of this; it had to blaze a trail by investing millions to build the order and transaction management capabilities to handle online business. This investment was necessary as processing orders and payments are obviously a priority process, and at the time there were no sourcing alternatives. Amazon is now a value network sourcing alternative in itself for other companies; it provides a new revenue generating service to other Web companies and directly via its z-Shops.

Find Other Priority Assets

We can't offer any list of general priority processes beyond the three mentioned here because every company situation is unique, but we suggest that you define them for your company in terms of the trust brand. Find priority assets through addressing the following questions:

► How do you attract and retain customers?

► How do you track operational performance across the value network?

► What do customers perceive as being at risk when they make a commitment?

► What will keep customers coming back and back and back?

► What can damage the trust relationship?

The answer to these questions moves many processes out of the background category they were in as part of the company's old business. For eCommerce, they become a priority to the customer. While there's no cookbook list of general priority eProcess capabilities, there are several broad areas of commonality. Consider how many of them have little to do with Web sites and everything to do with relationship design:

Marketing Customer acquisition, customer segmentation, personalization, customization, and pricing

Alliance management Joint planning and shared information

Organizational mobilization and renewal Incentives, team-building and coordination, and training

Infrastructure management Capacity, operations, scalability, and security

Companies win the branding game through identity eProcess capabilities. They win the day-by-day operational performance game through priority processes.

Background Capabilities

Background processes support daily operations, but do not directly contribute to or enable the business model. They are almost all by definition a liability that adds costs, people, and administration. They show up in the figure on the income statement that is generally shown as SGA: selling, general, and administration. This may be politely termed overhead and less politely waste. It's background processes that consume so much of a company's resources and create its complexity.

And it's background processes that in so many ways are transforming the entire economy and raising U.S. productivity levels by rates that puzzle economists who don't understand business dynamics—but not anyone who understands eProcess. Two of the most powerful forces in our economy now are

Self-direction Through embedding processes in software, back-office processes previously handled through people, workflows, paper, and layers of coordination, with delays and errors everywhere, are turned from expensive background liabilities for the company into front-office priority assets for the customer.

The logistics revolution It's no exaggeration to say that this has most transformed business productivity and efficiency: procurement, supply chain optimization, and business-to-business interactions.

We've discussed each of these many times in this book and won't add more comment, except the obvious: no company can afford to ignore them—it's almost literally crazy to do so.

Mandated Capabilities

Mandated capabilities are the ones legally required for operation, including corporate counsels, regulatory compliance and reporting, and tax filing. Companies don't choose to do these of their own accord, and they are a major source of complaint. They are a cost burden.

While it is easy to see that, as such, they will be relatively low on the executive agenda, this is not always the case. Consider the situation of a startup eCommerce company preparing for its initial public offering (IPO). In this case, mandated capabilities such as legal, finance, and accounting temporarily become identity assets for this crucial transaction. How well the new company handles them establishes its credibility, buzz, and market momentum. Here, a mandated liability can demonstrate business competence and become a priority asset.

A common problem mandated processes create is that they can get in the way of the online relationship. Account opening in securities trading, for example, as we mentioned earlier, is a cumbersome process with plenty of regulations designed to protect customers from fraud—and also from themselves and their inexperience. That's a plus in many ways, but the minus is that it can require physical forms and mailing delays that conflict with the instant-service nature of the rest of the relationship. There's no easy answer as to what to do to ensure that mandated processes don't interfere with the relationship. Managers have to keep in mind that the future of eCommerce over the next few years certainly will add, not remove, mandated processes, as concerns over jurisdiction, taxation, consumer protection, and others grow along with eCommerce.

Operational Sourcing

The operational sourcing portion of the eProcess capability matrix determines how a capability will be sourced across the value network. This requires managers to think about how they will gain access and use of these capabilities. The external sourcing options—embedding rules in software, out-tasking, and in-sourcing—are discussed in more detail in Chapters 7 and 8.

There is not a one-to-one relationship between relationship importance and operational sourcing, as Figure 6-4 shows. This creates the opportunity for innovation, as each company can pursue different sourcing options for its capabilities. It is no longer acceptable to simply say "out-task everything that isn't important."

Relationship Importance	Operational Sourcing		
	Embed	**Out-Task**	**In-Source**
Identity	X		X
Priority	X	X	X
Background	X	X	
Mandated	X	X	

Figure 6-4: Relationship importance and operational sourcing

We have focused our discussion in this chapter mainly on sourcing priority capabilities. Our message for handling mandatory process is out-task them fast. That leaves the most complex sourcing order: identity processes—the eCommerce brand-builders and background processes, the value drain.

Identity eProcess Sourcing

Identity capabilities create unique—not me-too—relationships and form the basis for your online brand. In traditional commerce, identity capabilities are closely controlled as a primary source of competitive advantage. That's Coca-Cola's and McDonald's advantage in their marketing, distribution, and promotion. Great brands and great companies. The imperative for such companies is to put every resource behind the brand. This made sense in the manual economy where vertical integration required companies to source processes and technology in-house. It still makes sense in eCommerce, where capabilities rest on unique intellectual assets and operations. But in eCommerce, value networks erode company-specific identity assets. We've mentioned Priceline.com several times. It's an identity asset eProcess company that hides the identity of the businesses its customers buy from. We've observed that almost none of the many articles we've read about Priceline's forage into the travel and supermarket business ever mentions the names of the airlines and grocery chains. Priceline's the identity, not they.

These companies bring their identity assets to market by embedding business rules into software. Consider ChemConnect, which uses software to track, manage, and complete market-making transactions in the chemicals industry. Market making is ChemConnect's identity asset, brought to life through software rather than creating a physical trading exchange. Embedding identity assets into software represents a new sourcing alternative for eCommerce companies that enables them to leverage intellectual property directly to customers and suppliers at scale.

Background eProcess Sourcing

Background processes can be in-sourced, out-tasked, or embedded. In-house operations represented the norm in the traditional economy, as coordination and contracting costs were high. Internet and related technologies changed all of this, lowering the costs and barriers to sharing processes across companies and creating entire new industries, such as integrated third-party logistics.

Background capabilities make a minimal contribution to your brand or critical relationships. Given their minor impact and opportunity, the sourcing decision calls for moving these processes outside the company through out-tasking or embedding the related rules in software. In most cases, the sourcing action will involve out-tasking provided there is a credible supplier that meets the company's performance requirements. Embedding the capability in software is possible where the background process can be readily leveraged by being directly linked to and self-directed by individual customers and suppliers.

Background assets offer a potential exception. In this case, the capability creates economic value for the company, but it is not core to its brand and customer strategy. This situation presents a potential new source of revenue, as the company can offer its background process to its customers and suppliers in order to build a new business in this area. This strategy seeks to extend customer and supplier process bases through sharing these background capabilities. Customers and suppliers gain as they get access to the company's process infrastructure. The company gains as it is able to reduce the capability's unit cost though increasing transaction volumes. They also gain as sharing background capabilities establishes strong relationship incentives. This is among the strategies that banks are using to provide services to their small and medium-sized commercial customers. These capabilities can include benefits administration, payroll processing, accounting services, and others where:

- Customers and suppliers have a smaller process base than your organization

- They require world-class performance in the area, but lack critical mass to warrant the investment

- They could obtain value through using your capability

- You can segment capability operations on an individual company basis

- You can provide the capability via an online interface

Background capabilities consume capital, organizational resources, and management attention. Careful sourcing of these capabilities increases the company's operational efficiency while reducing organizational complexity.

A Portfolio of Capabilities

A company's entire operational base and ongoing cost base are a mix of these capability assets and liabilities. Very roughly, the typical company's process portfolio has a few key identity assets. Those are its brand. In eCommerce, Amazon's differentiation has been built more on its product selection and shopping processes than on, say, pricing. It made its patented one-click payment process, by which customers do not have to enter the same information over and over when they make purchases, into an identity asset.[9] Pricing is not its identity asset, but a priority process. For the first few years of its existence, Amazon handled shipping as a background process—a necessary support to the business and a liability in the sense that it was an administrative expense that cut margins without bringing Amazon any value. It was also a CFF, not CSF: a failure factor, not a success factor. The best that could happen was that nothing bad happened—the book was ordered and promptly delivered.

Amazon recognized earlier than most retailers that *to the customer* timely and accurate shipping wasn't background but priority. It invested accordingly and built in distribution centers, a reversal of its previous strategy, all because fulfillment increased in value to the customer. Now Amazon stands out compared to almost all online retailers in this regard. It's turned a background liability process into a priority asset process. This is why Amazon entered the toy business over the summer of 1999 and stocked up on extra inventory for the 1999 holiday period—inventory which added an expensive cost burden to the firm. These were investments in the customer relationship, not in financial performance. Amazon was very explicit about why it did this: the company had to learn the toy business, ensure the customer relationship, and make sure customers were not let down by late shipments or orders not being fulfilled because of out-of-stock situations.

Online retailing during the 1999 shopping season was a major transaction success for many companies, but a relationship fiasco.

For many of them, order fulfillment and customer service processes were handled as background, and because they were liabilities, companies tried to minimize investment (it's called efficiency). One of the key differences between eCommerce and traditional business is that processes that were of minor importance to the company become priority or even identity assets to the customer. Indeed, eProcess might be defined as "process design on the behalf of the customer." Most processes have been designed on behalf of the company.

Customer Credit: A Business-to-Business Relationship

Consider, for example, business-to-business commerce in manufacturing. Sales, marketing, and manufacturing are identity, but handling credit and financing for new customers are background. So the finance department is very careful—and slow—in approving credit for a small company that wants to purchase, say, $30,000 of equipment. It may take two weeks to make the approval. The finance department is rewarded for minimizing write-offs, whereas the sales department is urged to sell, sell, sell. This built-in check and balance is needed to ensure that sales are made only to reliable customers.

Then the manufacturer moves online. It has excellent marketing and selling eProcesses and a fine Web site. The would-be buyer of the $30,000 of goods now can browse through online catalogs and make a fast choice. Click. Click. Stop. What happens about the credit approval? The Web screen informs the customer that it needs the following financial information and a mailed copy of the form it now displays on the screen. The process is the very same as before, for the very same reason: the sales-finance check-and-balance routine.

But entire business priorities have been turned upside down. To the customer, online credit management is a *priority* process and not at all background. It's a differentiator among all the equipment manufacturers the customer can choose. It's essential to the relationship, and it has to be made an asset. But the company can't achieve this. In this case, the purchaser is a small retailer with a good credit history, but relatively low profits and small margins. Whereas an Amazon or an eBay doesn't have to worry about credit because the customer pays by credit card and the card issuer makes an immediate yes/no decision through an electronic link from the Web site, the in-house credit decision is far more complex for the manufacturer. It needs references, must evaluate the company's balance sheet and cash flow, and in any case doesn't know much about small retailers (versus, say, consulting companies or restaurant chains with about the same revenues).

Using our eProcess capability matrix, the situation is as shown in Figure 6-5. Today, the credit process is offline, managed through people and procedures, and is definitely a background liability. Tomorrow, for the manufacturer's online business to be effective in attracting new customers, this must become a priority asset. The company has to decide how to source this capability. It can't be fully embedded in software because the business rules for commercial credit are so complex and require judgment as well as information. It can't be left as an offline process because that gets in the way of the online relationship.

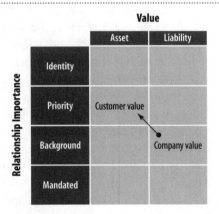

Figure 6-5: Sample capability matrix (partial)

The next issue, after determining the value of the process, is to decide on sourcing. In this case, the first task is to see if there is a potential value network partner to handle the capability. If there is, and it can provide the required service at scale, then out-task it. In the example of customer credit, eCredit.com is a relatively new company that fills this business-to-business electronic commerce gap. It provides the manufacturer with a capability it could never build by itself. eCredit also extends the equipment maker's value network. It is a pure software eProcess provider that uses proprietary data analysis techniques to evaluate the commercial buyer's credit riskiness by comparing it to profiles of comparable companies in its industry. Figure 6-6 shows the completed matrix for the customer credit capability and the shift from an in-house background liability process to an out-tasked priority asset.

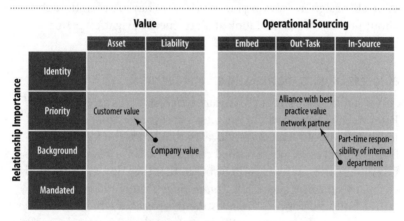

Figure 6-6: Completed capability matrix for customer credit

Assess eProcess Capabilities

It's essential that eCommerce companies be very clear in their assessment of current and required eProcess capabilities. These are not fixed. For instance, it's only as more and more companies offer goods online that shipping has become a priority eProcess. By definition, identity processes are unique to a company. The competitive arena defines which processes will be priority. What is background for one business may be priority for another. For example, as we showed above, credit is just a background embedded software feature for the retailer handling consumer credit card transactions, but may be a priority asset eProcess for one that sells to small businesses. eProcesses are thus a management assessment of strategic value. They define the priorities for action. To incorrectly assess an eProcess is to mis-prioritize it.

There must be a lot of retailing executives sitting around wishing they'd paid a little more attention to order fulfillment processes for their company's Christmas online launch, for instance. There are just as many who still think that their company's existing brand strength and operational strengths will transfer automatically to the Web. The hypothetical ACMEretailer.com is the same as the physical store, ACME, but with a Web site. And there are plenty of Web site designers working for ACME who haven't even thought about processes, but boy! look at all the neat navigation features they're adding to the home page!

eProcess Extends the Assessment Framework

As we said earlier, our eProcess capability matrix is an extension of Peter Keen's framework for business process investment presented in his 1997 book, *The Process Edge*. In that book, the focus was on business processes in established companies. It viewed processes as invisible economic assets—invisible in that they don't appear on the company's balance sheet. *The Process Edge* identified a number of "value builders" for process investment, several of which are further enabled by the Web. What's different about the eProcess edge today versus the 1997 process edge? Just two simple facts that change the agenda for defining the portfolio of capabilities: customers and creating a new business.

In 1997, customers were very important. Now they are everything. So, in the 1997 process world, companies could design their processes largely to meet their own requirements first. The most popular business school framework for business strategy, Michael Porter's well-known value chain (shown below), defined strategy in terms of a linear chain that began with raw materials and eventually ends up with the customer and after-sales service. Today, for eCommerce, the chain begins with the customer and works back to the company. It's also not a chain anymore, but a hub.

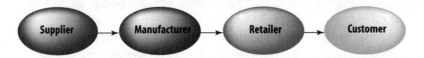

Chains are linear, with each step passing on to another. They are tidy and highly sequential. The sequencing introduces delays and, in many cases, errors as documents are handed off along the chain. Consider a mortgage application, for instance. This starts with the customer filling out a form. The form goes to the bank, which checks it for completeness. Then it goes to the administrative unit that checks out the customer's creditworthiness, then to underwriting, and eventually through to completion. This typically takes a month. If there's a problem at any stage in the chain, it can be difficult to locate the relevant work unit and repair it.

The chain is increasingly inappropriate for process design in eCommerce. Here, simultaneity and parallelism are key. The mortgage application is handled in minutes. A web of players, inside and outside the bank, communicate through software. Obviously, adding steps to a chain elongates the process. Adding them to a Web does not do so. So, for example, if an online mortgage service provider adds, say, features for title insurance application, mortgage insurance, and locating an inspector, these are just extra spokes in the value network hub, not additional links to a chain. There's a limit to how long any process chain can be. There are very few limits to a hub.

The move from a chain to a hub involves a jump from a production focus to a customer focus—from how you move things along the chain to how you meet needs via a network. The shift is fundamental; value chain vertical integration gives way to a value network. A value chain isolates suppliers and manufacturers from the customer as the retailer holds direct customer contact through the Web site relationship interface. This leads these companies to focus on their internal priorities rather than the customer priorities, as they see their job being to pass products and services "up the chain."

A value network forms around the enterprise, meeting customer needs, as shown on the following page. Customer needs drive the enterprise's capability priorities. The enterprise uses these priorities to determine the importance of its capabilities and the best source for the capability across the value network.

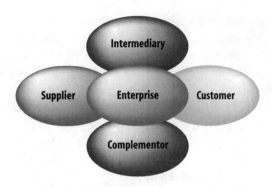

Create a New Business

The second major shift from the era of *The Process Edge* to that of *The eProcess Edge* is that in 1997 processes were largely addressed in terms of reengineering. "Re-" means try again. The challenge that reengineering explicitly addressed was the re-ing of processes in large companies. It was a massive attack on the bureaucratization, complexity, administrative growth, and eroding productivity that marked most of the *Fortune* 1000.

There's no room for "re-" words in eCommerce because there's nothing to try again—it's all new. An eProcess company seizes the opportunity to invent a new business through sorting out the value and relationship strength of its capabilities to define the areas for investment. The eProcess company then takes full advantage of capability sourcing opportunities to target high-value customer assets and out-task company liabilities. The result is an asset-efficient company that invests its capital wisely in identity and priority assets while leaving its potential liabilities in the hands of their best-in-breed value network players. Figure 6-7 provides a sample completed capability matrix.

Customer power plus eProcess invention offer both a formidable challenge and a massive opportunity. Either way, it's not something a company can overlook or handle by default. There needs to be a top-down business management evaluation of the eProcess portfolio to be built and sustained, starting with identity processes.

	Value		Operational Sourcing		
	Asset	Liability	Embed	Out-Task	In-Source
Identity	Marketing		Enable customers to select sales recommendations via the Web store	Market through alliances with portals	Direct-market through mass media to build awareness and traffic
	Sales		Enable customers to generate orders via the Web store		Provide sales support through call center operations
	Service		Enable customers to serve themselves for standard transactions		Manage customer service
	IT development				Maintain control of Web store functionality and business interfaces
	Product/service development				Partner with value chain to develop and deploy new offerings
Priority	Alliance management				Build based on the number and complexity of value network
		Order processing			Consolidate orders across multiple suppliers in warehouses
		Accounts receivable		Payments to financial intermediaries	
		Inventory management		Transfer supplies	
		Logistics and order fulfillment		Transfer logistics companies	
		Manufacturing and materials management		Transfer to suppliers	
Background		Finance			Manage investment to track company & alliance performance
	HR: Recruiting				Manage the pool of talent internally
		HR: Compensation and benefits		Partner with an HR BPO company	
		IT operations		Partner with an application service provider	
Mandated		Regulatory reporting		Hire point expertise	Manage investment in internal capacity

Figure 6-7: Sample capability matrix

The importance of a process-centered capability is largely a subjective judgment governed by the business model, customer demands, and resource requirements. The breadth of businesses and business model types destroys old rules of what constitutes an asset or a liability. Abandoning these old rules enables innovative new forms of business, just as eCommerce enables new forms of collaboration and sourcing.

The next issue is how to source the eProcess capability. Very roughly, here are our guiding principles:

▶ Wherever a process is routine, background, or mandated, and is a liability to your company but a priority to your customer, get it into the software interface and make it value-adding for the relationship.

▶ If it's a process that must be carried out superbly for the customer to benefit, but you don't have the capacity and capability, out-task it to the best-practice company.

▶ Look for every way you can to in-source priority asset processes you don't have in-house.

All this addresses the recurrent and the routine. Focus your in-house eProcess investments on handling the exceptions to the routine and making your company distinctive by how it deals with the non-routine, ranging from troubleshooting and problem-solving to pervasive collaboration.

Part III

Delivering eProcess Results

In this part

Chapter 7

Embedding Business Rules in Software

By now you agree with us that a business is more than just a Web site (or you would not have gotten this far in our book), but a Web site is also far more than a graphical user interface (GUI). It's the customer's front-office and relationship interface with the company's value network. A Web site establishes the company's visible presence for eCommerce. An effective one blends the usability of a GUI with support for business rules, creating a vital source of eProcess capability. A business process fundamentally is comprised of its business rules plus the sourcing of the capability to implement those rules. What most distinguishes eProcess from traditional business process design is the sourcing options; the very same business rules can be handled in many different ways—embedded in software at the Web site relationship interface, out-tasked to a best practice company, in-sourced to create a new capability, or handled in-house.

Earlier we defined a business process in the following terms:

An eProcess is a set of business rules to answer a recurrent request via the Web site relationship interface that requires some degree of interaction between parties. Think of business rules as the script for the dialogue.

The capabilities to carry out those rules must be coordinated across the value network for both parties to benefit. That's a major shift from traditional process design, where most of the company's capabilities were coordinated internally, and many were either not effective from the customer's perspective or not value generators for the business. That's been the case for many background processes that are liabilities (an expense) for the company and for the customer ("bureaucracy").

Business rules can be coded—the script defined and refined over time and the dialogue personalized. By extension, an eProcess is the choice of how to coordinate and source a process that combines the best of contribution to value network relationships and company profitability.

A Brief Academic Exercise

This may all sound rather academic, but we've had to pick our terms carefully in order to establish our very non-academic framework for practical management action. Bear with us for a few pages while we explain not so much the terms but rather their implications for eCommerce success.

The Relationship Interface

Commerce rests on relationships and is coordinated through a relationship interface that is the means of exchanging value. In the manual economy, that interface involved direct contact through a meeting or over the telephone or through letters and documents. In eCommerce, this interface is the Web site software that drives the flow of information and processes required to turn customer requests into company responses. In the simplified model shown in Figure 7-1, notice that the company performs a process in the sense that it is responsible for transforming the input (request) into the output (response). Recall too, that in the traditional view of processes as workflows, the link between input and output is a set of tasks and activities that constitute a linear flow of steps. For eProcess, the link is the business rules that may be software, an electronic link to an outside provider, or workflows. Input-process-output changes to request-source-respond. The company makes this transformation by using its capabilities sourced either through the interface, its value network, or within the company itself. Regardless of the sourcing, business rules govern the transformation of request to response.

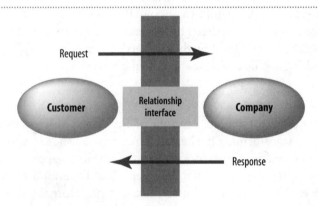

Figure 7-1: Components of the relationship interface

Process as Business Rules

The core of eProcess is our concept of "business rules." One of the reasons many companies appear to be process blind is that they overlook the importance of business processes in eCommerce when they separate the Web site from process and vice versa. From their perspective, Web sites are all about features, and processes are all about workflows, steps, tasks, and activities. They don't see that the Web site itself can be a process manager. This view estranges processes from technology. It positions application software as the recorder or accountant of business activity rather than the eCommerce relationship coordination engine it is. A Web site isn't a set of workflows. It's software. There are many processes behind the click on the screen—ordering, inventory management, shipping, pricing, payment, and so on—but the site is separate from these for most companies. So for many business managers "process" means non-Web, and Web means non-process. What a waste of eProcess opportunity that is!

Business Rules and Relationships

A business rule is a statement that guides the interaction between parties. Business rules define the basis for commerce and the terms of business for coordination within the value network. Rules begin with customers and what they want to accomplish. How rules are sourced defines the economics and responsibilities required to meet the customer request. The rules establish the relationship type, business interface, and capability sourcing. Business rules embedded in software conduct commerce at the business interface itself, linking the customer-requester directly to a needed eProcess capability. The entire script for the dialogue is handled by the software.

EPROCUREMENT: AN EXAMPLE

Consider the most obvious example of embedded business rules, the one that is transforming the basics of business logistics and business-to-business relationships: procurement of services, supplies, and office equipment, and maintenance, repair, and operations (MRO) purchases. These can be highly resource intensive, organizationally intensive, and expensive as requesters work through purchasing departments and suppliers to place their order and wait for its completion.

It used to be that ordering goods required getting authorization from someone to make the order, submit a purchase request, and send it to Purchasing. Purchasing had a mass of tasks to handle, including locating a supplier, sending the order, checking on shipment status, handling all the associated paperwork, and dealing with payments. This process is illustrated in Figure 7-2.

Now this is all routinely handled by software. The software is the process, and the process is the software. But that can't be true given the traditional definitions of process and the notion of software as an "application." Web site designers don't think of themselves as being in the business of process design, and process managers don't think of themselves as being in the software business. But they are.

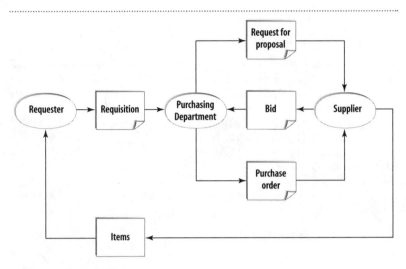

Figure 7-2: Sample MRO procurement process

eProcurement changes the rules and relationships among requesters, the purchasing organization, and suppliers. eProcurement uses Internet technologies to connect requesters and suppliers through online catalogs. This creates a new interaction between the requester and the supplier. The online catalog presents the products available for purchase. The purchasing application software contains the information-based rules negotiated between the purchasing department and its suppliers. These rules clarify purchasing decisions, limits, and product prices. These may include specific requirements about, say, which company to order office supplies from, which purchases need a supervisor's authorization, and the minimum and maximum units allowed in a single purchase.

The purchasing department uses the online catalog to aggregate standard purchases for a single supplier, giving the company the power to negotiate favorable terms with suppliers. This reduces purchasing department workload as a standard request flows directly to suppliers via the catalog. While non-standard transactions continue to be handled in terms of a request, bid, and purchase process, the volume flowing through the manual channel is dramatically reduced. Figure 7-3 shows a sample eProcurement process.

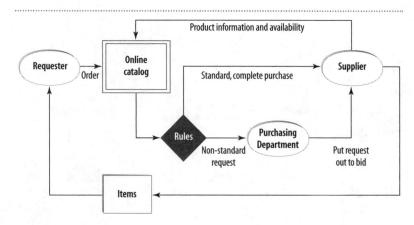

Figure 7-3: eProcurement for MRO purchases

Process as Rules, Software as Interface

Companies achieve process and business breakthroughs when they merge their process and technology perspectives. If we view a process as a set of business rules, the issue is as follows: can we define the rules and interactions between the requester and the agent in such a way that software can do a better job than people?

Sometimes, the answer is "No way." Try defining the business rules for, say, choosing a tie or dress at a level of precision and completeness for a software applet to pick out the garment for you. Sometimes, the answer is "Of course." Consider consumer loan processing, for instance. Software takes data from the applicant, links to credit record information, applies statistical rules, scores the application, and comes up with an accept-reject decision. Build a link from the Web site to the existing software system and your company can process loans online, as many financial services institutions now do.

Business rules define the *interactions* between players through the procedures required to meet the request. They involve more than validation edits on a Web page, a rudimentary form of a rule. Rather, they define the terms of business. In the case of a consumer loan, they are highly structured:

▶ Ensure that the applicant provides all the necessary information. If any information is incomplete, ask for more detail. If it is not forthcoming, reject the application.

> ► Apply the following formula for evaluating, income, debt, and other information: we will lend to a customer that has a credit score of X, a debt to equity ratio of Y, and so on.

> ► Inform the applicant of the loan status and decision. If approved, establish the closing requirements; if rejected, alert customer service to make the appropriate response.

In other instances, the business rules are more about interaction and conversation than procedures. They can apply to "softer" processes that involve recommendation and consultation, processes that previously were thought to be possible only by skilled personnel. So, for instance, you can't automate the tie-buying process in the way you can the loan applicant. But you can still specify interactive business rules:

> ► Look at the customer's profile of interests. Look at his recent history of purchases. Look at his current context and expected needs, as indicated by that profile and history. Compare these with tie purchases by customers with similar profiles, the current shopping basket, and the customer's purchasing history.

> ► Make a suggestion: "How about this one? A lot of our customers who appear to be very much like you have bought it." Show a picture.

> ► Use the reply to identify ties that more closely meet the customer's criteria—for instance, show the same pattern in different colors.

"Ask," "show," "suggest," and "compare" are as much business rules as "apply the following formula," "inform," or "check" *given* knowledge of the customer and interaction with the customer. The basic difference between the tools of eCommerce and the long history of automation of procedures is that the Internet provides for personalization of everything and interaction about everything.

That means that processes that previously rested on people because the business rules could not be precisely defined can now be handled as an interactive conversation. The software handles the dialogue in the way an adviser, agent, or consultant would. The business rules form the etiquette of polite conversation in that dialogue.

Recurrence: The Value of Embedding Rules in Software

Software is cheap to run. It may be very expensive to build, but if a company can design the business rules for helping a person choose a tie through advice, comparison, demonstration, and dialogue, the cost of electronically handling the process is basically the same for dealing with 50 people or 50 million. It's pennies. By contrast, the cost to offer comparable personal grooming advice in-store is highly dependent on the number of customers and how much time the salesperson spends with each customer. Some of the person-to-person interaction can be handled over the phone through a call center if the customer has the company's catalog, but that's expensive and unreliable.

So the software edge comes from recurrence. The more a process is part of the fabric of everyday business, the more customers who initiate it—and the more frequently they do so, the more likely the payoff from software.

A figure that is widely cited in the eCommerce press is the cost of handling a simple banking transaction. It's around $1 if it's processed by a teller, 30 cents via a call center, and 1 cent via self-direction through the Web. The originator of the figures is Wells Fargo, the bank that gets about 60 million customer inquiries a year for account balance information. That's a cost of $60 million for looking up the figure in the bank branch, $12 million for call center service agents to answer the question, and $600,000 for customers to do it themselves on the Web.[1]

What this means is that the primary target for embedding rules in software is to look for processes that have the following features, as they comprise an obvious and immediate opportunity for embedding them in the relationship interface:

▶ They are sufficiently well defined in terms of their business rules that only a few exceptional situations can't be handled through an interactive dialogue between the requester and a software "agent." That applies to most of the routine and everyday interactions between customers and suppliers. They may not support the full texture of the interaction and therefore can't be fully automated, but given information about the requester and given a simple question and answer interaction, they can be at least as well carried out in this manner as through alternative process options.

▶ They are recurrent enough to justify investing time, money, and brainstorming to work out the best way to design this dialogue and provide the interface. There's no point in committing these scarce resources for a process that only 1 percent of customers initiate just once a year.

▶ The requester—typically a customer—benefits from self-direction by using a software-based eProcess versus alternative modes of process, such as call centers, face-to-face contact, physical location, and so forth.

▶ When there's any breakdown in the software eProcess, the company can cost-effectively provide an alternative eProcess service. This is important, as embedding rules requires capabilities to handle customer crisis and exceptions that the interface does not support or when customers prefer not to use the software interface.

Scalability

A company has scalability when it can support increasing sales and transaction volumes without additional investment in people, equipment, or facilities. Software provides scalability, because it is not consumed as part of the transaction process as are inputs, time, inventory, staff availability, and other resources. This allows the same piece of software to support a theoretically infinite number of transactions.[2] Embedding business rules in software creates scalability, increasing asset efficiency found in eCommerce capabilities.

Embed rules in software to handle high volume requests like the Wells Fargo example cited earlier of 60 million requests a year for account balances over the phone. Or consider the business-to-business equivalent of Cisco, where customers request copies of invoices; having this processed through self-directed software saves the company around $6 million a year—and makes the customer happier.[3] Compare this with how slow and difficult is it for any company to get such copies immediately from its suppliers through traditional process mechanisms: a phone call to their accounting departments, a request to the sales rep, or a fax to the company.

Personalization

Personalization means that customers are handled in the context of their preferences, profiles, and requests. This involves delivering more than a tailored MyWebsite.com. It requires conducting business according to customer terms and preferences. Embedding business rules for this customer interaction versus using the same rules for all customers tailors the interface, creating personalization by managing the interface according to the customer and business context.

There are now many companies offering software that helps personalize the relationship interface. Ones like Broadvision build customer profiles, both directly from the information about themselves that they choose to provide to a company and from deductions the software makes about their interests from their pattern of purchases. Others, like DoubleClick, track which Web sites they go to, and many firms provide fully personalized sites, like My.Yahoo and MySchwab, which collect and use information from the customer interaction to provide information and offers unique to the person.

In all these instance, the software in the relationship interface knows exactly who you are and accumulates information about you, your preferences, and your purchases that over time creates a level of convenience, flexibility of enquiry, and access that, say, a call center operator can't immediately provide. Call centers suffer from two major constraints on such service: (1) they are designed to handle simple questions and requests, and (2) the staff doesn't have the information and authority to handle complex exceptions to their routine scripts. Personal contacts—with sales reps, in the store, or via fax—suffer from two different constraints: (1) knowledge ("Let me get back to you, I don't have the information but I'll get it") and (2) competence and experience ("Sorry, I don't know anything about that, but I'll ask around"). Ironically, the software interface provides more customer intimacy and personal service than a human can. Augmented by a human handling the exceptions to the software routine, both the eProcess firm and its customers get the best of all worlds in terms of service and cost.

eProcess, Not Process Automation

We emphasize these last points because they are what makes the difference between eProcess and automation. Perhaps we might call it the Schwab rule. A major factor in Charles Schwab's success rests in simultaneously exploiting the software opportunity that supports customers managing their own trades and the personal service that established full-commission companies already offered. This is a key element in eProcess. Use software to handle the routine that is more robust and context sensitive than ever before. Make sure the exceptions are just as well handled and provide integrated support across the channels.

All this opens up innumerable opportunities to embed processes in software, making them personalized and customized for the relationship. Many companies don't take up the opportunities, which is a waste. That's because a software-embedded process immediately enhances the customer relationship and directly contributes to improvements in the economic and organizational performance of the company.

Electronic Process Sourcing

Figure 7-4 shows eProcess options, ranging from embedding in software to coordinating through people and workflows. For most companies, this is a matter of either/or—either automate and go online or preserve the processes that ensure the personal contact and flexible response. The eProcess company finds ways through its sourcing to offer high-touch and -texture services at scale and cost. It must source its capabilities well up the complexity/efficiency scale in order to meet time-to-market and capital usage requirements.

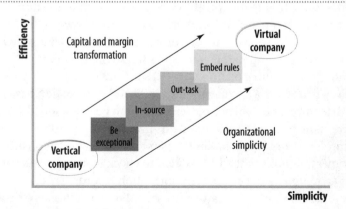

Figure 7-4: eProcess sourcing options

Sourcing must be an issue of both/and (not either/or) workflow coordination, in-sourcing, out-tasking, and embedding. The logic of eCommerce pushes toward embedding as much of the process base in software as possible, especially when that creates the win-win situation we described in the previous chapter of this book. Sourcing enables the eCommerce provider's background liability process to become the customer's priority asset eProcess. However, the move toward software must recognize that it has its limitations. For one, software is lousy at handling exceptions. People can be great at that. That means that wherever a company moves people processes into software, it must consider where it needs to add new people processes, too.

Process-Enabled Software

The continued rise of application software, such as enterprise business systems, and the emerging class of eCommerce tools speak to the value of embedded rules in software. These tools, unlike operating systems and network software, contain embedded rules for specific capabilities, such as procurement, credit management, shipping, accounting, and inventory management. Companies implement the software in order to gain access to these capabilities; in effect, they buy the process base of the software provider.

The importance of application software packages has grown in eCommerce as companies access the best of market functionality through buying rather than building. Companies such as Ariba, Commerce One, Broadvision, Blue Martini, and Vignette, to name just a few, all provide them with specific business functionality that enables new capabilities at low cost, ranging from how you buy things to how you market at your online storefront. Each is based on business rules and parameter values that build flexibility.

Enterprise resource planning (ERP) software such as SAP, Oracle, and others provide a standardized process and information base for the back office, onto which front-end tools can be easily added. So, for instance, the back-end ERP maintains inventory and ordering information. The front-end handles the personalized interaction with the customer and links to the ERP system to check on inventory availability and update the customer information records. This combination unifies the back office around a shared understanding of data and defined processes. It enables the Web relationship interface to provide back-office functions such as billing and order management to the front-office Web site with minimal complexity.

There are three structural components of this eProcess technology base. The ERP, legacy systems that process transactions, and operational databases are the substructure—the foundation that supports everything else. The main eCommerce structure is the Web site itself. The superstructure is the front-end software and information tools that add functionality and personalization. Making these work together is complex, obviously. Older legacy systems (the term is a misnomer—they are often more ancestral curse systems; a wicked fairy cursed the company with its 1980s accounts payable system until the fifth generation of managers) were built on an entirely different technology base from that of the Internet. There are also multiple processes and data entry interfaces (such as the five copies of a form that all go to different departments and into different computer systems). There are problems in ensuring that information flows between systems and that they are synchronized. For example, what should happen when a customer places an order through the Web site in terms of updating the legacy systems that handle orders and inventory management, updating the call center customer records, and updating the customer profile records? There's no simple answer to this apparently simple question. It demands an in-depth review of processes, operational constraints on handling heavy telecommunications and computer systems traffic online, and ensuring consistency in data definitions and data quality assurance.

Because of all of these complex problems, many companies do not build their Web site interface relationship structure on the ERP and legacy systems substructure; they literally don't communicate with each other. In that situation, the Web site is a Web site and not the relationship interface to the eProcess base. The rules that are embedded in software must be able to access the substructure resources since it is there that most of the firm's operational information resides—inventory data, customer records, accounting information, and supplier history.

The Cost and Complexity of Process Workflows

Embedding rules in software and linking them to internal systems and external partners for out-tasking and in-sourcing deliver efficiency through greater coordination and reduced complexity. The more that any process meets the traditional conception of process as workflow, tasks, and activities, the higher the cost and complexity of coordination. They are interrelated. The cost comes from the multiplicity of steps, duplication of data, all the paper, and all the staffing and administration those involve. The complexity comes from the levels of staffing, supervision, and management from the many cross-checks, control mechanisms, and procedures required. The scale of complexity is indicated by a 1980s study by Exxon that found that on average every single document in its head office was copied 40 times, with 15 of them stored permanently. As we've mentioned earlier, the average administrative cost to process a simple purchase is around $100. It's organizational complexity that generates this burden.

And it's eProcess that removes the burden. It's not at all surprising that the fastest-growing component of eCommerce has most recently been to simplify B2B relationships. That's where the cost and complexity have been high for both customer and supplier. Using a procurement example, Table 7-1 provides a reminder of just how far-reaching embedding processes in software have become and how huge have been the payoffs.

Table 7-1: Performance Comparison[4]

	Traditional	eProcurement	Savings
Average cost to process and indirect purchase	$100	$15	85%
Time from order to receipt	7 days	2 days	73%
Price discount for direct purchases	0%	20%	20%
Percentage of members buying outside strategic partners	40%	25%	38%

Complexity: A Creator of Cost

Embedding rules in software improves process efficiency through managing complexity. Complexity can be measured in terms of the number of activities required to complete a process. The greater the complexity, the greater the number of steps, and the greater the cost. Assume for instance that each step of a complex process chain, such as procurement, has an average 95 percent success rate—that is, only in 5 percent of cases does something go wrong, such as incorrect or missing paperwork, misunderstandings, miscommunication, or mistakes.

How many steps does a process need to involve before the average success rate drops to 75 percent? The answer is just 6 steps, as shown in Figure 7-5, and for a 50 percent efficiency level, 14 steps. Raise the success rate per step to 98 percent and the overall performance goes up from 50 percent to 75 percent. Raise it again to 99 percent and the figure is 86 percent. Take a process that involves 50 steps and there's just an 8 percent chance that it will be done right the first time.

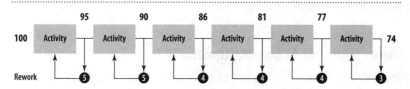

Figure 7-5: Efficiency: Six-step process with 95 percent accuracy in each step

Of course, such figures underlie the ethos of Total Quality Management and reengineering. Small incremental shifts in individual task success—moving from a 95 percent to 98 percent rate—translate to huge improvements. The figures also explain why good companies so often produce poor results in the masses of administrative background processes that dominate their head count, overhead costs, and organizational complexity. It's no wonder that, on average, 20 percent of invoices contain some error. Or that almost all reports of the cost to process an order of goods and corresponding payments amount to anywhere between $50 and $120.[5]

The clearer the business rules, the more recurrent the process. And the greater the complexity, the more likely the process should involve software embedding. We use the somewhat cumbersome term "embed" to stress that this is not *automation* of the process. The software doesn't replace the process or substitute for it. It does not eliminate the interaction and personal nature of the process; rather, it governs the flow of information and interaction in context.

The Iron Clad eProcess Rule

Of course, many complex process chains are anything but interactive and personal. These processes rest on inflexibility—rules that cannot be broken—and customers that must understand that a rule is a rule regardless of their situation. This is not eProcess. It is the "Have a nice day syndrome" that substitutes politeness for responsiveness. It's a process designed on behalf of the company, not the customer. It automates work rules under the reengineering mantra of efficiency; software can often outperform workflows in basics of service. But that said, it's not enough to convert business rules into software. That's automation, not eProcess. It's fine to improve the efficiency of a transaction, provided that you also increase the effectiveness of the relationship.

Guidelines for Embedding Rules

Embedding business rules in the interface turns your processes into products. Your process base then becomes a vital part of your revenue generation and operations. Realizing the potential of process as a product asset requires looking at business rules from a customer-centered, relationship-building, and information-intensive perspective. This perspective reflects the eProcess style of process as business rules, interfacing, and sourcing. Here are the guidelines for moving fast to exploit the opportunity.

Start with the Customer Experience

Producing a win-win situation is the goal of an eProcess. The customer wins because of better service, greater convenience, and a higher touch-texture experience, which encourages the relationship. The company wins because it gains the benefits of reduced complexity and cost coupled with increased productivity and efficiency. This means that the relationship interface—the Web site itself—must be designed to build relationships through supporting the customer experience rather than processing transactions. This is not at all easy to accomplish. McKinsey provides some figures that should scare managers responsible for eCommerce. It reported in early 2000 that the average large-scale eCommerce Web site gets 1.8 million hits a month. Of these, 127,000 lead to a customer transaction (around 15 percent). But the number of repeat customers is just 24,000. So just 1.3 percent of the hits translate to relationships.[6]

Call Centers: An Analogy

With traditional catalog sales, the call center is very often the customer's moment of first impression about a company. With eCommerce, the Web site is the moment of first interaction. Think of the very best toll-free phone services you have used and then think of the worst. The difference in first impression is immediate and striking, as shown in Table 7-2.

Table 7-2: Call Center Characteristics

Strong Call Center Characteristics	Challenged Call Center Characteristics
Understands my need	Only answers standard questions
Problems resolved with a single call	Problem requires multiple contacts
Available whenever I need them	Available only during company operating hours
Knows who I am	Needs account information
Has the information at their disposal	Needs to search for information

A challenged call center makes you aware at once that the agent is an hourly contract employee in one of the call center businesses that works on a contract basis for the company you think you're calling. The company got the bid through promising a given average number of calls answered per hour and related targets for cost and volume. No wonder the "agent" or "customer service representative," who is really neither of these, sounds distant and uninterested.

Look at the Full Customer Experience

You really don't want a distant or bored Web site for your company. Nor do you want one that is hyperactive, disorganized, unreliable, unavailable, slow, and difficult to interact with. Most companies have learned since the early days of static and cumbersome sites the importance of ensuring ease of navigation, security, intuitive interfaces, and the like.

It's outside the scope of this book to go into the details of Web design, but from the eProcess perspective, we stress that usable and natural interfaces are not a feature of just the customer interaction at the Web site but of the whole customer experience—before and after the click. Here are some questions for managers to address:

▶ What type of relationship are you trying to build with customers?

▶ What makes for a good experience, starting from what happens when someone hits the Web site for the first time through fulfillment of the request?

▶ What are the software features that help make the experience useful, comfortable, and safe?

▶ What should happen the very first second when customers come back to the site in terms of the full experience: recognition, special services, personal treatment, and so on?

▶ At what point is it appropriate to start gathering the information and taking the eProcess steps—using embedded software—to formally offer a relationship rather than just more transactions?

▶ How much of the back-office administrative and service processes can and should be embedded in the software for the customer and eCommerce provider?

▶ What has to be added to these in terms of the customer follow-up experience to handle breakdowns, email queries, and preferences for other modes of contact, such as through a call center or internal marketing, support, and technical staff?

▶ How do we gather information at the Web interface or through other sources for customer relationship management (CRM) that is win-win for customer and company? (The obvious issue here is privacy and confidentiality, key aspects of the trust bond, too easily put at risk.)

Make It Easy to Begin the Relationship

The first move in the customer experience is recognizing when and how the relationship starts. *Defining* when the relationship starts is an important business rule and early design issue. Some sites view a relationship as repeat visits to the Web site, others count customers when they register their identity (credit card number, email address, and so on), others when they make a purchase. Regardless of when you believe a relationship starts, initiation should be simple, timely, and advantageous to the customer.

Unfortunately, this is not always the case. Consider opening an account. That should never be a problem or involve bureaucracy. Sometimes, as with securities trading, there are legal and regulatory rules that prevent an immediate activation of the account. In that case, tell the potential customer right up front. Handle every single aspect of the first steps in relationship-building at the interface and make it as easy to do as is *possible*—not just practical. Keep in mind the figure that only 1.3 percent (24,000 out of 1.8 million hits) will turn into the business you want. The harder it is for the customer to start, the more you drive these numbers down.

Turn Every Customer Inquiry into an Interaction

A relationship is two way. Many online companies make it one way. That's often because they separate the Web site from the process base. This is a legacy view of process and technology, one inherited from the company's history. It has to go. So, for instance, when an order is placed, there should be an automatic software check on the availability of the goods, followed up by an emailed confirmation message. The software should maintain its monitoring, so if there is any delay in shipment, another alert is sent.

Relationship as Conversation

Think of these as relationship conversations. They are of two types, both of which affect the touch and texture of the relationship: (1) feedback and closing of any open loops, and (2) alerts and welcome surprises. Closing the loop means keeping customers informed and making sure there are no unwelcome surprises. Alerts are keeping customers up to date about problems, and welcome surprises are information and offers.

The more tightly the Web site is tied to the eProcess base, the more timely and valuable the conversations that can be held. The alternative is detachment: the conversations are detached in the sense of being limited and impersonal and also in that there can't be a conversation about many aspects of order fulfillment, status, alerts, and so on, because the site isn't linked to the relevant process base. By moving that base from the back office into the software itself, the Web interface knows the business rules and can use them for the two-way interaction.

Make the Exception-Handling Difference

The further the company moves to embed the routine business rules, the more it needs to consider what to do when the rules don't work or if there's a request it can't handle. Our strong recommendation is that managers design the exception-handling eProcesses along with the routine ones. There's no point in providing an email address for customers to send messages to if there's no organizational process for responding to them—a common problem in most eCommerce. Making the relationship difference requires designing the Web site for the routine and, from there, linking information and communication back into the company, so that its process base and employee skills handle the exceptions. That means appropriately layering the components of the eCommerce business, so that they are "seamless"—they work together smoothly and without interruption. Figure 7-6 shows the two directions required for an eCommerce design, top down—from the Web site to the network players—to handle the routine and backwards to ensure exception-handling capabilities.

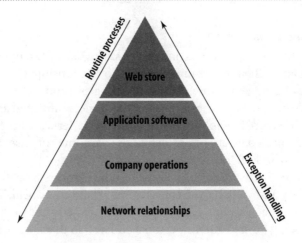

Figure 7-6: Layers of eCommerce components

Create a Conversation Factory

Companies build a conversation factory as they put more and more of their process base into the software interface. It will work well most of the time and probably be far more reliable (at the 99.9 percent level), simple (if the technical design of the Web site is well handled), and fast than workflow alternatives. But workflows have to take over for the 0.1 percent that fail. That is the moment of truth where the relationship and the investment in customer acquisition are on the line.

Exceptions Build the Promise and Your Brand

How a company handles exceptions may turn out to be a key to differentiating itself in a marketspace where more and more of the routine will be well processed by online convenience machines. Schwab has not just made this part of its brand, but has been able to charge a premium over the online transaction, a buy/sell order for a trade. Customers are well aware that if things go wrong, the company itself takes the initiative to repair the problem. They do this by linking customers to account representatives if the site is down so the customer's trade is carried out anyway. National Semiconductor's handling of emails is another example; it guarantees full resolution of the problem within a working day.[7] Software embedded in the interface evaluates the message and chooses from a list of employees the one who appears most qualified to resolve it. That person has formal responsibility to get this done and authority to draw on help from across the organization to do so.

In both these instances, it's people and workflows that handle the exceptions *because they are by definition not routine.* Here's where our eProcess approach differs from the ethos of automation. The more you embed processes in software, the more important it will be to carefully consider the people processes that complement them.

Self-Organize Processes

Self-organizing processes mark the difference between process automation and enabling eProcess. Traditional processes follow a chain of inputs-process-output that links the activities required to handle customer requests. These chains are replicated, much like strands of DNA, to handle different customer, product, or service lines, creating mutually exclusive process paths that create complexity as the business grows and diversifies. A sample of one of these chains is shown in Figure 7-7. When you look at it, you may think that it doesn't provide any insight into the process; it's just a set of boxes and arrows. You're right. It says nothing about the customer-company conversation, the customer experience, the historical relationship and relationship building, or the value network that supports and enhances the eProcess.

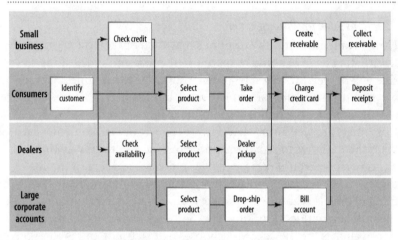

Figure 7-7: Sample order to cash process flow segmented by customers

Notice that each customer segment—small business, consumers, dealers, and large corporate accounts—is designed to have its own basic process flow with little sharing of process rules across segments. This occurs when executives focus narrowly on improving the operational efficiency of a specific segment. Projects that "improve the efficiency of in-store sales" often lead to single track processes that work in the "small," but increase organizational complexity and cost. This happens as the business focuses on inputs, processes, and outputs rather than looking for recurrent business rules, leveraging the interface, and sourcing. A rules-based perspective helps identify and create self-organizing processes.

Self-organizing processes break these chains into modules and then link them together according to customer intention and context. This involves bringing component and object development techniques to the discipline of process design. Those disciplines focus on understanding a business component and its behavior according to methods (business rules). The result is a process that has greater modularity. This approach gains flexibility and manages complexity as new products and services create different paths through existing modular processes rather than whole new streams. These streams are defined to a "broker" process that manages the different paths, based on context and condition, creating the self-organization shown in Figure 7-8.

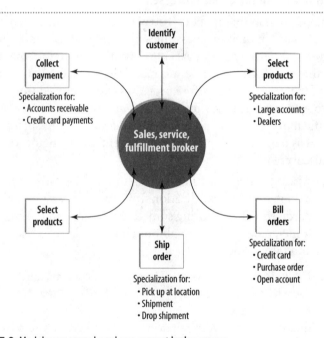

Figure 7-8: Modular processes based on a request broker process

There is a substantial difference between the two processes. The traditional process specializes its rules through creating separate process flows while a brokered process places specializations within individual processes. The genius behind this comes when the process changes, say adding a new form of payment or shipment. In the traditional, input-process-output approach, the change would require new process steps and additional flows. A self-organizing process, on the other hand, simply needs to add new rules to its existing flows, shown as text in Figure 7-8.

The broker process provides a single point of coordination for product and service process parameters. This greatly improves process flexibility, supports the reuse of processes, and is only possible through embedding rules into software. If traditional processes create chains of DNA that replicate into strands, modular self-organizing processes are RNA that recombine, based on context, to meet the need.

Clean Rules Make for Clean Processes

Software is cruel in that it obeys instructions, and those instructions must be "clean" in their business rules: no ambiguities, conflicting procedures, duplicated steps, varying definitions of requirements depending on which department is handling, and all the other muddying of the process flow. Before processes can be moved from workflows to software, the following cleaning-up process is often essential and difficult to achieve, as companies that cleaned up business processes as part of total quality management and reengineering often discovered:

1. Assess the degree of standardization of the process and its potential standardization. If it isn't and can't be standardized without losing something of value to the customer, redesign it to combine value and clarity of rules and information.

2. Evaluate the business rules to remove decisions and options "downstream"—this is a variant of the TQM mantra of "get it right the first time." For eProcess, this is "get it done the first time, at the Web relationship interface." If you have to touch it, inspect it, review it, or approve it, this is not standard and can't be routine. Redesign the process or complement it with exception-handling eProcess capabilities.

3. Identify all the information needed to complete all the eProcess. Capture it once only, and both guard and use it relentlessly to design software eProcesses that capture the information in as few steps and as naturally as possible. Use information from all sources to ensure that once the Web interaction is complete, there won't be some later ambiguity or information conflict or incompleteness.

4. Remove all reliance for the routine on manual interventions, interpretations, and variations in procedure. If you give the process business rules to three people and get more than one answer, this is not a clean process. If your non-technology-oriented spouse, parent, or child can't explain the business rule to you, it's not clean. If you can identify the need for a decision as part of a process but can't state the business rules, it's not clean.

Remember, too, that as you move processes into the software interface, your back door is wide open. Back-office processes that were previously hidden are exposed by eCommerce—like your somewhat cumbersome account-opening process and investment management system, which relies a lot on supervisors' judgment and crisis management or the sometimes improvised delivery schedules. While the Web site may bring in the business, it's behind the Web site where you do the work and pay the bills.

Embed Rules: Create the Relationship Through Software

Embedding rules provides a powerful source of eProcess capability, as the relationship interface enables you to "jack" directly into the value network. The results in terms of increased efficiency and cost are self-evident and a powerful enticement to creating a wholly virtual company. That would be the case if we were just processing transactions, as with an ATM. However, transactions alone do not create eCommerce success. Embedding business rules in the interface can build relationships and efficiency when they are designed from the customer's perspective, respond to needs, and recognize the need for in-depth support. Embedding rules can be difficult, but, when you get it right, this back office becomes the customer front office and provides the relationship base and the profit base. Transactions only provide a revenue base.

Chapter 8

Out-Tasking and In-Sourcing

Embedding processes in software brings the internal operations and capabilities of the company forward into the relationship interface. In a sense, this concentrates the business into the software; it transforms purchasing, credit, shipping, and customer service from departments spread across locations and time zones to capabilities at hand, now and anywhere. This is an inward move—taking what was outside the customer's immediate contact point and pulling it into the Web site.

The same eProcess principles extend the company outward to expand its boundaries. That expansion begins by extending both the relationship base across the network and the eProcess base by out-tasking capabilities. Out-tasking demands a capability view of the business that breaks a company into a portfolio of process-centered operations rather than interlocking departments or functions. That eProcess portfolio is built on electronic collaboration—the exchange of services across capabilities in the conduct of commerce.

Out-tasking is enabled through application program interfaces (APIs) that electronically link—immediately and automatically—to another company's eProcess capabilities. Out-tasking is our term for using APIs to have another company handle a task on your behalf. This extends the relationship interface and operation from the Web site beyond the company and adds the capabilities of value network players. Figure 8-1 shows the interactions across a customer, the company's business rules, and the supplier's capability for an order request process. Note that here the company is transferring responsibility to an agent—that term again!—that provides best-practice process capability. We emphasize "best practice process" because that's the real eProcess opportunity—to provide the very, very best service without having to build it and, indeed, without having to pay much to get it. We've cited UPS as an example here and could add FedEx and the U.S. Postal Service. All three of these companies handle shipments far better and at lower cost than a company could do by itself. That's the value element in a value network.

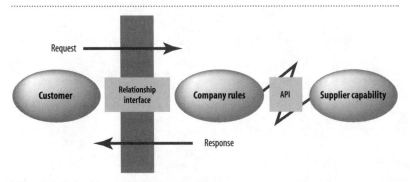

Figure 8-1: Out-tasking a capability using an API

Out-tasking creates vertical disintegration and is a hallmark of eCommerce companies that do not want to spend the time or the capital to invest in background or liability capabilities in order to make them eProcess assets. By vertical disintegration we mean that the firm unravels itself; it doesn't have to source capabilities in-house and can source 20 different functions from 20 different companies if it so chooses. Indeed, it can source a thousand functions or ten thousand—its organizational structure remains the same. It needs only to have access to online players that can handle the processes through electronic messages. This has created new niche markets for companies who make one company's background liabilities their own identity assets, as in our example of shipping.

Companies out-task capabilities for several reasons, including market availability of first-class process capabilities, internal capacity and skills, and cost. The market availability of providers of world-class level capabilities, particularly in the area of logistics and payments, means a company can lease these services, turning an asset-intensive fixed investment into a variable expense. These examples are obvious general opportunities, given the prominence of eCommerce enabling companies in the logistics, payment, and information technology services areas. It just doesn't make sense for a company to build its own capabilities when, in these areas, it's literally a waste of money.

Companies also out-task when they have insufficient capacity to drive down costs or to warrant the required investments to reach world-class performance. In this case, they look to pool their transactions with a service provider who can justify the investments required to provide the operational performance required at speed and scale. This is the case for many background and back-office processes such as payroll, benefits administration, and other similar activities. The issue here is how to get best service and best cost. It's rare for background liability processes that the solution is to build.

Clearing Out-Tasking Hurdles

Out-tasking in eCommerce rests on being able to directly and completely process a request sent through an electronic agent to a shipping company, manufacturer, retailer, bank, or broker. There is a catch here. All the players in the emerging value network must have the technology platform and eProcess base that ensures clean business rules and clean interfaces. They need a robust set of applications centered on a messaging architecture that enables the API. Many companies just do not have the degree of integration or message-based architectures that give them the ability to collaborate in real time. If you have to pass batch files between companies, you are not ready for the degree of interaction or performance requirements necessary to succeed in out-tasking. This may seem like a technical point, but it's more than that, even though it requires a technical solution. The underlying issue is coordination-coordination of process, information, and dialogue.

We will not downplay the size of each of these hurdles. The problem is considerable for established companies that have multiple computer processing systems, databases, and communication links, as well as complex workflows and corresponding business rules required to have these systems interact. They can't just hand off, say, a customer order to a third-party logistics company like UPS and manage the information flow automatically and directly. This gives a huge edge to companies that do not have legacy systems and who can design their eProcess base from scratch. Many of the new value-adding intermediaries and trading partner hubs like Ariba benefit from this first-mover organizational advantage. That's why more and more companies are out-tasking their procurement processing to them.

Whether a company is an established pre-eCommerce player or a new online one, the issues are the very same: the entry fee for creating or joining a value network is clean interfaces and clean business rules. That demands hard work by the company's technology development team and business units. Again, this is not just a matter of designing a Web site—this is as complex in terms of technology and business as any initiative in the 40-year history of computers in business.

Leveraging Value Network Assets

A value network generates value for all its members. If the problem is large, so is the opportunity for someone in the network. The foundation for investments in the eProcess portfolio of capabilities is win-win—everybody gains. Embedding processes in software is win-win for customer and provider, as we discussed in Chapter 7. Out-tasking—getting rid of a process—is win-win-win. The company wins by being able to interact with a best-practice eProcess capability without having to make investments itself in the process base. The customer wins by the very fact that this component of the relationship is being handled by a best-practice provider. The provider wins by extending its revenue base and market reach.

Figure 8-2 illustrates this point using "T" accounts of asset and liability capabilities. T accounts are the base of financial accounting, with debits to the left and credits to the right, with each debit entry requiring a matching set of credits and vice versa. The core accounting rule is that debits equal credits. Always.

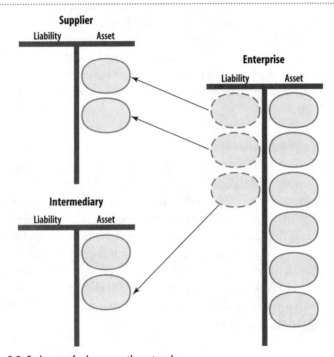

Figure 8-2: Exchange of value across the network

Out-Tasking Is Not Out-Sourcing

We do not use the word "out-sourcing" to describe this for four reasons. First, the term is generally associated in managers' minds with getting rid of a function, such as information technology operations. Out-tasking is much more selective in its focus; the issue is how best to source an eProcess that matters to the customer relationship *and* the company's productivity and performance. Second, the term downplays the interactive nature of the API dialogue, which is dynamic. For instance, when a company just out-sources shipping of goods, that may save costs and simplify operations by shifting transactions. However, when it electronically out-tasks them, it leases provider capability. This gives the company access to provider eProcess assets, such as order tracking, increased information flows, and broader use of the provider's process knowledge. The difference between payroll processing and benefits management services illustrates this difference. Payroll processing services handle the transactions required to cut checks and transfer funds. Information flows are fixed between the company and the payroll provider as this is an out-sourced process. Compensation management services, on the other hand, provide transaction processing and additional services to enable employee self-management of their benefits. This requires a dynamic flow of information and services beyond handling the specific out-sourced transaction.

Access an Extended Value Network

Our third reason for not using the term out-sourcing in this context is that the company *adds* something, not just gets rid of something. Out-tasking gains access to a partner's value network. For example, eCredit handles the financing of orders made through an eCommerce site, as shown in Figure 8-3. That is comparable to out-sourcing to a bank or leasing company. But eCredit brokers the opportunity out into its own value network of financial institutions. The API to an intermediary like eCredit is a link to a complex financial supply chain of lenders, leasing companies, risk underwriters, company reports, and credit rating information providers.

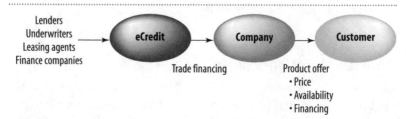

Figure 8-3: Using a supplier to gain access to its value network

The same is the case with trading partner hubs. It's this value network reach that makes company A much more competitive than company B even where they are roughly the same in internal capabilities, products, and prices. The difference between companies rests on the fact that company A is part of a strong supply chain value network and company B is not. This gives company A an advantage, as it has access to a greater capability base through APIs and its resulting expanded value network.

Companies like company B are very much still in the majority, with inflexible and restrictive operations that make it difficult for them to collaborate online. The National Association of Manufacturers reported in late February 2000 that 90 percent of the 2,500 member companies it surveyed that month report that they do not have their current business process technology systems fully automated. Table 8-1 shows other findings that indicate just how wide the gap is between the value network players and just the "manufacturers."

Table 8-1: The eCommerce Gap[1]

Year	Small Businesses in U.S.	Businesses with Web Sites	Businesses Doing eCommerce
2000	7.7 million	2.7 million	1.6 million
1999	7.6 million	2.1 million	0.8 million
1998	7.5 million	1.2 million	0.4 million
1997	7.4 million	0.5 million	0.1 million

Capital Preservation

The final reason for not talking about out-sourcing is central to eProcess versus traditional business: capital. When a company out-sources a function like information technology operations, it generally transfers a capital item over to an outside party; it moves from one balance sheet to another. Staff move from the company that hired them to the one that wins the out-sourcing contract, worrying about their job security. Facilities are transferred. This is why the contracting process for out-sourcing can be so complex.

In contrast to this type of out-sourcing, out-tasking adds a capability rather than transfers one, without the adverse balance sheet impact associated with out-sourcing. In this case, out-tasking has a disproportionate benefit for startups as they are able to "lease" the legacy asset bases of their value network partners. This allows them to design their eProcess base from scratch, leveraging as much as possible from their value network. For example, they don't need a finance, shipping, or even accounting department. All they need to do is locate a service provider and establish the API link.

Out-Tasking Potential

APIs make it relatively easy to make switches as needed. A new partner can be added to the eProcess technology platform in a few months or even less. It is impossible to exaggerate the scale of the out-tasking and in-sourcing opportunity—and the cost of neglecting it. We are not talking here about future possibilities, but about present actualities. If we look just at companies that are already profitable as large-scale eCommerce players, they all exploit the three software-centered elements of eProcess: embedding, out-tasking, and in-sourcing.

Recall the old adage that if a job's worth doing, it's worth doing well. Our eProcess adage is that if a job's worth doing and someone else can do it better, let them. Years ago, the concept of the "virtual company" became popular in the business literature. This is a company—like Nike, for example—that handles only a few core functions, such as design, and contracts out manufacturing, shipping, and related operational processes. Verifone provides another example as the leader in credit card authorization terminals without a formal office infrastructure. Verifone, now owned by Hewlett Packard, is a global communications network relying on email for communications, information sharing, and process coordination. A third example of a virtual company is Galoob, a toy "manufacturer" that out-tasks manufacturing, shipping, storage, and even payments.

These examples date from the early 1990s. In many ways, the eProcess opportunity is an acceleration and intensification of the move toward the virtual company. As in the Nike, Verifone, and Galoob cases, a company can concentrate its resources, internal skills, and attention: design for Nike, development and sales for Verifone, and merchandising for Galoob. It then sources everything else from the outside. It greatly reduces its capital investment demands and simplifies its company. It gains flexibility and speed, and it can choose suppliers based on best price, best logistics, and best product.

Out-Tasking: Building Scale @ Speed

As so often in eProcess, there's nothing new about the out-tasking/in-sourcing opportunity, except that the scale, speed, and flexibility are so exponentially higher that everything is new in terms of the management opportunity and challenge. Business design and organizational structuring have always been constrained by geography, physical location, workflows, time, and the link between these and capital investment demands. eCommerce lowers these barriers to the point where a company can gain ready access to world-class capabilities in months rather than the years required to build them in-house.

The results can be dramatic. It took Wal-Mart, one of the fastest growing companies in the history of business, ten years to become a billion dollar company. It took just four years for Amazon to reach that point. Once a company has a first-rate technology platform and, much more important, a solid base of repeat customers, it can add more and more capabilities at less and less capital cost. In the case of AOL and Yahoo!, companies paid more than half a billion dollars in fees in 1999 to be an API from their sites.[2]

Out-Tasking Stands on Its Own

It is rapidly becoming clear that the entry fee for large-scale eCommerce is far, far higher than early enthusiasts assumed in terms of marketing, technology, and operational support. The estimated costs in early 2000 were $40.5 million to launch and $48.8 million to operate and remain competitive.[3] Add to this the consensual estimate of $100 to $150 million to build a new eCommerce brand.[4] Executives thus have plenty of reason to be very cautious in approving the expenditures required to launch an eCommerce business. After all, imagine listening to what we might call the neo-Amazonian business justification: "We are aiming at 20 million customers and revenues of $2 billion a year...Oh, and by the way, we will be losing a few hundred million dollars a year for the indefinite future. And many analysts don't believe we'll make it."

Our personal opinion is that the established company doesn't need to look at justifying its eCommerce in these terms. That's the whipped cream on the sundae. Out-tasking alone can *fully* justify the investment in the eCommerce platform. If the company is able to out-task even a fraction of its eProcesses that are background liabilities, it lowers its invested capital per dollar of revenue, and it lowers its operating costs. If it does this in a way that attracts and retains customers, it has a win and the customer has a win. Table 8-2 shows the estimated cost savings from engaging in business-to-business (B2B) eCommerce. Keep in mind as you scan these that the average net margin for manufacturing companies in the U.S. is 3 to 5 percent and for financial services 8 to 12 percent. Can you think of any opportunity other than B2B eCommerce that is likely to provide the same margin improvement? We can't.

Table 8-2: Sample Savings from eCommerce[5]

Industry	Estimating Savings from B2B eCommerce
Aerospace machining	11%
Chemicals	10%
Coal	2%
Communications	15%
Computing	20%
Electronic components	39%
Food ingredients	5%
Forest products	25%
Freight transport	20%
Health care	5%
Life sciences	19%
Machining (metals)	22%
Media and advertising	15%
Materials, repair, and operating suppliers	10%
Oil and gas	15%
Paper	10%
Steel	11%

Within the next two years, the impact of out-tasking will become obvious to every company. That's because increasingly—almost by the week—more and more value networks are emerging to provide service via APIs. The most visible and accelerating example is business-to-business management of what we call "stuff"—inventory, shipping, office supplies, reverse logistics (a fancy term for what to do about returned goods), auctioning of surplus stock, payments, and the like—all the stuff that companies deal with as part of everyday business.

Out-task them to the best-practice online API partner. It doesn't make sense to do anything else. Consider the following best-practice eProcess company, which really could be your own, given the API-ready platform:

- ▶ It has some distinctive competencies and differentiation in the marketplace—this could be its products, services, reputation, prices, history of innovation, or some other set of capabilities.

- ▶ It doesn't have a large sales force, but it generates demand by carefully and selectively contracting for links to portals that extend the reach of its name and marketing.

- ▶ It doesn't have a large purchasing department either, but it's a superb one that has lowered the average price paid for supplies by 10 percent, again through its API links to trading hubs.

- ▶ It reduces its software development and operations costs by using application service providers (ASPs) that in effect rent software by the unit, person, transaction, or time period.

- ▶ It has a superb financing unit operating through links to banks and other institutions such as eCredit.

- ▶ It benefits from customer self-direction of more and more aspects of account management, research and evaluation, and handling of questions.

Or, alas, the following could be your company. It has a Web site, but it doesn't have clean eProcess business rules or clean interfaces, so it has no choice but to continue its business as usual. This involves building layer upon layer of administration to company processes and workflows to cover for poorly integrated applications, investing in value-wasting liabilities, and starving core innovation assets.

Out-Tasking Capabilities: Raising Efficiency and Operations

Going back to our eProcess capability matrix, presented in Chapter 6, the choice of processes to out-task rests on assessing the value of the capability and its contribution to the value network relationships. Basically, red flags go up wherever a capability is a priority in the relationship but a liability for the company. This situation indicates a capability that is consequential to eCommerce success, but does not create sufficient value for the company—no matter how well it handles the eProcess. Performing such a capability well does not create a gain for the company in terms of its reputation, repeat customer business, or brand. These types of capabilities are highlighted in the matrix shown in Figure 8-4.

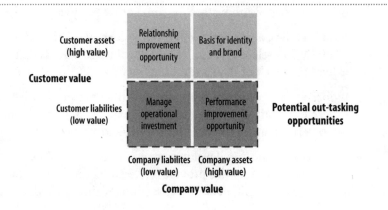

Figure 8-4: Identifying potential out-tasking capabilities

Customers care about security, for instance, but they don't in general value a company for having it—it's in this sense that the process is a liability, all expense and no value-adding contribution. The best that can happen for security is that nothing happens. The transaction is accurately handled, customer information protected, and fraud, pranks, and would-be thieves kept away. It can be value-losing, in that handling it badly can cause damage to the company, but doing it well leaves it where it was before and not ahead in the competitive game.

Similarly, customers don't care about many of the operational and support processes companies are burdened with that are background liabilities—relatively unimportant in themselves but part of everyday routine: insurance, payment processing, record keeping and accounting, reporting, order tracking, and the like. Mandatory processes, such as regulatory compliance, tax handling, and conformance with trade and consumer laws are examples. By definition, these are liability processes and in some instances, they are of negative value to customers. For example, they are able to get up on a stock trading site and sign up immediately, but then they are informed they must print out and sign a form and mail it or fax it to the company. The time to process the application may be as long as six weeks.

All these liability processes are targets for out-tasking. It just doesn't make sense in terms of economics, relationships, or operational efficiency to handle these processes if they can be far better handled by a company with specialist capabilities. Those capabilities populate the shaded areas of the capability assessment matrix shown in Figure 8-5.

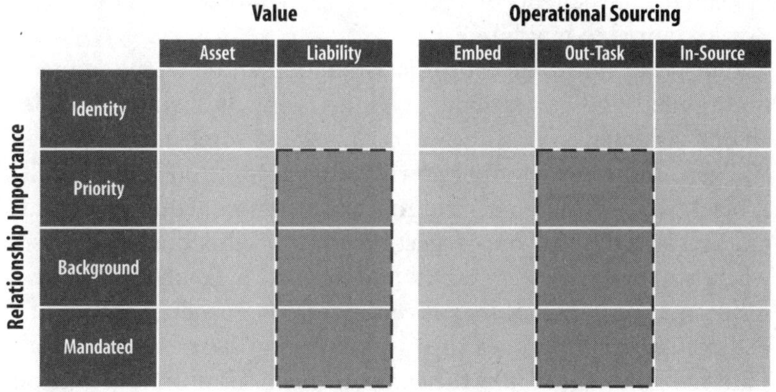

Relationship Importance	Value		Operational Sourcing		
---	Asset	Liability	Embed	Out-Task	In-Source
Identity					
Priority					
Background					
Mandated					

Figure 8-5: Capability assessment matrix (out-tasking opportunities shaded)

Out-tasking liability capabilities decreases balance capital demands, time-to-market, and executive attention invested in liability operations. Executives then focus on the parts of the business that matter most to acquiring customers, building relationships, and establishing their online brand. Out-tasking is not a fire sale, with companies seeking to shed all their operational responsibility. Rather, it is a deliberate decision to leverage the value network.

The challenge is to go beyond the basics and add more and more value-generating options through out-tasking. For example, eBay announced in March 2000 that it had reached an agreement with Wells Fargo for winning auction bidders to pay the seller directly via credit card, instead of having to deal with all the problems of sending checks or money orders, handling currency exchange, and processing very small payments. eBay's a stronger relationship player as a result of this value network collaboration, and Wells Fargo gains a new source of revenues. It's win-win-win. The customer gains, eBay gains, and Wells Fargo gains.

Implementing the Out-Tasking Decision

Out-tasking creates a Web of services across the value network, linked by APIs and operated in a coordinated fashion for the benefit of all concerned. Achieving these goals involves a multi-step process of definition, selection, implementation, and operation that results in realizing the benefits of a provider's capability without the investment required to build it for yourself.

Out-tasking is no excuse for ignorant out-sourcing; the company must understand the capability it is out-tasking. It is tempting to view an out-tasking relationship as a black box; fire some information in and get a response without knowing what is going on in the middle. A black box is the engineer's term for some unit of equipment that is in effect sealed from your inspection. Process black boxes are those where you pass a message across and that's it. Your interest is in the result, not the details of the process required to produce the result. FedEx is an example; does anyone who uses its superb service ever want to know exactly how the company meets its promise of guaranteed online delivery?

The decision to out-task requires the company to open up the black box. It needs to define business rules, performance requirements, and API links to the out-tasked capability. The black box, often associated with an out-sourcing arrangement, must become a gray-box definition for out-tasking a capability—a box the company can look inside. That gray box definition would include the following items:

Outcome This is the service or result produced by the capability. In the case of eCredit, the outcome is a financing proposal.

Information exchange In terms of the information you must provide to activate the capability as well as the information returned as part of the outcome, these information requirements define the nature of the APIs shared across companies.

Responsibilities between the company and provider Who is responsible for operation, issue definition, issue resolution, management, and improvement of the capability and service?

Performance criteria These criteria cover aspects of responsiveness, accuracy, availability, and scalability.

Applicable standards What are the industry, national, or other compliance standards applicable to the capability? This is an emerging key area as the supplier and third-party performance are criteria for environmental as well as quality certifications.

Investment requirements An out-tasking relationship involves mutual investment to develop the capabilities and markets for both companies.

Economic model This model covers the cost structure and transaction volumes associated with the out-tasking relationship.

Defining the capability establishes the terms for selecting a sourcing partner, the next step of this process. The definition should also be used to define the service level agreement with the provider. The service levels form the operational definition and management of the capability.

Selecting a value network provider is a strategic decision, as the company becomes wholly dependent, at least in the short term, on the provider for the capability. It would be easy to assume that selecting a provider is similar to selecting package application software. After all, if the company is routinely making a multi-year decision to go with a single source for application software, how could selecting a capability provider be much different?

It is very different, in the sense that an eProcess out-tasked capability provider holds the assets, skills, and process knowledge that the company leases. Compared with a purchase package where the company often retains source code and the database, selecting the wrong service provider has a greater impact on company performance. The selection process differs based on your executive team and industry considerations. At a minimum, we suggest the following assessment criteria for selecting a service provider:

Ability to perform at best-practice level, not adequate, low-price level Here the company examines the current state of operations and service levels. If the candidate providers are offering the service now, how are they doing, what is their financial and non-financial performance, and what is the quality of their people and service levels? If they are new entrants, what's the evidence that they will meet comparable standards?

Scalability How fast can the provider handle volume growth from you or other customers with similar services?

Extensibility Does the provider have the ability to expand its services to co-evolve with your changing products and services?

Exclusivity Here the company looks at the service provider's other relationships. Are they a strategic provider to your competitors? If so, does that affect your ability to offer products and services? In some cases (payment and logistics, for example), it is not critical to have an exclusive relationship.

Concentration Will your account represent a strategically important part of the provider's business? You want to be significant enough to command the best service and response levels while not being the sole source of provider revenue.

Competition To what extent can the provider establish a direct relationship with your customers? If it does, how will that affect your customer relationship?

Complete service Does the provider have an eProcess competence? Does it provide a full relationship, including support services and access to a broad capability base?

Technology compatibility Will your applications and information flow cleanly between systems, or is the provider using a proprietary system?

Intangibles Here the issue is how you feel dealing with the provider at all levels of the company. Remember, you are leasing part of your operation from the provider. If you feel uncomfortable or feel the provider is hard to do business with, you may be better off looking for another business partner.

Selecting a service provider can be obvious; in the case of logistics, there are just a few companies that provide superior service and scale. In other cases, the capability search involves looking at traditional and non-traditional providers. These criteria provide some ideas for making your choice.

In-Sourcing: Building Identity and Priority Assets

In-sourced capabilities extend the core of operations and services that you invest in, build, and control. The capability matrix is very different for in-sourcing (see Figure 8-6). Here, the goal is to create assets by exploiting the opportunity of an existing value network, by extending your own, and most of all by enhancing key relationships.

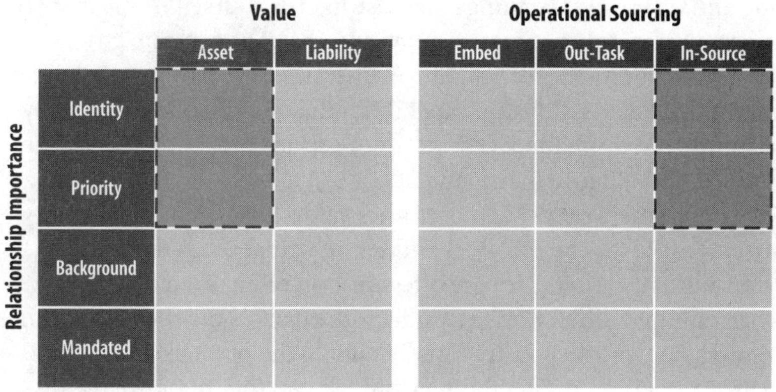

Figure 8-6: Capability assessment matrix (in-sourced opportunities shaded)

The main target of opportunity here is the priority processes that differentiate a company from the rest of its competition and that draw customers and lead them to come back. For consumer-to-business relationships, many of these relate to pricing, availability of items, catalogs, and other basics. All first-rate eCommerce players are strong in the basics—they have to be.

In-Sourcing Relationship and Development Capabilities

In-sourcing a capability should not be the decision of last resort. "If all else fails, in-source," is a poor management mantra. Rather, a company must in-source its key relationship and development capabilities, the ones that form the basis only for its current identity and build its future brand. In our review of multiple eCommerce companies, the one in-house sourcing decision we see with some consistency is retaining relationship capabilities—the identity assets that directly contribute to the customer relationship and experience—as well as the development capabilities the company uses to build and deploy future products and services.

Relationship Capabilities

The capability assessment matrix identifies the company's identity assets—the things it must get right to build relationships and brand in eCommerce. That part is common sense; you concentrate on building and operating the things that distinguish yourself in the marketplace. Then augment them as much and as fast as you can; grow some in-house, but in-source, in-source, in-source. We have consistently seen three key relationship capabilities that are often in-sourced by eCommerce companies: core product-service capabilities, customer service, and alliance management.

The business model and customer values determine the identity assets that form core product and service capabilities that define your business. e-retailer core offers rest on sales, service, and purchasing capabilities. Key success factors involve how they attract customers, present the product, and facilitate the purchasing process. Any experienced online shopper can tell you that these are the distinguishing capabilities for an online retailer. A business-to-business auction market rests on the capabilities it uses to certify buyers and sellers, make markets, and ensure the integrity of auction contracts. Follow the business model and customer values to find the core product and service capabilities. Table 8-3 provides some example business models along with their identity and priority capabilities.

Table 8-3: Identity and Priority Capabilities by Business Model Type

Business Model Type	Example	Identity Capabilities	Priority Capabilities
Customer Aggregator: Concentrates on being a portal for online customers. Economic model based on selling access to users via banner ads or click-through purchases.	Yahoo! AOL Information Web sites	Content acquisition, management, and presentation Community- building services Customer acquisition	Technology operations to maintain system availability Alliance management
Customer Lifetime Value: Concentrates on building deep relationships and leveraging the customer's long-term purchases through superior service. Economic model based on repeat purchases and referrals.	Amazon Charles Schwab	Merchandizing and purchasing Fulfillment	Customer acquisition Customer service Fulfillment
Junction Box—Auction Market: Concentrates on bringing buyers and sellers together to transact business. Economic model based on receiving a percentage of business transactions.	eBay FreeMarkets Vertical net ChemConnect	Market making Buyer and seller acquisition	Market assurance, the quality and sincerity of buyers and sellers
Transaction Factory: Concentrates on facilitating buying and other transactions; the storefront. Economic model based on sales transacted over the Web.	Bized.com Staples.com	Customer acquisition Merchandizing	Fulfillment
Specialist	ecredit.com Qpass	Specific area of process expertise	Alliance management to link service to other sites

Customer Service

Customer service is obviously a critical relationship capability as online service demands and standards continue to rise in eCommerce, making "good enough" no longer good enough. A central potential problem in in-sourcing is the very fact that it is targeted to strengthening relationships and branding in priority asset areas. This means that eProcess failures by the company providing the in-sourced capability damage the brand. A relationship is a promise, and a company can't pass along the blame. So the customer service capability becomes critical to the integrity of your relationships.

Alliance Management

A typical eCommerce company announces two to five new alliances per month as it builds its value network at a frenetic pace. New marketing, service providers, and investments make alliance management a critical organizational capability where executive skills and well-structured workflows contribute to ability to compete. Those skills must move toward a portfolio view that looks at alliances as a set of options coupled with a process for definition and creation of new alliances. This gives them the tools to compete at speed across the scale of a value network.

Build your alliance capabilities, using the eProcess sourcing options based on the type and nature of the alliance. The value of mass trading exchanges such as eBay and Priceline rests on the size of the market of buyers and sellers in the exchange. These exchanges embed a significant part of their alliance processes (registration, certification, and so on) as business rules in front-end software to handle speed and scale. Compare this with the larger specialty exchanges where portions of the registration process are handled online, with critical parts of the process in-sourced.

Alliance management defines the processes and skills required to collaborate with suppliers, intermediaries, and other providers across the value network. The alliances and partnerships in themselves require an eProcess discipline. Contracting and pricing are part of the alliance eProcess base. So, too, are collaborative processes that include joint planning, information sharing, and teaming for development, support, and marketing. These are not processes to be handled by embedding them in software, out-tasking, or in-sourcing. They are part of what we call process crafting: shaping the capabilities that make a difference in handling the non-routine and the exceptions. The challenge is to be exceptional in the exceptions. Your alliance capabilities need to address the following areas:

- ▶ Alliance identification, evaluation, and negotiation establish the approach for assessing and implementing alliance opportunities. This process used to take months; now it must occur in weeks or even days. It must include both the alliances the company wants to create and the alliance opportunities others present.

- ▶ Performance management establishes the criteria, trading partner service levels, and the alliance's progress and performance. The quality of management rests with the sharing of information that allows both parties to resolve issues.

- ▶ Operational processes to address performance issues and co-develop capabilities across the value network players. This process concentrates on strengthening the weaker links in the value network by providing better information sharing, supporting changes in sourcing, and sharing process knowledge.

Alliance operations involve more than strategy and negotiation in the executive suite, as each has eProcess implications. This is where having the right eProcess base pays big dividends. Clear business rules and a well-defined set of application program interfaces provide the flexibility to readily add new alliance partners and operations. Consider marketing alliances that track click-throughs and referrals generated from an alliance with customer aggregators and reference sites. These are often implemented through application program interfaces between the aggregator and your site. Alliances with suppliers, intermediaries, and complementors also involve APIs as the means to share information and transaction responsibilities. In this way, your eProcess base determines your capacity to form alliances and compete at the value network level.

Product Development Capabilities

Continuous competition in eCommerce requires renewal of products, services, and the relationship interface. Your product and application development capabilities form the basis for renewing your interfaces and customer value proposition.

Your company's long-term viability rests on your ability to distinguish the firm through its products and services. Product development is almost always an identity capability and one that is handled in-house, given its proprietary importance. It relies on the skill and intuition of the product development personnel, but also makes heavy use of the alliance in-sourcing opportunity. Product development may be the Achilles heel of many startup and "one trick" eCommerce companies that make an initial splash without the breadth of offerings to generate repeat business and an extended relationship.

There is an analogy here with novelty restaurant businesses, like Planet Hollywood, where initial strong sales growth created by the striking distinctiveness of the offering dissipated over time as there was little extension or refreshing of the customer offering to rekindle interest and repeat business. eCommerce companies must have a robust product development process in order to compete for customer attention and competing offerings.

Product development in eCommerce means a continuous stream of extensions, enhancements, and new products across a wider range of customer interactions. An eCommerce company needs to think of the "product" as the full range of items offered to the customer, including those provided by complementors and intermediaries. Service is not just what the company does for a customer. It is the full customer experience, ranging from the Web site interaction through fulfillment and problem resolution. The full experience is the service, making it all part of the product development opportunity. Delivering this steady stream calls for an overlapping cycle of product and service development that continuously evaluates and reevaluates the viability of current and future offerings.

An eProcess company enjoys a product development edge over traditional companies in two areas: information and organizational flexibility. An eProcess company, particularly one that concentrates on customer service capabilities, has an information-rich relationship with its customers and prospects. Direct email, Web site navigation data, and cookies all provide data on customer preferences and behavior that help guide the development process. Ignoring these types of customer information partially blinds your product development process and its effectiveness.

An eProcess company uses sourcing to increase its flexibility and reduce complexity; that combination of capabilities greatly enhances its ability to deploy new products and services. Embedding rules in software provides a single point of deployment for product information, pricing changes, product selection, and other merchandising activities. Out-tasking simplifies operations and improves service. In-sourcing enables the company to add new products and services by creating alliances with suppliers and complementors. Harness the skills and abilities of value network players through joint design sessions throughout the product and service development process. This increases the texture and touch of relationships within the value network, strengthening the operational and strategic bonds.

Build In-House Capabilities

In-house capabilities form the operational basis for the company—the things they directly control and operate. Use eProcess techniques to choose where and how to focus your in-house capabilities, rather than throwing people at your internal workflows. This means linking activities together through information with a high degree of employee self-direction. The requirement here is to

- ▶ Enable people with knowledge and access to work effectively by making databases and information widely available using Web technology

- ▶ Support knowledge work with high-touch and -texture interfaces that provide ready access to company information and the facilities to take action based on that information

- ▶ Embed company rules into these software interfaces, particularly at points of customer service and contact

- ▶ Build internal systems that provide high-value functionality using an eCommerce-enabled infrastructure, with agents, and APIs

The "Net" Effect: What an eProcess-Enabled Process Looks Like

We have now covered all the software-related eProcess sourcing options, from embedding rules to out-tasking to in-sourcing. We have talked about the pieces and individual decisions. Now it is time to put these together in order to get an idea of what an eProcess looks like. To do this we will use an obvious example to illustrate how capabilities change through applying new rules, sourcing, and interfaces.

The customer order-to-cash process is the perennial example from a process reengineering standpoint. Often labor intensive, hand-off ridden, and error prone, order-to-cash has been a target of new processes and technologies. It also provides a clear illustration of what is possible for an eProcess company. Consider a typical order-to-cash process shown in Figure 8-7.

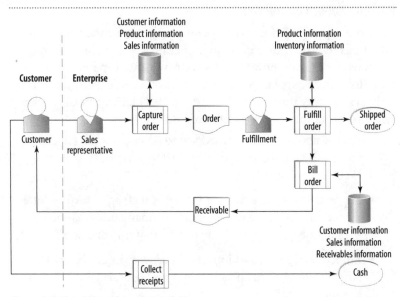

Figure 8-7: Order-to-cash process: A sample

The process is self-explanatory and straightforward, as customer needs transform into orders, then products, then an invoice, and finally cash. Moving this process from manual commerce to electronic commerce involves applying the eProcess framework in terms of addressing the following questions and potential actions:

▶ What relationships are involved in the process?

▶ How can we enhance the customer experience by increasing their involvement or contribution to the process?

▶ What parts of the process are we less than qualified to handle and should be given to others?

▶ What are the identity processes that form the basis for the relationship?

▶ Where can we strengthen the processes through improved information or enhanced capability?

▶ What are the business rules that govern the relationship?

► Which rules are essential to maintaining control of the relationship and business transaction?

► How can these rules be standardized to enable choice through configuration?

► Which rules can be embedded in software?

► Which rules require the flexibility provided by human skills?

► What are the information flows within the process?

► How can we use information to enable the relationship and experience?

► What is the required information to operate the process across the value network?

The answers to these questions identify the relationships, the required relationship types, rules, interfaces, and sourcing that transforms an existing process into an eProcess. The result can be dramatic, as we will show in the next section.

Identify Processes Within Order-to-Cash

The order-to-cash process is the basis of economic viability as it generates sales and cash. "Capture order" is the win-win identity process within order-to-cash, with "fulfill order" a priority asset. These become an area of focus for the process redesign, as they represent the relationship-building assets. A sample capability assessment matrix appears in Figure 8-8.

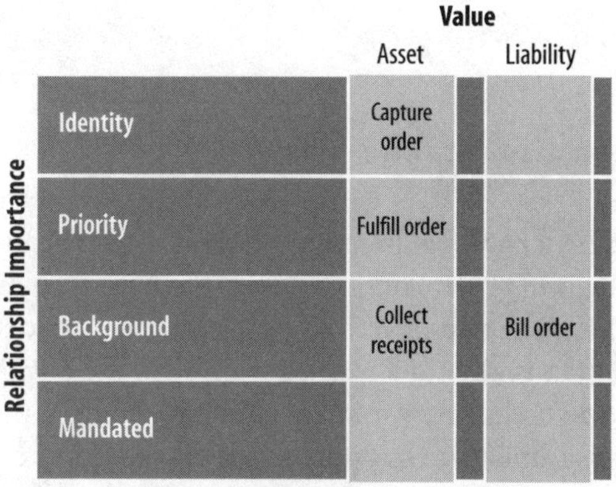

		Value	
		Asset	Liability
Identity		Capture order	
Priority		Fulfill order	
Background		Collect receipts	Bill order
Mandated			

(Relationship Importance — vertical axis label)

Figure 8-8: Capability assessment matrix: A sample order-to-cash

The process of priorities contained in the matrix guide process sourcing decisions as well as the flow of information across the value network.

Changing Relationships

The value network enables an eProcess company to source capabilities and responsibilities across a range of players and relationships. In this case, the traditional customer-to-enterprise relationship can be extended to capabilities provided by suppliers and intermediaries that bring their own specialized skills and processes to the order-to-cash process. Figure 8-9 illustrates what an eProcess version of order-to-cash processes might look like.

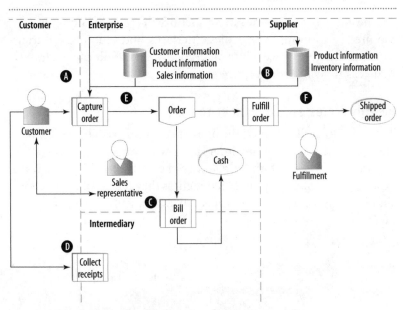

Figure 8-9: Order-to-cash process: An eProcess sample

The company enables a direct interaction with the customer through embedding merchandising and purchasing rules in the Web interface (A). This creates a Web store. That places process responsibility for product evaluation and selection with the customer. This sourcing option entails new information flows among the customer, company, and suppliers to support product selection, configuration, and fulfillment.

The company out-tasks order fulfillment to its suppliers (B), harnessing their inventory management and manufacturing capabilities. It also out-tasks its receivables risk to a financial intermediary (C), who assumes the risk and responsibility for billing and collections (D), two traditional background processes. This has a dramatic effect on the cash flow cycle.

The net effect of these sourcing decisions reduces company process complexity by sourcing the capabilities through the use of value networking. This increases company focus on its identity processes, while moving its other processes to players who are best able to provide strong service, including changing the role of company personnel from order takers to service providers.

Change Rules and Information

New sourcing options are meaningless without changing the rules and information flows. Embedding merchandizing and purchasing rules in the Web interface enables customers to serve themselves (E), including accessing product information through suppliers (F). Customer, order, product, and inventory information flows through integrated applications from suppliers to the company Web store.

Order-to-Cash Summary

eProcess rules, interfaces, and sourcing create new relationships that reduce company complexity, cost, and economics. Consider the order-to-cash example (shown in Figure 8-10) which realign the company process units responsible from handling the entire four processes to managing a single process.

	Customer	Enterprise	Supplier	Intermediary	Note
Capture order	X ⟵—• X				Embed rules in the interface to enable customer self-direction
Fulfill order		X •—→ X			Out-task inventory management to leverage supplier capability
Bill order		X			Retain within the company to manage customer relationships
Collect receipt		X •————————→ X			Out-task to intermediary to free up cash flow and leverage capability

Figure 8-10: Summary sourcing changes: Order-to-cash

These sourcing changes increase customer convenience and control, reducing inventory requirements and changing receivable collection. The net result is improvements in cash flow, customer service, inventory management, and capital efficiency. These points illustrate the potential changes associated with giving your company an eProcess edge.

The Out-Tasking and In-Sourcing Agenda

The opportunities we described in this chapter are surely too important to be missed by any company. Many won't be hubs and power brands that dominate their value network complex. Instead, they will be spokes in someone else's value network. There won't be more than a few portals like Yahoo!, AOL, Schwab, Travelocity, and eBay in the consumer market, though there will be a large number of specialized business-to-business hubs. In either case, though, *any* company that wants to be part of a value network has to pay the membership fee, whether it wants to be a hub or a spoke. That fee includes a first-rate technology platform and clean business processes and interfaces.

It doesn't make sense for most companies to try to build and operate the technology platform themselves. They need close alliances with the elite technology service and tool providers that specialize in building and hosting integrated "mission-critical" eCommerce services. They will out-task most operations—or should. It is becoming harder and harder to locate and retain skilled staff across the ever-broader, ever-innovating spectrum of telecommunications, computers, multimedia, data management, and IP tools.

But the company must take charge of business prioritization for the design and use of the technology platform. That's why our eProcess capability matrix really amounts to business prioritization. The sequence we have outlined provides the base for the management agenda in this regard. Here are the principles we recommend for getting started on that agenda.

Defeat Complexity

Defeat complexity through out-tasking background liabilities. This removes a morass of administrative processes with all of its well-known faults and costs. It removes capabilities that generate waste and get in the way of speed. It makes sense, regardless of your eCommerce revenue strategy.

Look at the best way to reduce complexity and the cost of complexity: embedding processes in software. The obvious two main targets here are the company's own logistics and procurement processes and customer self-direction. There is no excuse now for not taking advantage of the number, quality, and reach of business-to-business trading partner hubs. Similarly, there is a win-win payoff for customer self-direction. The company wins when it makes it easy and convenient for the customer to manage the more complex aspects of the relationship. This allows the company to remove costly administrative expenses and costs from the company. Cisco and Dell are the examples here. Just as Toyota set the standard for car manufacturing and quality management processes and entirely transformed the rules of competition, companies like these have redefined the base level of company performance by their eProcesses. So, move fast to get in this game and be a major league player. It is not at all an exaggeration to say that companies have at most a year to do this; if they do not, they are confining themselves to the minor leagues.

Look to Out-Task Capabilities

The second task in eProcess prioritization is to take a cool, hard, and dispassionate look at where to out-task capabilities. It does not make sense for most companies to handle their own shipping and distribution, for example, when the third-party logistics players are so superb at handling every link in the chain. Financing and routine technology operations are likely candidates here for most companies. The management questions to ask here are

- ▸ If we were the very best in the business in handling this, does it really matter to our profitability or customer relationships?

- ▸ *Are* we the best at handling this?

- ▸ If we never, ever handled this ourselves, would we be put at risk?

If the answers are no, no, and no, locate the best provider and get moving on the alliance.

At this point in the agenda, the company has addressed what is mainly a matter of cleaning up its act. It has tidied up its processes, rationalized its costs, and improved its productivity by slaying the complexity dragon (or at least knocking it down so that it now has time to rescue the eProcess princess who has been bound in chains).

The third step in prioritization is to look outward and ask the question: which value network partners should we work with to extend our own brand and capabilities *and* theirs? This is not at all simple to answer. It really translates to the offers and promises you want to make to your customers that will make you indispensable to them and get *them* wanting to build the relationship. Is the answer centered on touch—more self-direction, customization, and personalization? If so, which value network capabilities can you add through in-sourcing? Is it more a matter of texture—breadth of offers, collaboration, and range of choices? Again, which value network partnerships should you be looking at?

The Difficult Truth: You May Only Have a Web Site

Addressing these questions on the eProcess prioritization agenda will generate some very disconcerting findings. Typically, the company will find that it does not have an eCommerce technology platform, just a Web site. That its business rules and interfaces are muddy, fragmented, unclear, and multiple. It will also realize that no one has thought much in these terms, so that eProcess is handled on a case-by-case basis rather than as a top-down enterprise design responsibility. Senior management involvement in decisions becomes more critical as the company moves its capabilities from vertically oriented toward the virtual capabilities. In-sourcing, for example, has many strategic implications: alliance partner relationships, co-opetition—allying with competitors—and branding.

Top-Down and Enterprise-Out

So our recommendation is to think top-down and enterprise-out. There are plenty of bottom-up actions that can be taken across the company. For example, once the company recognizes the opportunity of embedding rules in software, logistics and customer self-direction become priorities that many units can work on. The company that systematically prioritizes and electronically sources its eProcesses is well positioned to look at the last of our categories: crafting eProcesses where people make the exceptional difference. It can focus its resources in this regard. It is here that identity asset processes are built: the ones that make this company stand out.

Chapter 9

Be Exceptional: People Plus Process Plus Technology

Embedding rules, out-tasking, and in-sourcing are the first three options for sourcing capabilities across the eProcess portfolio. These options all depend on technology. They transform a company's costs, streamline its productivity and efficiency, and strengthen its relationship touch and texture. But these advantages are all gained at a potential cost: they use technology to make a process routine and automatic. That's fine, but what does the company do to handle the exceptions to the routine? It's here that companies establish their service brand and reputation.

What Does It Mean to Be Exceptional?

Most companies still neglect the need to be exceptional—our term for both handling exceptions and standing out in how they do so. Table 9-1 shows just a few examples.

Table 9-1: Exceptions to the Rule

The eProcess	The Exception	How It's Usually Handled
Order delivery and handling of returns	Incorrect shipment	The customer has to find out how and where to return the product, often to the retailer's physical store, where, unsurprisingly, the sales staff and manager are underwhelmed at having to handle a transaction that wasn't a sale for themselves, involves extra work, and takes time away from serving customers who may actually want to buy something.
Web site interaction about a problem	Customer email	Most companies either don't reply or do so with a form letter type of response.
Order-taking situations	Out of stock	The customer finds out only when the goods haven't arrived.
Network operations	Network crash that blocks service	The company is not in business for the moment and you are on your own.
Troubleshooting via Web site tools	The user can't resolve the problem	Well, you could try the call center, which is staffed by part-timers and run by an outside company that won the contract on a low bid and a guaranteed number of phone calls handled per hour.

What stands out in all these instances is that whenever a company moves a process into software, it should ensure that there is an exceptional process to complement it. Look at what disservice is being created and how much damage the company is doing to itself otherwise. It's spent money and effort to build its online presence and brand. It has a good Web site and has been able to attract more and more customers. Of its, say, 2 million transactions a month, 99 percent are routinely processed. That means that 20,000 a month aren't, and then, as in the examples above, the Web site becomes a barrier to service. (Figures show that the success figure is closer to 80 percent than 99 percent in retailing.) The customer is stuck with the wrong goods and can't work out how to get the company's attention or is sitting watching the price of one of her stocks drop by 16 percent (this happened to a friend of one of us) while her online broker's network is down.

There's far too much of such online disservice. Table 9-1 cites examples that could be expanded into a whole book by themselves. What happens, of course, is that customers move to the company that stands out from the crowd. It's the old case of once bitten, twice shy, and it's not at all difficult for customers to find another provider of most services. As more and more companies build comparable eProcess capabilities in terms of software, it can only be the exceptional that makes them stand out. Going back to the examples in Table 9-1, the sections that follow discuss how the best eProcess companies handle them.

Exceptional Order Delivery

As so often, Amazon is an exemplar here. First of all, its entire eProcess base is so focused on customer relationship and customer interaction that you get a flow of information about your order, from the confirmation when the order is placed to automatic information on any problems. It provides delivery upgrades (next-day delivery versus two- or four-day service) when it screws something up, as it sometimes does—every company makes errors sometime. It even arranges for heavy and large return goods to be picked up from the customer's house.

Because Amazon is so controversial in terms of its stock being overvalued (or not) and whether it will ever be profitable, many commentators don't pay attention to its eProcess skills, which are simply extraordinary and provide many object lessons for companies everywhere. Consider what looked to many investors like an Amazon mistake in the Christmas 1999 selling period. The mass media had been touting online shopping as being the thing for the end of the millennium. Amazon knew that the time was right for the Internet to move from a novelty to being accepted as the new economy. Amazon stocked up on inventory to the degree that its turnover increased from 17 days in June 1999, prior to stocking up for the holidays, to 29 days in December. That "mistake" was an intentional smart move. When many other retailers failed to meet their promise to deliver goods by Christmas Eve, Amazon had the highest success rate in online retailing, around 99 percent.[1]

Another eProcess leader in this regard is Webvan, which is mislabeled in most observers' minds as an online grocery supermarket, just as Amazon is mislabeled as a book retailer. Webvan is a process-driven delivery company, not an automated grocery store. Its entire strategy is built around "the last mile" delivery problem—getting goods to the customer's house at the promised time, which the customer chooses and which has only a half-hour window. If the driver is later than that, Webvan refunds $3. Given that the service may require deliveries every 10 to 30 minutes along complex routes within the city even during rush hour, this requires superb process design and implementation.

This design and implementation is creating Webvan's identity asset processes—the ones that will differentiate it from the other online groceries aiming at capturing a sizeable part of the grocery market. And because these are based on exceptional process capabilities, they will be hard for others to match, unlike marketing and price discounting. A *Wall Street Journal* article described the meticulous combination of people, process design, and technology that Webvan is committing to. Route-planning software tries to give each driver a feasible route and timing, but as the *Journal* said of one driver, "He thought he knew the delivery business after more than a decade of driving trucks for FedEx, Frito-Lay, and Wonder Bread. But since joining Webvan in February, he has reworked almost every routine."[2]

Webvan faces some very real challenges as it positions itself to be something different from a grocer. It is working to deliver anything customers would like to get at short notice: rental movies, dry cleaning, or books ordered online, for instance. Clearly, in this instance, it's not the Web catalog that will make for success or failure, important though that is. Instead, it's Webvan's eProcess base, with delivery the very core of its strategy. That point was made clear by its absence among so many retail companies that overlooked the need to link Web site with fulfillment and customer service eProcesses.

Exceptional Web Site Interaction

We described earlier how National Semiconductor handles customer email. Most companies don't. Survey after survey shows that. Given that the very core of Internet eCommerce is the interaction at the Web site as a relationship interface between customer and provider, and given that email is the very core of the Internet in general, this is bewildering. Why on earth do companies undo many of the merits of their site through lack of response to customers' follow-up messages? After all, around 20 percent of all customers have some sort of after-sale query.

Here's our hypothesis: the more attention—and investment—that a company commits to the software elements that handle the routine of the customer relationship, the less likely they are in general to make a comparable commitment to handling the exceptions if those exceptions require equal attention to non-software eProcesses. Their entire view of eCommerce makes software the driver and coordinator, so they ignore whatever aspects of the customer interaction can't be routinely handled by it.

By contrast, companies like National Semiconductor handle customer email as an *organizational* issue. They rely on software analysis to screen the messages, which may include an inquiry about an order, a complaint, a request for something to be mailed, a dispute about a payment, interest in getting technical information…just about anything. The purpose of the analysis is to look for key words and phrases that indicate what the topic of the message is. The software selects a real human being from a database of information about skill areas and responsibilities and sends the message on. That individual has a given period of time to respond to the customer and has the authority to contact others in the organization for assistance.

Here is one of the most common aspects of effective eProcess exception-handling: people plus organizational processes plus technology support. This amounts to a cultural development, one of coordinated customer service built on personal responsibility across the organization. If you work in marketing and get a customer email that indicates a problem you can't solve, but you believe someone in engineering or production might be able to, you and the people in the rest of the business all have the joint responsibility to work together as needed. That's because the company's eCommerce operations make the customer the priority.

This is a very difficult cultural shift to sustain and make work. But it makes the company exceptional.

Exceptional Order-Handling

Another area of widespread weakness across eCommerce is simple order-handling, which ought to be literally routine. Surveys by

Andersen Consulting and other companies show that around a quarter of all customers abandon their shopping carts and don't make a purchase.[3] Much of this relates to poor Web site design and navigation—filling out more and more information, having problems working out how to change an order and the like. But most of the inadequacies go deeper. Here's a concise summary of the lack of eProcess thinking, from E-Commerce Times, a Web site that reports on eCommerce facts and figures from a large range of sources:

> Most retailers view customer service as a problem-solving action after the sale. In e-tailing, however, customer service begins the moment a customer enters the Web site.

It reports that 19 percent of customers request help to find products and get answers to questions about product attributes, and 21 percent have questions during the buying process about billing, receipts, and the checkout process itself. After the order is placed, 58 percent check on order status and shipping. After the item has been received, 19 percent of buyers have questions about returns.[4]

Andersen Consulting carried out a study in early 2000 of the quality of the shopping experience. Its team tried to buy 480 gifts online from the top 100 retailers. They succeeded in only 350 of the instances—that's close to a 25 percent failure rate. Around a quarter of the sites crashed, were under construction, refused to accept an order, or were just inaccessible. Where the team was able to make a purchase, just 20 percent of the purely online companies failed to deliver goods on time, whereas 80 percent of the traditional retailers missed the promised date.[5]

One more survey, to which dozens could be added, comes from *USA Today*: "Few retailers sent notices that returns had been received. Computer systems in bricks and mortar stores were not in sync with Web sites. Prices were not consistent."[6]

What these figures show very clearly is that most companies regard order-taking as order-taking. It's a procedure to be designed and routinized. For the exceptional companies, it's not at all that. It's the core of the customer *experience*. The eProcess successes come from designing that experience, with order-taking an integral and key aspect of the experience, not the procedure.

This point is one that all managers involved in their company's eCommerce implementation must take to heart and mind—to heart in the sense that "experience" means attention to every aspect of the customer's personal contact with the company, which obviously goes well beyond just the formal procedures of order-taking. They can check out the quality of the experience by becoming a customer themselves; managers should routinely make purchases at their company's site, send email queries, check follow-up services, and so on.

They must also take the customer experience to mind in the sense that it's very easy for the focus on that experience to get lost. Technical designers and computer programmers think procedures, screens, links, and data requirements. Accounting and financial control worry about security, marketing focuses on catalogs, pricing, and advertising, and so on across the business. It's not that any of these parties ignores the obvious point—that the whole purpose of eCommerce is to attract and serve customers—but the customer is a long way away from the data center, multimedia Web design team, and head office.

Designing the Customer Experience: Who's in Charge?

Order-taking is about the very basics of a transaction-centered site. Delivery is about the basics of customer satisfaction. Interaction is the entire purpose of online business. What chance does a company that can't handle these basics even adequately have in becoming a relationship site? None.

So the next question is, what are companies doing wrong and why? Why, too, did the Andersen Consulting study find—and other analyses support its conclusion—that traditional retailers do worse in handling these basic eProcesses than purely online ones? You'd expect their expertise to make them very alert to the importance of order fulfillment, returns, and shipping.

The answer to these questions is that no one is in charge of designing and supporting the customer *experience*. The routine elements of the transaction eProcess components are parceled out among many parties, most obviously the Web site design team, which may include staff from the company's own information technology unit, specialty service providers, IT vendors, consultants, and marketing and operations people. Their focus is on designing the site and handling the routine elements of all the eProcesses. There's no one group with the authority and focus to make the whole work together—that means no one is designing for the exceptions *and* the routine.

Exceptional Troubleshooting with Web Site Tools

By definition, an exceptional element of the customer experience is troubleshooting. This is especially the case when installing and using personal computer hardware and software in the consumer marketplace, and more generally in the equivalent areas in business-to-business customer-supplier relationships: telecommunications and computer, manufacturing equipment, materials, and complex products.

The Web itself is an obvious vehicle for troubleshooting: answering questions that are part of a special situation for the customer but routine to the supplier, or providing simple diagnosis steps to walk customers through a problem. Many such cases are what have long been termed FAQs (frequently asked questions) in the wider Internet community. They generally have the following format:

- ▶ My X isn't working? What do I do?

- ▶ Who do I contact about Y?

- ▶ I'm having some trouble and I don't know what's causing it. Can you help?

Here, the whole spectrum of eProcess sourcing applies. Many FAQs are simple to answer. One example is from American Airlines' survey of customer phone calls to its toll-free reservation number. Among the most frequent FAQs is "What do I do to take my pet with me on the plane?" Such a question is an obvious candidate for being put on a list of FAQs that are part of the software tools embedded in the Web site.

That approach can be extended for many more complex Help menus that might include a diagnostic Q&A for diagnosing a printer problem or a step-by-step walkthrough of how to install a new piece of software. Such tools are often much more effective than using the company's call center. The call center agents or service representatives are mainly trained to handle routine problems, such as what to do about a broken part. They can't see the item and have to ask many questions.

This is especially the case with personal computer problems, where the technical support representative has to ask the customer to "try this and then tell me what's showing in the upper right-hand corner of the screen," then get more information from the customer about the system, what's installed, and what other symptoms there are that might give a clue to what's happening. It's a cumbersome and often frustrating process for the customer, who is frequently unable to get through and then put on hold for an indefinite period. Quality of technical knowledge and diagnostic skill also vary widely among call center tech reps.

For companies, this is a very expensive burden that many of them now charge for above a prespecified number of service calls or for a given period after the purchase of an item. So, all in all, this is an unsatisfactory situation for both parties. Thus, everyone gains if FAQs and troubleshooting aids can be moved into the software interface. But lurking in the background of the routine is the exception that can't be handled that way and that requires skilled judgment. In many instances, after the customer can't solve it through the software help and the call center rep can't solve it either, the only solution is to return the item back to the company for examination and then to wait an unknown number of weeks to get it back. In the meantime, either the company will send an empty box for the item to be packed in or the customer must do the packing and hope it doesn't get damaged in transit.

Here's a classic example of an eProcess opportunity—*if* there's an eProcess focus on the customer experience. The scenarios we've sketched out above are decidedly not contributing to a warm experience. The FAQ and self-direction approach is limited to standard problems with straightforward diagnosis and solutions. The call center too often leaves a bad memory even where the tech rep has done his or her best. And of course having to go through the inconvenience of losing your personal computer for weeks can make that bad memory a long one.

What's it worth to the customer for the company to find a better way? Obviously, in this example it's worth a lot in terms of the overall experience and its impact on the relationship potential. What's it worth to the company? That's a tougher question in that if the relationship is not right at the forefront of concern, the answer is "not much, if anything."

For the exemplars in this area of customer relationship management, excellent eProcess exception-handling combines people, software, and the links between them. For instance, Dell provides its business customers with an icon on the Web site screen that shows a telephone. Touching on this automatically links to a technician who sees exactly the same screen as the customer. The two can now work the problem through over the phone as if they were in the same room at the same machine.

The Technology Side of Exceptional eProcess

It's outside the scope of this book to review the technology of eCommerce, which in itself demands complex technology management processes: design, software development, data management, customer relationship management tools, operations, security, and so on. But clearly this is not just about technology. Technology quality and performance have major impacts on the customer experience. Here again, the issue is duality. The use of technology for handling the routine—access, transaction management, enquiry, and search—must be complemented by eProcesses for handling the exceptions.

If a company's success rate in processing 1 million customer transactions a month is 99 percent, that translates to just 10,000 exceptions or around 300 a day. That could be viewed—not *should* be viewed, of course—as within acceptable limits and probably isn't even brought to management's attention. If, though, network service availability is 99 percent, that 1 percent failure—which is just 7 hours a month when the Web site is inaccessible—is seen by every single customer who tries to visit the site during those hours. The results can be spectacular and often are caused by congestion created by a sudden surge in demand. In other words, the very success of the company's marketing and the product it has to offer creates the traffic jam. Two cases in early 2000 that are likely to be widely quoted for years are Encyclopedia Britannica and Stephen King:

▶ Britannica offers a superb free service on the Web. Initial demand was immediate and huge—and so was the collapse of the site. It took several days to address the issue during which all the company could do was post a letter of apology from their CEO.

▶ Stephen King was the first author to test the enticing opportunity for authors of publishing over the Web. He offered a short novella, a horror tale of 85 printed pages, for $2.50. Readers could download it to their PC or any of the new electronic books like the E-book or Rocket book. You could also order it from Amazon. You can guess the result. The demand was so high that the servers could not keep up with it. Amazon had to offer to send it later by email for free.

These are just cautionary tales, fairly simple and limited in their disruptive impacts. But as eCommerce volumes increase, it's harder and harder for companies to avoid network crashes, loss of service, and congestion. The problems are compounded by the increase in hackers attacking networks, with the first months in 2000 seeing some well-publicized invasions of major eCommerce sites.

All these situations are obviously about exceptions. They require exception-handling processes. There are four eProcess questions for managers to address here:

► What coordination processes must be developed to minimize the likelihood of such problems?

► What technology management planning, monitoring, and crisis response processes must be in place, including both within the company and in collaboration with its technology service providers?

► How does the company handle these situations to ensure the enhancement of the customer relationship instead of putting it at risk?

► What should be its sourcing strategy?

The final point brings us back to our original eProcess capability sourcing framework. In general, it makes most sense to embed network monitoring, fraud detection, and security in the software itself. It makes even more sense to out-task key functions to best-practice specialist services that offer economies of expertise. They can afford to hire the ten best people in a given area (such as network operations) and scale up their services (with backup systems, duplicated copies of software, and so on).

This sourcing offers many solutions to the complexity and risks of eCommerce network operations, but in the end everything comes back to how the company handles the exceptions versus the routine. This is what establishes its identity—its trust brand.

Conclusion: Designing the Customer Experience

Who in your organization has the authority and accountability for designing the customer experience? What do you do when there is a service failure or issue? How are you exceptional at handling the exceptions? These are critical questions for building the relationships necessary to create an eSuccess.

Designing the customer experience means ensuring an end-to-end focus on the relationship. The Web site transaction—a purchase, request for information, comparison shopping, and the like—is in the middle of the experience. It's preceded by what brings the customer to the site: marketing, promotions, referrals from other sites or banner ads on their Web pages, and search engine results. It's followed by after-sales queries about payment, order status, and return policies. All this is enveloped by the wider value network that enhances and supports every element of the experience.

In this context, the design of the customer experience rests on clarity of business model, quality of technology, alliances, and organizational imagination and collaboration. Who leads this? It can't be just the company's chief information officer, who has authority and expertise in handling the technology platform. Nor can it be the chief marketing officer or head of operations or the senior human resource executive. When a company designs its operations to maximize its own efficiency, it can easily keep all these functions separate. But once it starts to look at its entire eCommerce strategy from the customer's perspective, that situation has to end. Marketing, technology, and logistics become so intertwined that neglecting one damages the others. It's very easy to call for cross-functional teams, collaboration, knowledge management, and all the other enablers of organizational innovation, but in reality most companies find it difficult to create this new style of working together.

We hope that our eProcess frameworks help our readers build a blueprint for cooperation. The very conception of sourcing an eProcess portfolio should help bring together the efforts of all the parties that individually have a responsibility for some part of eCommerce but that may not recognize the interdependence of their own work with that of other groups. In particular, we hope that our nontechnical readers will see the immense opportunities that embedding processes in software opens up for the company and collaborate with their technology experts to realize it. Similarly, we hope that technology and marketing professionals will recognize the business opportunity of out-tasking and in-sourcing and work together to prioritize eProcess investments and build external alliances. It's a truism that the customer is king in the new economic environment of eCommerce, globalization, and deregulation. That pious claim simply has to be turned into reality very quickly for a company to be a successful player in eCommerce. So, our recommendation is to design the customer experience collaboratively and then the relationship eProcess capabilities just as quickly.

Chapter 10

Managing an eCommerce Business

Running an eCommerce business requires integrating processes, technologies, and organizations across the value network. Operating a company that involves multiple players, a dynamic Web site, and intense competition may seem a challenge. It is.

The pace of change and competitive factors alone make running an eCommerce business new, urgent, and complex. That challenge can become insurmountable when managers use traditional tools and techniques. Budgets, span of control, and management oversight were created for a vertically oriented company, not a value networked one. This raises the issue of how you integrate, operate, and manage an eCommerce business. Fortunately, there are techniques for managing the eProcess executive agenda. These include:

▶ Managing business and technology

▶ Managing a networked organization

▶ Managing a brand

▶ Integrating the business

▶ Managing multiple channels

Managing eCommerce involves managing relationships and their performance. It has more to do with understanding the process lines that bind the value network together than the organizational boxes that comprise the network. You run an eCommerce business by running its eProcess capabilities, not its corporate entities.

Managing Business and Technology

An eProcess company competes on its ability to blend technology and business to create new forms of commerce and relationships. Technology was for decades just a support to business activity. It was separate from the core business and given its own domain under the CIO. It's a tough job that requires someone who can act as chief technology officer and business ambassador at the same time.

The vicious cycle consequences of poorly managing the relationship between business and technology are massive in eCommerce. That ought to be a truism, but the entire history of IT has been at best an awkward dance, with each party treading on the other's feet as business and IT try to get in tune and be partners.

eCommerce demands a business-oriented and technology-integrated applications suite between the Web components and legacy systems, as well as an IT platform specifically designed to provide lines across today's value network and enable its continuing extension. Otherwise the company cannot tap into the benefits of eProcess sourcing and interfaces. Creating a business-oriented eCommerce application involves rediscovering how business drives technology to

▶ Process business transactions in terms of the orders, requests, and other interactions or outcomes technology must support. Technology must be able to support these transactions, particularly those embedded as rules in the interface. The management question here is how does technology help coordinate our business transactions?

▶ Meet business performance criteria in terms of cost, time, capital intensity, satisfaction, and security. The technology must provide an infrastructure to deliver these transactions within the required business. How can we use technology to do business at speed, at scale, and with security?

▶ Create an environment for future flexibility in terms of infrastructures that are readily able to deploy new products, services, and interface functionality with minimal redevelopment effort and time to market. How can technology provide us with future flexibility?

Technology enables new business models and transaction types by changing the use of information and computing power. The obvious example is the use of the Web to create customer self-service. The more subtle and powerful opportunities rest on how well the company brings together business and technology to

▶ Extend relationships by providing texture and touch using information presentation, transaction enablement, and adaptive online dialogues

▶ Create new relationships by using new sources of information and access to customers, markets, and suppliers

▶ Enable new forms of process sourcing and collaboration with customers, suppliers, intermediaries, and other third parties

▶ Open up access to back-office assets to the value network and customers

Business drives technology, technology enables business—the relationship seems so clear. However, it is also so misunderstood. An eProcess company understands how to embed business rules in software, taking advantage of technology scalability and capacity. It understands how to use increased access and communications to improve information flows and coordination across the value network. It also recognizes the value of new technology to increase texture and touch in order to build relationships and repeat business. In short, it understands that the business creates the economic justification for the technology investments, and technology creates new ways of doing business.

Managing a Networked Business

Throughout this book, we have talked about capabilities, sourcing, and how eProcess reduces complexity while raising efficiency. eProcess companies enjoy greater flexibility through innovative forms of sourcing that move operations from vertical integrated workflows to virtual processes coordinated across a value network. This sourcing approach can create more management nodes for an eProcess company. A management node can be loosely defined as an organizational unit of control or influence. Generally, the greater the number of nodes, the more people who need to be involved in management decisions.

Companies have created multiple management nodes in an effort to empower their organization. The philosophy of this move espoused that giving employees greater say in management would produce improved commitment and performance. Empowerment is a critical factor in organizational flexibility. However, its implementation through creating multiple management nodes has proven difficult, giving many employees a cynical view of bosses who cannot make a decision, which is expressed in the Dilbert cartoons as reality, not humor.

The multiple management nodes of corporate empowerment created matrix management, which defined the stakeholders, reviewers, and approvers of management decisions. Matrices are by their nature complex. That complexity in management has led many companies into a world with limited direct accountability, management indecision, and consensus paralysis. Matrix management works by Metcalfe's Law on networks in reverse. That law states that the value of a network grows exponentially with its connections. The reverse is that complexity and inertia do so, too. While a growing network of customers is beneficial, a growing network of management nodes becomes more complex and cumbersome, as shown below:

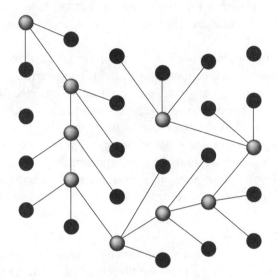

A matrix is too complex and cumbersome to compete at eSpeed. It results in everyone being involved in everything, with few people responsible for everything. Rather than a matrix, a value network can be managed as a collection of services. This establishes clear lines of responsibility that enables all players while avoiding the complexity of matrix management.

Service Management

A value network consists of players and the information and services they exchange. The strength of the value network rests with its ability to fulfill its service commitments and use information and communications links to improve its operations. The network is not defined by what it is or whom it involves, but rather what it can do to augment the role of each individual player in it.

Services abound across the players in a value network. A service is what is exchanged between parties in the value network. For example, your company has an implied mutual agreement with its customers. You provide the offer and product information in exchange for the customer's commitment to pay for your product or service. You commit to delivering on your part of the agreement. Fulfilling that commitment requires you to use the services of suppliers, intermediaries, and complementors. The value network is defined and managed from a service basis rather than traditional command and control. A service exists within a network. Service management works best when everyone recognizes that their business is networked and interdependent.

Service management is a natural discipline for an eProcess company, as capabilities create services. A service is governed by a service-level agreement that guides performance, incentive systems, and rewards. This agreement must be based on what it contributes to the value network. For example, manufacturing may be given incentives to meet cost-based budgets. For eCommerce to become the driver of its business value generation, the more appropriate reward is for meeting target levels of customer order fulfillment, including on-time delivery, minimization of returns, and repeat business revenues.

IT Sourcing: An Example

Many elements of IT operations must be out-tasked, not out-sourced. If it is out-sourced in the traditional sense of the term, it's lost to the business as a dynamic and strategic resource. That statement may sound dogmatic, but the scale and complexity of eCommerce technology platforms strain every company's skill base and management capabilities. eCommerce demands alliances. The win-win in IT out-tasking involves gaining access to a company that brings together system integrators, key IT service providers, technology vendors, and hosting services. This relationship makes IT a value network in itself. In other words, the company that builds its technology platform on alliances will outperform those that try to do everything themselves.

Service management value networks create relationships that are dynamic, ever shifting, collaborative, and extensive. The value of service management comes from observing what happens when a company views out-sourcing as getting rid of a problem by placing a contract with an outside company. In this situation, the company that out-sources its IT function often fails to recognize it has networked its business. When issues arise, the company views and treats the out-sourced IT function as if it remained part of the corporate whole. When requests are made of the outside IT department, the company expects it to jump as if it were still under corporate control.

These requests were understandable when the company owned IT. Now, they are detrimental to the relationship as the out-sourced

IT operation often seeks to work to the letter of the law (service-level agreement) in order to control service levels, scope, and cost. This creates a downward spiral in the relationship as the company feels it has lost control of the IT function, and the service provider becomes defensive of its capabilities and performance. The spiral begins when the company fails to recognize that it cannot have the same level of control in a business that has become networks of networks.

Working in a value networked business requires each player to recognize new realities regarding influence, control, and operations. Those realities concentrate management attention on the results and services shared across companies rather than the means used to create those results. Managing in a value networked environment relies on the following principles:

- ▶ Focus on service performance rather than service procedures

- ▶ Share performance information across the involved parties

- ▶ Recognize that service providers and your own business have multiple interests and incentives

- ▶ Assess the market to ensure the service remains competitive in terms of quality, timeliness, and economics

Service-Level Agreements

A service is exchanged between players in a value network. A service-level agreement defines the terms of the exchange. It is the instrument that defines the rules of the relationship among players in the value network. The service-level agreement specifies the components of the service, its performance requirements, application interfaces, business interfaces, and the responsibilities of each party. The agreement should have the force of a contract in that it establishes the rules and responsibilities. The components of a service-level agreement include:

- ▶ Service definition that precisely describes the service and its characteristics

- ▶ Roles and responsibilities of each player, including defining the single points of responsibility and accountability

- ▶ Fee and payment terms, including how fees are calculated, the form of payment, and the frequency of payment

- ▶ Information and interface requirements that define what each party must provide and/or share in providing the service

- ▶ Frequency of the service and terms when it is requested

- ▶ Performance characteristics for the service, required response times, capacity levels, and so on

- ▶ Rights and warranties that pass through the service to parties in the relationship

- ▶ Exception-handling procedures and contacts

- ▶ Remediation actions and notifications that describe how issues will be addressed and resolved

A strong service-level agreement is one that is clear and precise but also flexible. Clarity is necessary to build an operational rather than legalistic understanding of the service requirements and operations. Clean rules count in an effective service-level agreement. Flexibility is just as essential because this is about a collaborative relationship, not a contractual transaction. Service levels should avoid jargon and discuss the service and its intent in terms that enable collaboration rather than foster competition and control.

Manage to Service Levels

Service levels define the formal roles and responsibility between parties in the value network. These formal definitions are necessary for building the value network and establishing the relative relationships across players. However, a focus solely on the formal aspects does not create the flexibility and performance required to compete in the electronic economy.

Perhaps the greatest value of a service-level agreement is in the definition of measures used to manage the service. These measures provide a factual basis for raising and discussing issues. The measures and performance outside of targeted levels provide an unbiased basis for discussion of the relationship and its effectiveness.

A service-level agreement should define the boundaries of the relationship. It is the letter of the law; however, the business needs to operate according to the spirit of the relationship. A healthy service relationship is one that stretches and accommodates current business conditions rather than paying slavish attention to specific measures of performance and responsibility.

Effective service-level agreements and service management rest on an eProcess principle: be exceptional at handling exceptions. All sides of a value network must be committed first to the business objectives of the relationships. That commitment creates the flexibility necessary to handle the inevitable exceptions, crises, and things no one ever thought would happen. Service needs and issues must be addressed immediately and correctly. This places a high standard of performance and professionalism on all concerned. Recognize that activating an organization's "problem escalation" process is an admission of defeat in this environment.

Analyzing Service-Level Information

The information created in service management is the basis for managing the relationship between players in the value network. The information, or more accurately, the data generated from the service requires interpretation by the management of both organizations. Unfortunately, data analysis and interpretation is not the strong suit of many managers.

Use analytic techniques such as statistical process control (SPC) to analyze the data generated from the service levels. These provide an approach to understanding the meaning behind the numbers and how to spot trends rather than responding to noise. The data analysis disciplines associated with SPC are not as daunting as the name. The information generated from this type of analysis is essential to managing based on facts versus variance.

Service levels discuss how you manage relationships across the value network. They define the performance characteristics and flows between the capabilities and players required to create wealth. While service levels define how to manage the value network, they do not address how you manage and integrate the capabilities that are sourced within your organization.

Managing Brand

Brand is hot again. eCommerce creates new markets, companies, and channels that all call for new brands. Creating an eProcess edge builds your brand through relationships and repeat business, which in itself generates an eProcess view of managing your brand.

It's More Than a Name

A strong brand has name recognition and association. Say "Coca-Cola" and you recognize the red bottle or can and the association of refreshment. Say "Intel" and you either hear their aural signature (the little jingle) or see their logo and associate it with technology advancement. Say "DeLorean" or "Edsel" and, if you are old enough, another set of images comes to mind. In all of these cases, the name evokes an image, reaction, and thought.

eCommerce is often obsessed with building a dot-com name because it is the company's physical marker in a virtual world. True, the Web site is the brand's storefront, but without the name it is difficult for customers to find you. This has led companies to create cute names with "i" (for information or Internet) and "e" (for electronic) and new forms of spelling, all in an effort to break into this market. The importance has led to companies paying millions for the ideal dot-com name. The name obsession created a new cottage industry called cybersquatters—individuals who buy up Internet domain names in the hope of selling them to startup companies as well as established companies just coming online. Table 10-1 illustrates this phenomenon.

Table 10-1: eCommerce Domain Names and Acquisition Costs[1]

Company	Cost for the Domain Name
Business.com	$7,500,000
AltaVista.com	$3,300,000
Wine.com	$3,000,000
Wallstreet.com	$1,000,000
Drugs.com	$823,456
University.com	$530,000

The race to dot-com is largely over. While there will continue to be innovative companies launching, the market cachet of dot-coming yourself is starting to wane in favor of the viability of business models and operations. Your name is important in helping customers find you, but it alone does not create your brand.

A Brand by Any Other Name

We distinguish between name recognition and brand. Advertising can buy name recognition and online visitors. Online companies have invested billions in advertising that results in high traffic but limited business. Name recognition does not create a brand in the sense that it builds relationships and repeat business. Name recognition creates an idea and awareness that something is out there. A brand represents an implied promise that sets expectations of product, service, and quality. Those aspects of brand have little to do with who can remember your Web site name.

If a brand is a promise, your brand rests on the capabilities that deliver that promise. This makes process excellence a brand issue, particularly for your identity and priority capabilities, as these are closely identified with your positioning. This is what makes fulfillment such a critical issue to eSuccess. The relationship is based in part on the promise, and the promise is proven through repeat business. When fulfillment breaks down, the relationship and brand are at risk.

Fulfillment: The Tool for Brand-Building

The eProcess dimension of fulfillment is new for many marketing departments accustomed to promoting established brands that have an established track record (for good or ill). In these cases, brand identity is managed through communications, advertising, and product extension. In the eCommerce world, there is no historical basis for the brand, and therefore brand-building relies more on operations than on slick marketing. This applies for both established and startup companies, as consumers appear to view the online market as distinct. If you don't agree, consider the difficulty that traditional bricks and mortar companies have had in transitioning their brand into electronic channels. We believe that one reason for this is that eCommerce represents a new market where there is a relatively equal footing, giving everyone the opportunity to deliver on their online promise.

Target for Repeat Business

Target your customers, products, and services for repeat business. Recognize that when you try to be all things to all people, you often wind up being nothing special to anyone. Targeting doesn't begin with asking yourself who will come to the site. Rather, it should begin with asking why they will come back to the site.

Charles Schwab is an example worth mentioning again, as the company has built a dominant market share despite having the highest cost per trade in early 2000. One might think that all Schwab had to do was move its bricks-and-mortar clients online to gain this position. However, remarkably, the company doubled its customer base at the same time as new companies entered the marketplace. Schwab did this through targeting new customers by looking for individuals with larger investment balances who tended to buy and hold rather than day traders. Schwab accessed these customers through advertising that stressed service and availability rather than price. These ads often featured a computer room with a telephone ringing unanswered. The message was clear: you can trade with someone else, but if you want service you should trade with Schwab. The result is shown in Table 10-2.

Table 10-2: Online Trading Companies[2]

	Schwab	E*Trade	TD Waterhouse	Ameritrade
Cost per trade	$24.95	$19.95	$12.00	$8.00
Avg. annual trades	9	19	15	22
Avg. account balance	$91,864	$23,212	$56,311	$34,271
Total accounts	5,900,000	909,000	1,844,000	569,000
Market share	27.5%	12.9%	12.8%	8.4%

Targeting your customers, products, and services for repeat business is essential in building the customer engine for delivering relationships and value. Achieving this starts with identifying the customer types and working backward in identifying customer needs and the value network relationships required to deliver those needs.

Integrating the Business

What is the scope of your eCommerce business? In a world of value networks, intermediaries, and customer hubs, the question is a necessary one, in that the answer is no longer bounded by your internal organization and its resources. You can out-task and in-source everywhere and thereby greatly extend the scale and variety of your business offers and hence relationships. Deciding how far to push the reach of your business determines the value network opportunity and target. Traditional notions of a business as consisting of organizational units and functions give way in eCommerce to a business as a set of capabilities and services. These capabilities represent the points of integration and management for your business, as shown in Figure 10-1.

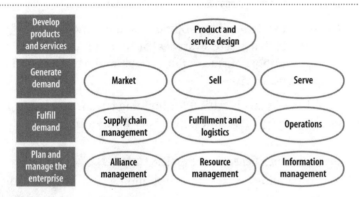

Figure 10-1: Sample eCommerce capabilities

These capabilities represent your scope of concern, but not necessarily your scope of control, as sourcing distributes the roles across the value network. While you may not control all capabilities, you are responsible for their integration and for the operation of the services in each of these areas. A brief review of each set of capabilities defines the breadth of activities involved in an eCommerce business.

Generate Demand: Market, Sell, and Serve

An effective generate-demand capability relies on several factors:

▶ Provide superior service levels via electronic channels in terms of convenience, enablement, and self-management

▶ Establish flexibility by developing self-organizing processes that combine and recombine to address customer requests and needs

▶ Recognize that the relationship foundation grows by supplying information intelligently to support customers' shopping and buying activities

▶ Encourage customer use by designing Web sites and capabilites based on customer perspectives, decision-making processes, and intentions rather than automating your sales process

▶ Enhance credibility when you provide access to a broad range of information, including competitor information, product reviews, customer reviews, and recommendations

▶ Generate the demand capabilities that are responsible for the services that create awareness of your brand, products, and services; support business transactions; and handle customer support and service

Each of these factors is critical for building customer relationships and fostering the repeat business necessary for creating wealth.

Marketing Capabilities: Generate Interest and Customers

Marketing capabilities are the base for building your image, acquiring customers, and generating interest in the brand. The success of this capability governs the velocity of your eCommerce business by building your customer base and transaction volumes. This is why marketing processes and capabilities matter so much and go way beyond just placing ads. Indeed, marketing is the vehicle for communicating and making real the business model and mobilizing the organization.

Key service-level measures for monitoring the success of marketing capabilities include:

Customer acquisition cost Customer acquisition cost monitors the ratio between marketing expenditure and new customers. This ratio is important as it helps determine where in the economic model your business operates. How effectively are you spending this most expensive component of the eCommerce investment base?

Customer retention Customer retention measures the ability of the company to hold the customer's attention and business.

It is a key indicator of relationship versus transaction effectiveness. How effectively are you turning customer acquisition investment into relationship payoff?

Customer acquisition effectiveness Customer acquisition effectiveness is related to customer retention and measures the relationship in terms of the number of times a customer comes to the site before registering or purchasing. How well are you turning hits into customers and customers into committed relationships?

Sales Capabilities: Generating Revenue

Sales capabilities support customer shopping and buying processes. They are based on providing evaluation and dynamic offer relationship types through the Web site. These capabilities build customer purchasing confidence by providing information on competing products and product referrals. Sales effectiveness is managed through one or more of the following measures:

Sales per enquiry Sales per enquiry looks at the hit ratio between shopping and buying activities. In general, it will compare the number of accesses against product purchases. It can be a leading indicator of customer interest as well as of the effectiveness of purchasing processes and technology.

Repeat business in dollars per customer Repeat business in dollars per customer measures the quality of revenues the eCommerce venture is creating.

Customer referral business Customer referral business looks to capture the effectiveness of peer-to-peer marketing. This metric should track the number of reviews and the effectiveness of sales to the number of referrals.

Service Capabilities: Delivering to Customer Needs

Service capabilities represent a substantial management challenge, as service activities draw on all value network eProcess capabilities. Customer service is crucial to building relationships. Customers seek out your service capabilities when they have an issue or problem. This takes customer service from a cost center to a value-building relationship tool, as good customer service—especially at a point of customer crisis—can cement the relationship and stimulate peer-to-peer referrals and recommendations.

Service capabilities often center on a customer interaction center that integrates services across all of the company's channels. This interaction center combines elements of call centers, customer service, Web site content management, and direct customer contact. Bringing these elements together requires integrating customer, account, and product knowledge along with highly skilled service representatives. This creates a customer service capability that is flexible and adaptable to a wide range of requests and is far removed from a "boiler room" operation associated with many call centers.

There is a multitude of measures that can apply to the service capabilities. The following provide some guidelines for assessing your service characteristics and their contribution to building deeper relationships and repeat business. You should notice that these measures do not concentrate on cost metrics, such as time required to handle a call or number of calls per person. Those measures, while important to your call center economics, often cause behavior that is counterproductive in building relationships. Our measures focus on customer interaction and relationship building:

Customer relationship intensity Growing customer relationships is critical to building more sophisticated and valuable relationships. The indicator here is the revenue growth rate of established customers who have an account relationship rather than just a transaction history.

Net cash flow value per customer transaction This measure addresses something that is easily overlooked: cash flow. eCommerce changes the cash flow cycle by shifting payment and inventory responsibilities.

Electronic channel responsiveness eCommerce opens new channels of communication. This measure simply tracks the percentage and time lag between receiving and responding to customer email messages, calls, and other forms of correspondence.

Fulfill Demand: Supply Chain, Fulfillment & Logistics, and Operations

Your company must deliver on its commitments. This links fulfillment issues to customer sales, service, and brand. The capabilities involved in managing your supply chain, handling fulfillment and logistics, and operations.

Supply Chain

The supply chain is responsible for acquiring products and services needed to manage manufacturing, production forecasting, and procurement. The performance of these capabilities dictates your cost basis and operational strength. Operating a supply chain at scale requires capital and assets, which is one reason why these capabilities are frequently out-tasked while companies concentrate on building customer relationships. Business-to-business eCommerce is most closely associated with these supply chain activities as organizations seek to improve business performance through:

- ▶ Improving the accuracy of information to eliminate errors, improve response times, and reduce manual re-keying of information

- ▶ Improving decision-making by using actual demand information rather than forecasts and estimates

- ▶ Reducing errors and rework caused by hand-offs by integrating information flows within the organization and across the supply chain

Fulfillment and Logistics

Fulfillment includes everything that happens from the second your customers place an order to the time they receive the product, return it if necessary, and are thoroughly satisfied. Fulfillment and logistics include inventory management, distribution, transport, and warehousing. As the name implies, many, if not most, of the decisions made in supply chain management converge in the fulfillment process. It is the essential last link between a company and its customers. In the world of eCommerce, it becomes even more essential, since it may well represent the only direct contact between the company and its customers. It is the fulfillment of a *promise*.

eCommerce is not just another way to take orders. Though fulfillment operations are similar to those of more traditional companies, eCommerce customers have different expectations of fulfillment and logistics. Customer expectations concerning speed and service reliability requirements generally rise when dealing with eCommerce companies. Customers associate the ability to see a product online with it being available for immediate delivery.

Customer expectations strain traditional fulfillment and logistics operations because there is less inventory in an eCommerce channel and therefore less slack to cushion. The height of these expectations can be summed up when you consider customer dissatisfaction with holiday shopping. In this case, there was customer dissatisfaction even with online retailers that delivered 90 to 95 percent of orders on time—a performance level any retailer would envy. Clearly customer expectations regarding fulfillment are high. The bar keeps getting higher in eCommerce fulfillment.

Fulfillment offers a difficult challenge for many companies. The Andersen Consulting study we discussed earlier showed that pure eCommerce companies achieved only an 80 percent fulfillment compared to the online channels of traditional retailers, who achieved only 20 percent.[3] Part of the challenge rests in the fact that most eCommerce companies carry significantly less inventory than their bricks and mortar counterparts as they are able to manage inventory based on actual rather than forecasted demand. Key performance measures in this area include:

Fulfillment rate The percentage and actual number of orders being fulfilled within the service requirements.

Delivery rate The number of hours required for a product to leave the warehouse and customer acceptance.

Cost of delivery The average cost to warehouse and deliver a product, measured in dollars. This addresses the operational cost of managing inventory throughout the fulfillment process.

Inventory velocity Standard measures of inventory turns that assess the efficiency of buying and warehouse operations.

Operations

Operations involve the back-office processes centered on the payment and cash flow capabilities. These capabilities "turn the crank" of the cash flow cycle and are essential to operations and maintaining strong supplier relationships. Managing the cash flow cycle is critical for many eCommerce startup operations, as they will generate positive cash flow well before recording accounting profits. eCommerce companies generate cash through exchanging inventory for information and transferring receivables risk to intermediaries.

An eProcess company exchanges inventory for information when it links its Web store to merchandise and inventory management applications. This changes the basis of manufacturing and purchasing from highly inaccurate sales forecasts to actual demand. This information, when shared with suppliers, replaces inventory and safety stock levels, freeing up cash normally invested in inventory stocks. In Figure 10-2, this results in a 35-day improvement in inventory purchasing through better forecasting based on actual rather than forecasted demand.

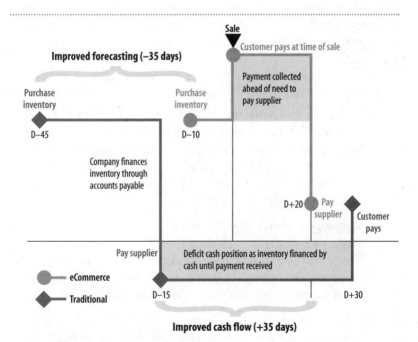

Figure 10-2: Traditional and eCommerce cash flow cycles

An eProcess company can also out-task its receivables risk to financial intermediaries, such as banks or electronic funds transfer services. A company can virtually eliminate accounts receivable risk as it creates an eProcess-based billing process. The net effect is negative cash outflow, a condition where the company collects its payment for products and services ahead of paying its suppliers. In the case of Amazon, this cash flow cycle helped account for a portion of the $700 million in cash and marketable securities on their balance sheet.[4]

Plan and Manage: Alliances, Resources, and Information

In a dynamic eCommerce environment, enterprise planning and management are critical. Planning and management capabilities involve more than the traditional finance organization, and these capabilities must be ready to expand to support new business models, participate in startups, and assimilate new technologies. Each major dimension of the management and governance capability will be challenged—from strategy to organizational capability and service delivery. As a result, each of the major process areas—governance, business decision support, and transaction processing—will be affected. Companies that proactively address new business challenges and embrace process efficiency opportunities should realize multiple benefits, including:

▶ Evaluating and managing value network relationships and alliances. This includes handling potential new alliance relationships as well as managing the company's existing portfolio. Potential new relationships must be evaluated at speed. Value networks constantly change, and existing relationships must be managed to deliver results.

▶ Managing resource allocations based on highly accurate information across the organization through integrated systems. The company uses this information to improve budget procurement and operations management decisions while eliminated resource intensive reconciliation and reporting activities.

▶ Supporting new business appraisal and mobilization required to make ongoing investments required to compete in eCommerce. This includes tracking investment effectiveness and operational performance in real time.

▶ Providing increased information accuracy through improved front-to-back-end application and data integration to improve the speed and accuracy of executive decisions.

Develop Products and Services: Renewing the Customer Value Proposition

Competition creates and erases market opportunities at a frightening pace, making your ability to develop products and services a critical part of competitive advantage. Products and services alone do not equate to profitability and success. The initial stage of eCommerce involved creating electronic sales channels for products and services. The next-generation eCommerce businesses are building relationships based on intentions, information, and trust. These relationships extend the company's competitive strength as they transcend any particular price-product combination. This makes development of products and services critical to building the content that connects customers in a relationship with your company.

Electronic commerce provides new sources of information, innovation, and inspiration for new products and services. Increased information exchanges across the value network raise the volume and value of information. The Internet enables companies to go directly to the market to test products and services with greater fidelity of information. Will you use this information to your advantage or rely on traditional marketing studies?

Innovation possibilities abound in eCommerce as the ability to mix products, services, and information create new value propositions and markets. Consider reverse auctions, micro payments processors, and other new businesses competing in eCommerce. Innovation provides products and services that change relationships between customers, companies, and others. The issue becomes not which new idea can you create, but how can you develop it to build relationships and value.

Inspiring new product and service development involves addressing important issues regarding your company, its customers, and the competition. The following questions provide some issues to address in developing new products and services:

- ▶ What types of relationships do you want to attract and build?

- ▶ What other products, services, and companies are competing for your customers' attention?

- ▶ What do you know about your customers' intentions and needs?

- ▶ What is your understanding of the service levels provided by your competitors within and outside your industry?

- ▶ What do you know that will be of value to your customers and suppliers?

- ▶ How can you tap into the capabilities of suppliers to extend your offerings?

- ▶ What customer capabilities can you strengthen or complement?

Competition requires flexibility that improves your ability to develop and deploy new products and services rapidly. Marketing and sales capabilities must be able to readily incorporate new products into your brand image and marketing approach. Sales and service capabilities must adapt quickly to identify and serve new customer intentions. Fulfillment capabilities require flexibility to deliver a steady stream of products and services. Key measures in this area include:

Speed to market The time it takes to conceive, design, and introduce a new product or service into production. The calculation should cover the time taken in product development as well as deployment time to bring the operations up to speed.

Cost to market The resource costs required to conceive, design, and introduce a new product or service into production.

Revenue from new products and services The percentage revenues generated from new products and alliances.

Managing Across Channels: Channel Harmonization

Electronic commerce represents a new business channel for reaching and servicing customers. This creates the opportunity for conflict as traditional and electronic channels compete for customer business and attention. Companies create this conflict through the design of relationships among the players in the value network.

A channel is the way a company reaches its customers. There are direct and indirect ones. A direct channel involves interacting directly with the company and its customers. Retailers have this type of access to customers through their physical stores, catalogs, and Web stores. A manufacturer and its suppliers view the channel as indirect since customer contact is handled by retailers, wholesalers, agencies, and other parties. The value chain illustrated below shows the direct relationship between the customer and retailer with all other relationships indirect through the retailer

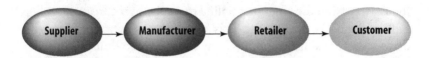

The first generation of eCommerce solutions concentrated on the promise of establishing direct relationships that cut out the retail-wholesale middlemen. The promise in the mid 1990s was that any company could create wealth by disrupting the value chain by getting rid of the players that stood between the company and its customers. Disintermediation became the call of many in eCommerce. This led to many companies willingly creating channel conflict as they sought to supplant traditional players and establish a direct relationship with customers.

Channel conflict is real and self-inflicted by many companies in their design and sourcing of their capabilities. Multiple channels compete when the company sets its partners in competition with each other. A common situation is a manufacturer who wants to sell "direct" over the Internet, yet maintains indirect channels through wholesalers, dealers, and retailers. Manufacturers want to capture some of the wholesaler-retailer margin and build a relationship and gather information about their customers. Wholesalers and others naturally want a fair return for their risks and react negatively. The two channels are in competition, one that all players see as a win-lose or zero-sum game.

The net effect of this conflict has undermined the brand value of consumer and commercial products by undercutting their emergence in electronic commerce. The initial appeal of strong consumer product brands led several companies to pursue a direct electronic channel. Unfortunately, this has proven to be challenging on several fronts. First, a manufacturer's economic model is tuned to bulk product purchases and shipments, which are ill suited for the demands of consumer retail sales. The second issue rests with the relatively low volumes generated in the early stages of eCommerce channels. These lower business volumes, coupled with high marketing costs, do not offset the current revenue streams created in the traditional channels. This enables traditional retailers to change their marketing and sales focus away from the emerging online manufacturer threatening the bulk of their sales and profits. This approach has been sufficient to drive several established brands away from direct online sales.[5]

Channel Harmonization

Viewing channels as competition rather than collaboration has made channel conflict a popular topic in eCommerce. However, "conflict" is the wrong way to think about channels and customers. Deciding to create a branch channel (or a call center channel or a distributor channel or a Web channel) is to look at the issue from the company's perspective, rather than the customers'. Customers do not see any channel conflict, only channel choice.

Companies that have built the strongest reputation for customer service in eCommerce tend to view channels from the customers' perspective. They use the customer perspective as the foundation for designing their customer service processes. These companies believe that the critical design goal is to ensure that the architecture enhances the customer relationship through superb meshing—harmony—of channels.

Harmonizing channels is a direction that many successful eCommerce companies pursue. "The customer should never be aware of channels" is the critical design criteria for eCommerce powerhouses such as Dell, Schwab, and others. The reasons are simple. Channels in conflict confuse the customer and complicate company operations, lowering customer service while increasing costs. To be effective, channels must operate in harmony with one another. That harmony begins with channel and capability design that concentrates on the following factors:

- ▶ What is the customer's view of these channels? Which will be most attractive to our customer segments?

- ▶ How can we provide a consistently high-quality service regardless of the channel the customer chooses?

Challenges of Channel Harmonization

Channel harmonization poses strategic and tactical challenges. The choice of sales and service channels is often strategic, as exemplified by Dell's success with a customer direct channel or by IBM's use of a professional sales force. Companies must think about channels strategically so that they complement each other. This requires the right channels to be selected for the right customers, products, and services. It also requires the integration of information, service levels, and responses across all channels.

Selecting the right channel requires companies to examine themselves from the outside in. Unfortunately, many companies do not seem to think from the customers' perspective. This leads them to view as product and revenue streams rather than relationship interfaces with customers, suppliers, wholesalers, and others. Management's focus turns to capturing revenue and information from other players, rather than how they can add value and leverage the capabilities of their related players, creating a win-win for the customer, channel, and themselves.

This view is understandable when considering channels from an internal perspective. For example, an insurance company can envision the savings from a direct-sales channel by calculating the "saved" agenda commissions. This sets the company against its agents competing for customers and revenues. The result is predictable; agents will move their recommendations to other companies with similar services and better commission structures. The effect is sluggish agent sales, which still make up a majority of the insurer's revenues, causing the insurer to pull back on its direct channel for fear of further enraging the agents. This example is in the insurance industry, but it is repeated every time a company sets two channels in competition. What the company and the sales agents fail to realize is that this competition is meaningless to the customer. Customers choose the best channel for themselves. In this example, that channel will probably be offered by a company able to harmonize and integrate sales agents and direct sales. That company is probably not the one in our example.

Harmonize and Mix Channels

Harmonization makes sense because it's what the customer wants. Companies too often ignore the customer perspective when they seek to blend channels into new business models. Many companies enter eCommerce by trying to introduce a direct selling and service channel while still relying on distributors for the majority of their current sales.

Mixing channels requires strong target marketing and clear communications across all channel players. Companies that look at channels as a means to push product fail to recognize that channels are only effective when customers pull the product through sales. Successful channel mixing rests on a simple premise: a diverse customer base will naturally select the channel that best fits its needs.

Channel harmonization and choice do not mean that one size fits all; rather, it means allowing customers to self-select the channels that fit them best. Mixing channels means target-marketing channels to the customers who are most likely to use them. Hewlett-Packard provides an example of handling this challenge. HP has strong channel relationships, to the extent that the company is known as "the channel's best friend." Recently, HP has faced the same margin pressures as Compaq, and commentators in the industry trade press argued that HP would have to consider at least some direct-sales options to keep up with Dell, Compaq, and IBM.[6]

HP did not try to fool its dealers in an attempt to have them buy into a HP direct channel. Rather, it worked with the channel partners to recognize how HP channels fit with their partners' strategies.

Channel Strategies

There appear to be several emerging channel harmonization strategies. These strategies define models for establishing new electronic channels. The first is channel unification. Dell Computer and Charles Schwab provide representative examples, as both seek to unify the customer relationship through multi-channel access. This strategy works best for diversifying existing direct channel relationships and unifying the customer experience across traditional and electronic service channels.

The second strategy concentrates on strengthening channels through value-added services. This is the strategy that HP and Sony have pursued. They add value to the distributor's channel by acting as a gateway for customers to be matched to the best distributors, resellers, and systems integrators. This strategy works best when the manufacturer has a strong brand identity that will draw customers to the manufacturer's site.

Channel Unification

Unifying the customer relationship across and regardless of channel is a long-term strategy that is fully consistent with the main eCommerce business and technology trends. These trends include customization, personalization, ease of access, and streamlining of the interaction (one- or two-click transactions).

The top technology trend is the use of software to unify the customer relationship dynamically—"apps-on-tap," agents, "bots," and the like. Software that routes the customer from Web site to call center or sales/technology specialist is becoming a major growth area for Net innovation. This also represents a major area of eProcess innovation.

Unifying the customer relationship requires a consistent level of process performance and customer satisfaction across all channels. The ability to give the customer the same information regardless of whether they phone the call center, visit a local office, or access the Web is the touchstone of a unified relationship.

Achieving this relationship requires

- ▶ Robust customer-centered processes that produce the same outcomes regardless of channel

- ▶ Customer, product, order, and status information available across all channels, including the call center, Web site, and field sales force

- ▶ Technology that provides a consistent view of the customer and the customer relationship across the organization and its information systems

- ▶ Highly trained personnel who are able to handle customer contact from and through multiple channels

Provide Value-Added Services

Using eCommerce to increase the value added to channel partners is another strategy for harmonization. This strategy involves the use of eCommerce to add value to channels that might otherwise feel threatened by a company-direct channel. This strategy is most effective when a company is working with established distributors and channel partners whose value the company must recognize. Again, this approach relies on having a good understanding of the company's customers and channel partners. That understanding enables the company to fit its channel design to the customers' and partners' needs. This often involves sharing and applying information with channel partners.

For example, Sony uses its Web site to strengthen its own relationships with consumers and business customers without weakening its distributors. It uses the interaction and information it gathers to assess which type of channel partner Sony should refer the sale to—retailer, systems integrator, OEM, or reseller. This prequalification of prospects helps the distributor retain the direct customer link, while at the same time Sony uses the Web interaction and data it gathers to increase its sales.

Sony has described itself as a channel marketing group. Sony views its relationships and partnerships as important, and it is using the Web to enhance its ability to work with their partners. Previously, the Sony Web site was product focused and tried to speak to too many customer segments at the same time. Telemarketing was the main source of leads, though a costly one. Now, the updated Sony site uses "needs-based" navigation to deliver a customer to the right distributor. Sony's aim is to "keep the sanctity of the distribution network."[7]

A value-added strategy means preserving relationships with existing channel partners in order to reinforce and extend their effectiveness. This enables the company to open new channels aimed at new customers and distributors without conflicting with value-added new channels.

Choose a Channel Strategy

Fundamentally, the issues of channel strategies have to be looked at from the perspective of the customer. The key question that must be answered is where is the relationship interface and what value does it provide to the customer? A secondary question is if the channel relationship is bypassed or augmented, will extra value be created along the entire manufacturer-to-purchaser chain?

In some instances, the answer to these two questions may result in counterintuitive results. For example, real estate and insurance look like obvious areas for online selling, but progress has been very slow. The real estate broker handles a large number of informal functions, such as locating a termite inspector and helping to coordinate the closing. Similarly, even though the insurance industry's agency system is very expensive, the complexity of many of its products makes people hesitant to buy online.

Once again, the best way to assess channel strategy options is to take the eProcess view. Which of the existing or potential processes add or erode value? The processes that should be examined include pricing, fulfillment, customization, service, support, and many others. To be effective, a company must work back from the customer relationship interface and ensure that the company's channels create harmony in that regard. Charles Schwab is the standout here in financial services, and Dell is the leader in distribution.

An eProcess Executive Agenda

An eProcess executive agenda summarizes the decisions and actions required to address issues of sourcing, structure, technology, channels, and the value network. The executive agenda sets the path for building an eSuccess based on relationships, process excellence, and capability sourcing. This agenda must address a core eCommerce question: How does the company attract and grow profitable relationships and repeat business?

The question is simple. However, the path to producing the answers can be complex. eCommerce changes customer, relationship, and process fundamentals. This complexity creates indecision and limited actions, requiring executives to take action and lead the charge to create their electronic business. Gaining an eProcess edge involves recognizing and taking the actions necessary to create new capabilities and relationships, as outlined in Table 10-3.

Table 10-3: eProcess Executive Agenda

Agenda Item	Tool or Approach	Things to Keep in Mind
How does the company attract and grow profitable relationships and repeat business?	eCommerce strategy	eCommerce success rests on building repeat business
Who do we want to do business with? What relationships do we want to build and attract?	Value network	It is more effective to play on a team than going it alone

Table 10-3: eProcess Executive Agenda (*continued*)

Agenda Item	Tool or Approach	Things to Keep in Mind
What type of relationships must we support?	Relationship types	The relationship type defines the scope of your eCommerce capability
How do we source the required capabilities to build these relationships?	Capability assessment matrix	Capability value is driven by the customer first
How do we build these capabilities?	eProcess sourcing options	Embed business rules to enable self-management
		Out-task to the value network to gain capability at speed and scale
		In-source identity capabilities that strengthen your relationship and brand
		Be exceptional in handling crisis and exception conditions. These make or break the relationship
How will we operate and manage the business?	Service management	Define the letter of the law in service levels and metrics well, but operate in the spirit of the business objective
		Manage real issues rather than the "noise" in the process

Addressing the items on the agenda enables executives to leverage eProcess relationship and sourcing options in order to transform their balance sheet and operating cost through innovative capability sourcing. This is achieved when executives concentrate their attention and capital on the identity capabilities that are the engine behind relationships and brand value. Taking every sourcing and alliance opportunity that comes along is not intelligent or innovative sourcing.

There is no set solution for the questions raised on the executive agenda; if there were, there would be little need for this book. eCommerce options and opportunities are more diverse than anyone could have predicted. However, we do know there are some emerging business practices that point the way forward:

▶ Leverage the value network by identifying and concentrating on core identity capabilities. The sourcing options available through the value network are too efficient to justify investing in processes others can do better, faster, and cheaper. The one caveat here is that you cannot out-source to the extent that you lose control of your relationships or the economics of the transaction.

► Design from the customer in, not company out. Customers matter, as we have said, and they are smart and now have choice. Designing from the company out will only make your back-office inefficiencies public through the Web.

► Design for relationships and repeat business, using information and knowledge to demonstrate that you know customers, suppliers, and others. A relationship requires context, and your company must have the flexibility to deliver information, products, and services in that context.

► Automate processes intelligently. While Internet technologies offer unparalleled possibilities, the ability to automate does not lead to automation of everything. This is one of the myths of being "virtual." Operations are important, and people are important. Their skills and abilities are critical to how you handle exceptions and change.

► Clean up your business rules and processes. Clean rules really do make for clean processes that are able to handle large transaction volumes without high operating costs. Ambiguous or poorly defined rules destroy eCommerce efficiencies and reduce quality.

► Manage the business as a collection of services rather than organizational units. Services are the management node of a value network. Data driven and defined, they provide a good way to manage the business across all of its alliances, relationships, and ventures.

Innovate or die! Execute or go broke! These were the challenges we set at the beginning of this book. eCommerce requires both innovation and execution. It requires process excellence that comes from thoughtful decisions and designs that build relationships and repeat business. Those designs leverage the capabilities within a value network and source capabilities through the Web site, alliance partners, and internally. Quite a challenge when you consider the need to do all of this at eSpeed.

One word of caution, though: Working at eSpeed is not an excuse for being eSloppy, making poor decisions, or wasting valuable attention and capital. There was a time when having a dot-com in your name implied being able to get away with a lot in the name of market valuation and the new economy. That economy will not be built through poor management decisions and excessive marketing. Rather, we see the new economy emerging from companies that avoided that temptation and stuck to the fundamentals of commerce: relationships, processes, rules, interfaces, and sourcing. Those companies have pursued eProcess excellence, building their futures on a strong network of relationships and intelligent sourcing that will grow their businesses by creating customer value and business wealth.

Conclusion

The Next Wave of eCommerce

At the start of the book, we talked about "white out"—the blizzard of information that is blinding executives with new technology, new markets, and new competitors. This book has been about how to see past the blizzard and into the future by taking the actions needed to create an edge in eCommerce. That edge, based on relationships, sourcing, and a new definition of process, represents a path to the future. The first wave of eCommerce is ending as the race to dot-com is over. Companies now view the Internet as a core business channel, which is driving companies into new markets, alliances, mergers, and operations. These moves are signs that the race is now about profits, operations, and process excellence rather than a mad dash to market capitalization. This makes the new race one about gaining an eProcess edge.

What will the eSuccess company look like five years from now? No one knows, regardless of when "now" is! But we can offer our speculative answers to this question. Take them as nothing more than that—speculations. If anyone tells you they know what the business of tomorrow will look like, ask them what they predicted five years ago about today's business environment—and ask them if in, say, 1995 or 1996 they foresaw Charles Schwab and E*Trade transforming the securities industry, AOL being in a position to buy Time Warner, or eBay becoming a primary vehicle for state governments to dispose of surplus goods and items confiscated from drug dealers.

All anyone can be reasonably certain of is that there will be at least as much change in the next five years as the last five. Some of the players of tomorrow don't exist today, any more than Priceline.com, AutoByTel, Ariba, Commerce One, or Exodus were around five years ago. That said, many of the winners of tomorrow are in business today, but may not yet be in eCommerce acceleration mode. Remember that Cisco, Dell, Intel, Southwest Airlines, and General Electric—all of which are billion dollar eCommerce firms—were well-established companies before they added the Internet to their sources of strength. Any company can be a leader in the new economy as eCommerce becomes more and more commerce and less and less just electronic.

What we do know is that, regardless of new technology, new markets, and new business practices, a few things will always be true:

- ▶ Customers will always be important, no matter the market structure or mechanism used to sell or serve. Those customers will continue to have choice and will have more information (although not necessarily better information). Companies that have a strong and growing relationship based on a win-win set of values should fare well regardless of what happens.

- ▶ Competition will continue to fuel the innovation and change necessary for the creative destruction we continue to see in the economy. The "need for speed" to bring new and better offers to market will continue to create change. Companies that create flexibility by being willing to change and look at their operations as sourcing decisions should be able to sense and respond to change.

- ▶ Market reach and sophistication will continue to increase and go global. The fronts on which a company serves and competes will continue to expand—in positive terms to new markets and customers, in negative terms to new competition. Companies that maintain a focus on their customers and innovative sourcing should be able to take advantage of both terms. A customer focus will lead to developing and tailoring offers to the local market while sourcing options can build a local presence at speed and scale. Looking for a model, consider Yahoo! and Amazon and how they have opened local operations in Europe.

While these constants seem innocuous, the challenge they pose to businesses is quite daunting. In this book, we have tried to provide some tools that will stand the test of time and help address these issues and challenges.

The Content Challenge

One of our concerns throughout this book is a focus on eCommerce content companies such as AOL or Yahoo! The concern is that companies will view eCommerce as the exclusive domain of these types of companies. We believe this is not an appropriate view.

The content challenge is one of awareness and visibility. We recognize that not every company sells content via the Web and that eCommerce margins are easy to explain when all the company does is sell its content. However, we would like to challenge that definition of content. It is true that chat rooms, stock research, product catalogs, and the like represent content that is often available from the Web. But your company, regardless of its business, is awash in content that has value and applicability in eCommerce.

Every company has content it can use and leverage to improve relationships with customers, suppliers, and others. The issue is not whether you have content, but rather, how you should best use it. Finding a use for content involves looking for the win-win in these relationships by finding how what you know—your content—can benefit customers and suppliers. Consider the following types of content most companies have at their disposal:

Customer preferences and profiles This type of information is latent throughout the company. How do you use it to create customized offers, deliver specialized service, and build a relationship beyond product availability and price?

Product information and specifications How can you integrate your products into those of your customer? How can you inject your information into the customer's design and development processes? In other words, how can you become part of the fabric of their products and offerings?

Inventory stocks and availability How can you make this available to customers so they can reduce their invested working capital? How can you get actual customer demand so you can change your working capital investments?

Maintenance history and experience How can you provide better service and availability by knowing when things need attention before you get a service call? How can you help customers address their own service needs to manage warrantee and repair costs?

Cost and time required to manufacture How can you use this to make better offers to existing customers or break into new markets?

Employee skills Are you aware of the talents and interests of your people? How can you harness their energy for their own benefit and that of your customers? How will you use these talents and interests to create new offerings, innovate new ideas, and build deeper relationships with your workforce?

These are but a few content areas that are often overlooked by most companies who do not see content as part of their offering. The potential value hidden in the answers to these questions should tell you that you have content and therefore you are not outside of eCommerce. You have knowledge and content that are more valuable than you may realize.

The Business Challenge

The core business challenge is relationships. How will you continue to reach, sell, serve, and build relationships with customers? How will you form and run the business relationships that are now networked and integrated across multiple players? How will you build relationships within your organization to improve flexibility, retain talent, and gain speed of response? All of these questions challenge businesses regardless of where they are in the electronic economy.

Relationships are at the core of an eProcess edge. Customer relationships are the first among equals, as customers set service and performance requirements. The business must look and design its operations from the customer in rather than the company out if they are to build deep and lasting relationships. This requires looking for the convergence of customer and company values to find the capabilities that build your identity and brand.

Relationships are more than a purchase; they must engage your entire business. Fulfilling your commitments with accuracy, speed, and scale build customer belief in your promise and brand. A smooth Web site, a great call center, or an eye-catching marketing campaign are of little value if you cannot pick, ship, bill, and collect the business. The challenge is to recognize that your back office governs your long-term growth and profitability potential as much as your front-end marketing.

Relationships are the way out of commoditization and competing only on price. People want to do business with companies that know them, tailor offerings to their needs, and deliver on those offerings. The business challenge is to find the right blend of product, service, and customization that will engage and solidify the relationships. The challenge is that your capabilities must be flexible enough to handle different price-service-performance requirements that are set by the customer. Such flexibility is necessary to deliver on the promise of customer self-directed commerce. The challenge is there, but the reward is as well.

Relationships exist across a value network of customers, suppliers, intermediaries, complementors, and others. These players bring a wealth of capability, information, and potential to bear on your business. Intelligent sourcing, service management, and channel harmonization represent the challenges of working in a networked business. Make sourcing decisions based on customer and business priorities to ensure you do not give away the store by out-tasking identity capabilities. Implement a service management approach with network partners to manage the relationship based on performance rather than perception. Harmonize channel relationships rather than putting them into competition.

These business challenges represent the eProcess hurdle an organization must clear in order to compete successfully in eCommerce. Use the value network, relationship types, and capability sourcing models to help address these challenges and create new eProcess capabilities.

The Executive Challenge

It's natural for companies to look at all these shifts and ask whether the most appropriate response is to try to evolve the new capabilities or to start from scratch. Like poor Hamlet, the CEO may then wander the boardroom asking himself or herself, "To dot-com or not to dot-com—that is the question." Like Hamlet, executives can become caught in indecision that ends in disaster for everyone. Without pushing the analogy too far, executive indecision about organizing for the world of eCommerce will kill off the careers of many people in good companies and paralyze the enterprise. When Hamlet asks himself if he should kill Claudius at his prayers, the audience's response should be "Do *something!*"

"Ah but..." is Hamlet's response for much of the play. It's not quite that simple. And it's not at all simple for the CEO. Opinions are widely divided about the relative merits of setting up a separate dot-com unit versus building an eCommerce capability within the existing business. There are many arguments pro and con for each option. The dot-com advantage is a clean slate, the opportunity to recruit new talent, and freedom from the constraints of existing structures, procedures, and organizational habits that get in the way of speed, flexibility, and innovation.

Gaining an eProcess edge comes from executive leadership and vision that bridge the gap between innovation and execution. Vision requires executives to look at their company as a collection of processes and capabilities rather than organizational units. That vision, focused through the eProcess sourcing options, involves looking at how to structure the company to take advantage of new technologies, build new relationships, and secure the future by creating a business with the right mix of vertical control and virtual operations.

While knowing what to do is half the battle, it is not half the effort. Executive leadership and hard work are required to turn the vision into operations. That is nothing new. What is new is that the changes required to gain an eProcess edge for your operations, processes, and relationships go to the core of your business. eCommerce changes the fundamentals. The sourcing options available in eProcess enable organizations to engineer their balance sheets and profit-loss statements to an unparalleled degree.

Executives who leverage the value network concentrate their management attention and capital on their identity capabilities— the capabilities that form their core asset base. Executives use the eProcess sourcing options to change thier structure and move their companies toward vertical integration through:

- ▶ Embedding business rules in software enables companies to lower their cost structures by hiring customers and suppliers to handle tasks where they have the information and interest. This leverages customer-supplier skills and knowledge, reducing the amount of error-prone form filling and translation activities.

- ▶ Out-tasking through APIs and software leverages best-in-class capabilities available in the market. This has a dramatic effect on the balance sheet as companies "lease" their partners' capital base and operations rather than bringing them in-house. Out-tasking also enables companies to redistribute business risks to suppliers, intermediaries, and complementors. The core cash flow risks are a visible example of this, and one that can have a dramatic effect on operations and the balance sheet.

- ▶ In-sourcing by using technology and eProcess principles strengthens your core operations. It also increases the use of information and business rules to make better decisions and improve coordination throughout the business. The result is greater asset efficiency.

- ▶ Being exceptional in handling exceptions secures your future as you are able to sense and respond to customer needs and crisis. That ability to perform beyond the rule and handle the odd situation is an often untapped source of customer relationships and innovation.

Now, some of you may be skeptical, but look at the business press to see the mergers, alliances, and consortia forming. Those decisions may seem to be isolated tactical moves. Look at them as a whole and you will see companies building their value network. Consider the operations and management activities you do now that add little value and consume valuable attention and resources. Is there someone who views your liability process as their core asset? What if someone else handled these liabilities for you? Find those companies and you will see the power of out-tasking. Look at your decisions, their accuracy, how well the information meets your needs, how often someone says "The data is wrong, I'll get back to you." These situations point to the need for better integration and use of information. Look at the situations that build customer loyalty and recognize innovation. Customers give you their repeat business based on trust that is proven when something goes awry and they need an exception. Those exceptions are a source of innovation, as handling exceptions often involves doing business in ways you never thought of before.

The Future Challenge

Fear, uncertainty, and doubt have paralyzed companies, created process blindness, and allowed whole companies to lose their way in a white-out of information and noise. The future challenge is to cut through these influences and act. We hope this book has provided some examples, approaches, and tools to help you make the decisions and take the actions you need to be successful.

We do not know exactly how companies will create their future eSuccess. But we do know what will matter: commerce, relationships, processes, interfaces, and sourcing. These fundamentals will continue to form the basis for success now and in the future.

Notes

Introduction

1. From the University of Texas Internet Economy Indicators Web site: <http://www.internetindicators.com/>.

2. "Earnings Review for America Online," *Washington Post*, April 24, 2000.

Chapter 1

1. The National Association of Manufacturers' members reported in a 1999 survey that only 10 percent can handle orders electronically. "New NAM Poll Shows That Despite Tech Advances, Most Manufacturers Still Not Using E-Commerce," by Rob Schwarzwalder and Jo-Anne Prokopowicz. Included in a press release by National Association of Manufacturers, February 22, 2000. You can find this article online at <http://www.namb2b.com/>.

2. Nike is a well-known example and represents the spirit of eProcess. See *Competing Against Time*, Stalk and Hout.

3. Financial figures based on an average of the four quarters ending October 31, 1999. See "The Internet Bubble Inside the Overvalued World of High-Tech Stocks—and What You Need to Know to Avoid the Coming Shakeout," by Anthony B. Perkins and Michael C. Perkins, *Harper Business* (November 1999).

4. "Suddenly, Amazon's Books Look Better: The e-tailer Is Raking in a Bundle—From Other Merchants," by Robert D. Hof, Heather Green, and Diane Brady, *Business Week* (February 21, 2000).

5. Ibid.

6. "Cisco Systems—Seizing the Internet Opportunity," by Cern Basher (list archives, February 8, 2000) <http://provident.listbot.com/>.

"Cisco Systems: The Paradigm of an e-Org, Strategy and Business," by Gary L. Neilson, Bruce A. Pasternack, and Albert J. Viscio *Focus* 18 (Quarter 1, 2000): p. 59.

"The Godzilla Companies of the New Economy," by Kenichi Ohmae, *Strategy and Business* 18 (Quarter 1, 2000): pp. 137–138.

The Clickable Corporation, Rosenoer et al.

"Embracing the E-World," *Wired* (February 2000): p. 11.

"Cisco Systems—Y2K Worry? Cisco Reports Second Quarter Results Above Street Consensus Expectations," by Paul Johnson, Ara Mizrakjian, and Robertson Stephens, *Networking Hardware Research* (February 9, 2000).

"Making Out: Outsourcers Were Bottom-Feeders in the Electronics Manufacturing Business. Now They're on Top," by Robert McGarvey, *Upside* (February 2000): pp. 136–137.

e-Profit: High Payoff Strategies for Capturing the E-Commerce Edge, Cohan, p. 30.

Customer Service on the Internet, Sterne, p. 247.

Cisco Corporate Financial Report, April 2000, <http://www.cisco.com/>.

7. *Competing in Chapter 2 of Internet Business*, Keen.

8. *Electronic Business Outlook*, Conference Board and PricewaterhouseCoopers.

9. "Holiday Purchases Show 27 Percent Failure Rate," by Chet Dembeck, *E-Commerce Times* (December 21, 1999).

10. *Competing in Chapter 2 of Internet Business*, Keen.

11. *The Process Edge*, Keen.

12. "Features/The E-Volution of Big Business/Online Report Card: 10 Companies That Get It," by Melanie Warner et al, *Fortune* (November 8, 1999): p. 115.

13. *Free, Perfect, and Now*, Ronin and Hartman.

14. *Competing in Chapter 2 of Internet Business*, Keen, p. 36.

15. "Embracing the E World—GartnerGroup's 'Three E Strategy' Paves the Way for Brick-and-Mortar Companies," *Gartner Interactive* (February 2000): p. 8, <http://www.gartner.com/>.

16. This analysis of eCommerce margin structures is discussed in more detail in *From .Com to .Profit*, Earle and Keen.

17. *Competing in Chapter 2 of Internet Business*, Keen, p. 36.

18. "New Winners, Net Losers," by A. Gary Shilling, *Forbes* (January 24, 2000).

19. "Amazon Promotional Deal Nets 145M," by Mary Hildebrand, *E-Commerce Times* (February 2, 2000).

20. Ibid.

21. *Competing in Chapter 2 of Internet Business*, Keen, pp. 20–21.

From .Com to .Profit, Earle and Keen.

Chapter 2

1. *The Process Edge*, Keen.

2. For an in-depth discussion of business models, see the following:

- ▸ *The Business Internet and Intranets*, Keen, Mougayar, and Torregrossa.

- ▸ *Competing in Chapter 2 of Internet Business*, Keen.

- ▸ *From .Com to .Profit*, Earle and Keen.

3. Figures extrapolated from America Online 1999 Annual Report, <http://www.corp.aol.com/annual/10k/index.html>.

4. "One Quarter of Attempted Holiday e-Commerce Purchases Fail," *Cyberatlas* (December 22, 1999), <http://cyberatlas.internet .com/markets/retailing/article/0,1323,6061_265191,00.html>.

5. McKinsey & Company ePerformance Index.

6. "Some Online Retailers Can't Handle Holiday Rush," by Stephanie Stoughton (the *Washington Post*), published in the *Detroit News* (December 24, 1999).

7. "Online Shopping Gets Real," by Blaise Zeraga, *Red Herring* magazine (September 1999).

8. *Customers.Com*, Seybold.

9. Conversation between author Keen and an anonymous manufacturing company executive.

10. "Commerce Sites Need Inventory Management," by John Evan Frook (*Internet Week*), published in CMP's *TechWeb*, Technology News (March 5, 1998).

Chapter 3

1. *Process Innovation*, Davenport, p. 28.

2. "Online Banking Hindered by Bureaucracy," PR Newswire, <http://www.prnewswire.com/>.

3. "A third-quarter 1999 study by Jupiter Communications found that 46 percent of the 125 sites surveyed either did not have an email address, never responded, or took more than five days to respond to email." From "Customer Service Continues to Decline," *The Internet Analyst* (November 1999).

4. "UPS Worldwide Logistics 'Tunes Up' Fender Guitar's European Supply Chain," UPS Logistics Group News Release (May 27, 1999).

5. The one-click process is so central to Amazon's strategy that it sued Barnes and Noble for patent infringement and won its case, though it could possibly be overturned on appeal in 2000 or 2001.

6. *Competing in Chapter 2 of Internet Business*, Keen.

7. "e-Bay's Top Cop," by Jean Shrive, *Wired* (February 2000): p. 76.

Chapter 4

1. "How Chrysler Created an American Keiretsu," by Jeffrey H. Dyer, *Harvard Business Review* (July 1, 1996).

2. *Competing in Time*, Keen.

3. Ibid.

4. IVANS: Insurance Value Added Network Services

SWIFT: Society for Worldwide International Funds Transfers

CHIPS: Clearing House for Interbank Payment System

CHAPS: Clearing House for Automated Payment System

FEDWIRE: U.S. Federal Reserve network

5. *Road Warriors*, Burstein and Kline, p.105.

6. "Yahoo!—A Cash Flow Monster," by Cern Basher (list archives, April 6, 2000) <http://provident.listbot.com>.

7. Provided by Reuters News Service, New York April 14, 2000 USA: Research Alert, <http://www.reuters.com>.

8. Ibid.

Chapter 5

1. "The Impact of Information Technology on the Organization of Economic Activity: The 'Move to the Middle' Hypothesis," by Eric K. Clemons and Michael Row, *Journal of Management Information Systems* 10, no. 2 (Fall 1993): pp. 9–36.

2. "All For a Good Cause," by Norma Vale, Canadian Centre for Philanthropy, *Front & Centre* 2, no. 2 (March 1995): pp. 1–2, 9.

3. "Co-Creation: A New Source of Value," by Ajit Kambil, G. Bruce Friesen, and Arul Sundaram, *Outlook* (June 1999): p. 38.

4. Ibid.

5. Personal conversation with Rik Maes.

6. *Free, Perfect, and Now*, Ronin and Hartman.

Chapter 6

1. Boston Consulting Group Survey, *Business 2.0* (May 2000): p. 451.

2. From a personal conversation with Mr. Flores.

3. "E-Trade Raises the Curtain on Its Own Internet Bank," by Amy L. Anderson, *American Banker* (April 5, 2000).

4. *Saving Big Blue*, Slater.

5. "It's About Time," *Business 2.0* (December 1999).

6. Andersen Consulting study, *Business 2.0* (March 2000): p. 428.

7. "Dell Sees No End to Strong Growth," by Jeff Franks, *Technology News* (May 13, 1999).

8. The ASP/Netsourcer Andersen Consulting has invested in.

9. Amazon.com patented this process and has filed a suit against Barnes and Noble for infringing upon its patent.

Chapter 7

1. "Relationships: The Electronic Commerce Imperative," by Peter Keen (December 1999), <http://www.peterkeen.com/>.

2. The scalability of the software is only bound by the capacity and performance of the company's technical infrastructure, which is a serious concern for most eCommerce companies.

3. "Relationships: The Electronic Commerce Imperative," by Peter Keen (December 1999), <http://www.peterkeen.com/>.

4. Analysis by McKinsey & Company, "Procurement 2.0: An Invitation for Innovation," *Business 2.0* (December 1999): p. 322.

5. "IT's Value Is in the Chain," by Peter Keen, *Computerworld* (February 2000).

6. Analysis by McKinsey & Company, "@ Your Service," Edited by Kim Cross, *Business 2.0* (December 1999): p. 427.

7. Ibid., p. 428.

Chapter 8

1. "New NAM Poll Shows That Despite Tech Advances, Most Manufacturers Still Not Using E-Commerce," by Rob Schwarzwalder and Jo-Anne Prokopowicz. Included in a press release by National Association of Manufacturers, February 22, 2000.

2. Fiscal 1999 annual reports from AOL and Yahoo.

3. Dembeck, Chet. *E-Commerce Times* (January 31, 2000).

4. Ibid.

5. *Business Week* (January 17, 2000): p. 37.

Chapter 9

1. "Suddenly, Amazon's Books Look Better: The e-tailer Is Raking in a Bundle—From Other Merchants," by Robert D. Hof, Heather Green, and Diane Brady, *Business Week* (February 21, 2000).

2. "How Webvan Conquers E-Commerce's Last Mile," by George Anders, *Wall Street Journal* (December 15, 1999): p. B1.

3. From Andersen Consulting Web site: <http://www.ac.com/news/newsarchive/1.00/newsarchive_011000.html>.

4. "Study: Top Customer Service Drives E-Commerce Sales," by Rob Spiegel, *E-Commerce Times* (December 1, 1999).

5. "Holiday Purchases Show 27 Percent Failure Rate," by Chet Dembeck, *E-Commerce Times* (December 21, 1999).

6. "Many Happy Returns? An E-buyer's Tale," by Lorrie Grant, *USA TODAY* (January 25, 2000): p. 12B.

Chapter 10

1. "Cybersquatters Banned from Holding Web Names to Ransom," retrieved from *UK Sunday Times* (January 13, 2000), <http://www.infowar.com/law/00/law_011300a_j.shtml>.

2. "E-Commerce Transforms Schwab from Hunter to Hunted," by Chet Dembeck, *E-Commerce Times* (February 3, 2000).

Cost, annual trade, average balances, total accounts, and market share information provided by *Money* magazine (September 1999): p. 154. Market capitalization information provided by Quicken.com, as of January 14, 2000.

3. Andersen Consulting study, *Business 2.0* (March 2000).

4. "The Next Amazon.com? It's Wal-Mart," by Jim Jubak, from the MSN Web site (August 17, 1999), <http://www.moneycentral .com/articles/invest/jubak/3519.asp>.

5. "Business Quick Study, Disintermediation/Reintermediation," by Julie King, *ComputerWorld* (December 13, 1999).

6. Ibid.

7. *Competing in Chapter 2 of Internet Business*, Keen.

Bibliography

Burstein, Daniel, and David Kline. *Road Warriors: Dream and Nightmares Along the Information Highway*. New York: Dutton Books, 1995.

Christensen, Clayton M. *The Innovator's Dilemma: When New Technologies Cause Great Firms to Fail*. Cambridge: Harvard Business School Press, 1997.

Cohan, Peter S. *e-Profit: High Payoff Strategies for Capturing the E-Commerce Edge*. New York: Amacom, 2000.

Conference Board and PricewaterhouseCoopers. *Electronic Business Outlook*. Conference Board Publications, April 2000. Publication ID: R-1267-00-RR.

Davenport, Thomas H. *Process Innovation: Reengineering Work Through Information Technology*. Boston: Harvard Business School Press, 1993.

Earle, Nick and Peter G. W. Keen. *From .Com to .Profit: Inventing Business Models That Deliver Value AND Profit*. San Francisco: Jossey Bass Publishers, 2000.

Evans, Philip, and Thomas S. Wurster. "Strategy and the New Economics of Information." *Harvard Business Review* 74, no. 5 (September–October 1997).

Greenspun, Philip. *Philip and Alex's Guide to Web Publishing*. San Francisco: Morgan Kaufmann Publishers, 1997.

Gulati, Ranjay, and Jason Garino. "Get the Right Mix of Bricks and Clicks." *Harvard Business Review* 78, no. 3 (May–June 2000).

Kaplan, Steven, and Mohanbir Sawhney. "E-Hubs: The New B2B Marketplaces." *Harvard Business Review* 78, no. 3 (May–June 2000).

Keen, Peter G. W. *Competing in Chapter 2 of Internet Business: Navigating in a New World*. Delft: Eburon Publishers, 1999.

Keen, Peter G. W. *Competing in Time: Using Telecommunications for Competitive Advantage.* Cambridge: Ballinger Publishing, 1988.

Keen, Peter G. W. *Online Profits: Every Manager's Guide to Electronic Commerce.* Cambridge: Harvard Business School Press, 1997.

Keen, Peter G. W. *The Process Edge: Creating Value Where It Counts.* Cambridge: Harvard Business School Press, 1997.

Keen, Peter G. W., Craigg Ballance, Sally Chan, and Steve Schrump. *Electronic Commerce Relationships: Trust by Design.* Englewood Cliffs, N.J.: Prentice Hall, 1998.

Keen, Peter G. W., Walid Mougayar, and Tracy Torregrossa. *The Business Internet and Intranets: A Manager's Guide to Key Terms and Concepts.* Cambridge: Harvard Business School Press, 1998.

Leonard-Barton, Dorothy. *Wellsprings of Knowledge: Building and Sustaining the Sources of Innovation.* Cambridge: Harvard Business School Press, 1995.

McDonald, Mark. "From Manual Commerce to e-Commerce: Business Practices for Building Relationships." *Cutter IT Journal* 13, no. 4 (April 2000): 12–24.

McWilliam, Gil. "Building Stronger Brands Through Online Communities." *Sloan Management Review* 41, no. 3: 43–54.

Perkins, Anthony B., and Michael C. Perkins. "The Internet Bubble Inside the Overvalued World of High-Tech Stocks—and What You Need to Know to Avoid the Coming Shakeout," *Harper Business* (November 1999).

Ronin, Robert, and Curtis Hartman. *Free, Perfect, and Now: Connecting to the Three Insatiable Customer Demands: A CEO's True Story.* New York: Simon & Schuster, 1999.

Rosenoer, Jonathan, Douglas Armstrong, and J. Russell Gates. *The Clickable Corporation.* New York: The Free Press, 1999.

Schrage, Michael. *Serious Play: How the World's Best Companies Simulate to Innovate.* Cambridge: Harvard Business School Press, 2000.

Schwartz, Evan I. *Digital Darwinism.* New York: Broadway Books, 1999.

Seybold, Patricia B. *Customers.Com: How to Create a Profitable Business Strategy for the Internet and Beyond*. New York: Times Books, 1998.

Slater, Robert. *Saving Big Blue: Leadership Lessons & Turnaround Tactics of IBM's Lou Gerstner*. New York: McGraw-Hill Professional Publishing, 1999.

Stalk, George, Jr., and Thomas M. Hout. *Competing Against Time: How Time-Based Competition Is Reshaping Global Markets*. New York: Free Press, 1999.

Sterne, Jim. *Customer Service on the Internet: Building Relationships, Increasing Loyalty, and Staying Competitive*. New York: John Wiley & Sons, 1996.

Stewart, III, G. Bennett. *The Quest for Value: The EVA® Management Guide*. New York: HarperBusiness, 1991.

Tapscott, Don, Alex Lowy, and David Ticoll, eds. *Blueprint to the Digital Economy: Wealth Creation in the Era of E-Business*. New York: McGraw-Hill, 1998.

Index